CREATIVITY

THE ENERGY POWERING
ALL PUBLIC SECTOR CHANGE

BELINDA TOBIN

Published by Understanding Press

UP

Paperback ISBN: 978-1-7638596-7-8
E-Book ISBN: 978-1-7638596-8-5

For permissions or enquiries, please contact:
Understanding Press
Email: up@heart-led.pub
Website: www.heart-led.pub/understanding-press
First Edition: November 2025

NATIONAL LIBRARY OF AUSTRALIA

A catalogue record for this book is available from the National Library of Australia

I acknowledge the Yuggera and Ugarapul peoples as the Traditional Owners of the lands and waterways where this book was written. I honour the wisdom that lives within the cultures of our First Nations peoples and celebrate its continuity. I pay my deep respects to Elders past, present and future and send my greatest gratitude for all they do for the life of this land. Always was, always will be.

Dedication

To the public servants who, with care, courage, and compassion, strive each day to build a better society for us all.

CONTENTS

INTRODUCTION

"Our most important national resource is the creative capacity of our people." ~ J.P. Guilford

You do not hear the word 'creativity' too often within the walls of our public sector agencies or government offices. However, there are plenty of other c-words commonly used, such as customer-centric, consultation, collaboration, capability, and confidence. Sitting quietly beneath them all, though, is creativity. Even if we do not hear it called out by name, there is no doubt that this essential power enables all these other crucial outcomes. Moreover, every government leader draws on creativity daily, whether it is recognised or not.

Creativity is not being ignored because decision-makers lack imagination. It is happening because, for generations, we have been misguided by a malicious myth: that creativity and government work are incompatible. We have held on to awful assumptions about creativity—that it is an 'airy fairy' concept and is all about boundary-breaking, excessive emotional expression, eccentricity, and egregious risks. We have upheld beliefs that it belongs solely in the arts, and has no place in the public service, especially not in leadership, which must demonstrate logic, reliability, seriousness and respect for the rules.

At the behest of these warped worldviews, we have built systems that systematically suppress creativity. We have focused on other c-words such as control, consistency, credibility, compliance, and continuity. We have created risk-averse cultures where those who think differently are seen as problems rather than assets—overlooked for promotion, quietly pushed aside. And we have convinced ourselves this is not only professional—it is for the public good.

What we have failed to do, however, is take time to understand what creativity actually is and to challenge the outdated notions that are preventing us capture its powerful potential.

At its core, creativity is *the ability to develop a "novel and appropriate, useful, correct or valuable response to the task at hand"* (Amabile, 1996, p.35). This capability—to deliver a new and valuable policy, product, service or system to your customers and constituents—is central to your organisation's purpose and pivotal to your continued performance. Moreover, your ability to adapt and change, to work in new and valuable ways is essential to ensure ongoing efficiency and effectiveness. Simply put, you cannot meet your organisational objectives or deliver excellent community outcomes without creativity.

The Cost?

The costs of not questioning our assumptions around creativity are high. Every time we choose to cling to outdated notions about creativity, we forfeit the privilege of enabling our people to live to their fullest potential.

Every time we refute creativity's relevance to government and its agencies, we reject the energy needed to bring about meaningful change.

And every time we constrain our people's creativity, we are preventing possible solutions for the complex challenges our communities face.

Why This Matters Now

Now is the time we need to be talking about creativity in the public sector because there are urgent issues and unresolved problems that are harming people and the future prosperity of our nation.

Every single one of these, be it housing affordability, mental health crises, climate change effects, low productivity growth or social inequality, require change. They are all demanding new and valuable responses, which is exactly what creativity delivers.

The longer these problems go unsolved, the more people are hurt and the more potential goes unfulfilled. And if we don't act now and invest in creativity in our public sector, then the risks of decreased legitimacy and relevance are real. Some may say the slip has already started.

Are We Already Going Backwards?

The latest Trust in Australian Public Services annual report presents a very positive picture, with 62% of Australians having confidence in government services, up from 56% five years ago. Moreover, nearly three in four people (73%) trust the specific services they have used, and several agencies have experienced increasing trust scores over time (Australian Public Sector Commission, 2025). These results are a testament to the work you do every day to provide excellent services and the wise investments you have made in their improvement.

Nevertheless, beneath this sturdy service base, there is cause for concern. The 2025 Edelman Trust Barometer reveals Australians perceive government as both incompetent and unethical. There is also a broad level of societal grievance, with 62% of Australians unhappy with the governments they see as not serving, or in some cases even harming, ordinary citizens. These factors have seen public trust in Australia's government decline sharply from 61% in 2021 to 47% in 2025 (Edelman, 2025). This reversal is particularly stark given that trust had been steadily increasing from a low of 35% in 2018, suggesting a fundamental shift in public sentiment over the past four years. This decline indicates a belief that current policy approaches are failing to meet citizen needs and is significantly reducing government legitimacy.

The premise of the Edelman survey is that any organisation's ability to succeed or fail is defined by trust in its mission and leadership. While rising confidence in specific government services is heartening, it cannot mask the growing perception that government does not serve the public interest. This divergence demands attention, not complacency.

The satisfaction with services must become the foundation upon which to build solutions to the wicked challenges of our time. Solid service satisfaction is a cause for celebration, but it is not the endpoint—it is a strategic asset that leaders must leverage to rebuild institutional trust and secure a sustainable future position.

For our world is changing too fast for playing catch-up and patching leaks to be effective public sector strategies. The rapid pace of technological advancement, coupled with escalating citizen expectations and mounting fiscal pressures, has created what organisational theorists call "complex adaptive systems"— environments where linear solutions no longer suffice and where effective solutions emerge from the dynamic interplay of multiple interconnected elements.

Leaders are faced with decision-making environments drenched in volatility, uncertainty, complexity, and ambiguity (VUCA), and this demands a new leadership model—one that is dynamic, engaging, adaptive and able to turn challenges into opportunities for meaningful change—and one that has creativity at its core.

Many are suggesting, though, that we are already losing the battle for ongoing legitimacy and that there has been a "whittling away of policy imagination" (Landry & Caust, 2017 p. 14). The Grattan Institute's analysis of policy reforms led it to conclude that popularism has overtaken public interest, and that in many areas, Australia's governments and political parties "are going backwards" (Daley, 2021, p. 58). The most recent Responsive Government Survey (Global Government Forum, 2023) also indicates public servants are becoming less confident in their organisation's ability to respond to the changing needs of citizens and that public services can be improved. This situation is one of great concern.

This is why creativity matters now more than ever. Not as a luxury. Not as something confined to innovation teams or strategic retreats, but as the fundamental capability that powers every change your citizens are demanding.

Guilford's Warning

This is not the first call for recognition of creativity's rightful place in the public sector. This battle has been fought before.

We live in a time of relative peace, so it may be difficult to imagine the horrific aftermath of World War II. Cities were destroyed, economies were struggling to rebuild, and millions were scarred, physically and mentally, from years of conflict.

Governments faced the large and lengthy task of national reconstruction, needing all the ingenuity they could muster to build a path back to prosperity. At the same time, they were facing a radically altered geopolitical landscape that was becoming increasingly menacing. The United States and the Soviet Union, once steady allies, were increasingly at ideological odds, and both were escalating the threat of nuclear confrontation.

It was within this Cold War context that J.P. Guilford made an impassioned plea during his 1950 Presidential Address at the American Psychological Association. He called on his fellow psychologists to stop treating creativity as an afterthought and to make it a central, credible scientific field of study. He called for clear definitions, reliable measures, and practical applications that could unlock creative potential in education, industry, and national development.

Guilford made this speech because of the desperate need he saw for innovation in science, engineering, education, and national leadership, and to help us learn how to cultivate, rather than suppress, our creative potential.

His message was urgent then, and it remains urgent now:

"Our most important national resource is the creative capacity of our people."

Additionally, he challenged his peers with a question that still echoes today:

"Why is there so little interest in creative thinking? We shall not solve the problems of our age without it."

Psychologists, public agencies, and researchers responded to Guilford's call for action. Since his rousing speech, there have been significant advances in creativity research. We now have proven methods to assess divergent thinking and a comprehensive understanding of the social and environmental factors that influence creativity. Like any field, it is becoming increasingly specialised, with researchers now focusing on the unique contexts of the public sector and the challenges leaders face in fostering greater creativity within government organisations.

Nevertheless, across all countries, industries, and sectors, researchers are reaching the same conclusions: creativity is the fundamental capability that drives innovation, productivity, problem-solving, resilience and strong community relationships. Guilford recognised this 75 years ago during a time of global crisis. Today, as we face our own era of wicked problems, his words carry even greater weight. The problems may have evolved, but the solution remains the same: we must finally take seriously what Guilford so passionately declared—that our greatest resource is the creative capacity of our people.

And more specifically, the creative capacity of leaders like you.

You Are a Creator

You may be thinking, *"But I'm not creative."*

Let me be clear: you are. Moreover, your work as a public sector leader is inherently creative. Every time you navigate competing stakeholder demands, redesign a process to improve service delivery, establish a collaboration or co-design project, or find ways to do more with constrained resources, you are exercising creativity.

> The belief that you lack creativity is not only misguided—it is dangerous, because it prevents you from recognising and developing this essential capability.

However, here is the more vital truth: you are also a creator of conditions. Research confirms that creativity flourishes or withers based on the environment leaders establish (Amabile et al., 1996). Your role is not just to be creative yourself—it is to build the space where others can develop and express their creative potential.

When you demonstrate curiosity rather than certainty, respond to unconventional ideas with genuine interest rather than immediate scepticism, and treat intelligent failures as learning rather than career-limiting events, you signal to your team that creativity is valued.

The profound influence that leaders have on creativity within their organisations is why experts increasingly agree that it is now the most crucial leadership competency, placed well above technical expertise or hierarchical authority. This recognition has compelled the Harvard Business Review (2023) to state that,

"Creativity is the most sought-after trait in leaders."

Moreover, the Institute of Managers and Leaders Australia and New Zealand (Gibbings, 2024) assert that,

> *"For leaders to be effective today and ready for tomorrow, creativity is a crucial competency to master."*

In VUCA environments where linear solutions fail and novel challenges constantly emerge, creative leadership—both your own creative capacity and your ability to cultivate it in others—has become the differentiating factor between irrelevance and meaningful change.

Why I Wrote This Book

I came to the public sector over 20 years ago after leaving a career in corporate consulting. My mother had just died, and like every great loss, it was followed by a period of deep reflection. I asked myself what I genuinely wanted to do with the rest of my life, and the answer was...? Something more meaningful than helping big companies make more money. I wanted to contribute to more noble outcomes, such as equality and social justice, and knew trickle-down economics could never deliver such things.

When a public service position appeared, I was thrilled. I joined a small team developing governance and strategy systems for a brand-new division. This place was dynamic, fearless, and forward-looking. We operated with deep respect for what each person brought to the table, and creativity flourished.

Then, over the next few years, I watched all the excitement erode. As the division grew, so did the number of frameworks, procedures, and reporting lines. The systems and structures also became increasingly complex, contributing to a sense of controlled chaos. The leaders grew distant, and decisions had to be routed through five layers, with answers taking forever and not always being filtered back down.

The leaders were too busy navigating politics to spend time with their people. Instead of sharing their visions in person during small-team meetings, they announced the department's strategy from a stage at infrequent town hall sessions.

I witnessed the slow demise of a purposeful, driven team to one that became just another cog in a colossal wheel. Structure distanced people from meaning, and with more resources to manage came the pervasive panic of making mistakes, compounded by leadership practices focused on securing control.

While these changes are symptomatic of any growing organisation, they are especially pronounced—and well-documented—features of the public sector, which must balance scale, accountability, and public scrutiny in ways few other workplaces do.

Years later, researcher Peter Coaldrake described perfectly what I was sensing: an *"atmosphere of fear"* across the public sector (Coaldrake, 2022).

By watching my leaders' behaviour, I knew that my creativity would no longer be appreciated. Like so many others, I hid it away, using my time away from work to research creativity, author books, establish a publishing company, and take on a role as a film producer. Creative energy insists on flowing; otherwise, we become unwell, and so I found a way to compartmentalise and let it live freely outside the office.

Looking back, I realise creation was still happening in my agency, just in unhelpful forms. What had been built were rigid hierarchies, excessive formalization, red tape, siloed departments, centralized decision-making, and risk-averse cultures—structural barriers that research has repeatedly shown to constrain creativity. Simultaneously, essential pillars of wellbeing were decimated: purpose, trust, and the safety to share ideas.

It took a mentor to help me see the obvious: over the years, I had built extensive creative skills outside of my career. Now I can apply them to help the public sector, which I still hold in great regard and wholeheartedly believe in.

I have had the honour of experiencing firsthand the conditions under which creativity thrives in government and have personally witnessed the forces that destroy it. It is this knowledge, along with my passion for creativity, that I bring to this book, which, in part, is a public declaration of what I believe.

What I believe is that every person in the public service is creative and deserves to live to their fullest potential. I also believe that leaders have a great responsibility and privilege to support their people to thrive, and that creativity is central to this achievement.

> I believe governments are critical creators—they shape the society we become, and so within it, creativity must be embraced, nurtured, and celebrated.

This book comes from my core belief that delivering excellent community outcomes requires us to recognise and unleash the creative capacity that has always been there. It is not dead, simply dormant, waiting for someone to read this book and decide that things can be done differently.

What This Book Delivers

This book exists to challenge the myths we have believed, to break down the biases we have held, and to prove, without a doubt, that creativity is core to public sector work.

It provides understanding and evidence that show creativity is a fundamental government and leadership capability, and a practical framework for unlocking creative potential in yourself, your team, and your organisation. This book reveals the true nature of creativity and its pivotal role in the public sector over four sections.

Section 1: What is Creativity?

We all come to this book with unique notions about what creativity is, how it works and who gets to be creative. Therefore, this section seeks to build a shared understanding of this concept and to contest outdated and erroneous beliefs. To do this, we begin with the fundamental question: What is creativity?

Too often dismissed as an airy-fairy notion confined to the arts, creativity has been studied comprehensively, with a clear, agreed-upon definition used both in academia and by public-sector practitioners.

> Creativity is the ability to deliver something new and valuable.

This something could be a new policy, process, service or system. It could also be a solution or a new behaviour needed to adapt to changing circumstances. Creativity is not just about bold ideas; it is also about how we respond to everyday challenges.

However, as with much of your work, the devil is in the details. We will explore the nuances of novelty and value, examining their various levels and dimensions. You will also see that navigating these nuances is not a simple proposition and requires the integration of the full suite of human intelligence.

Neither is creativity an isolated capability; it operates within a multi-layered social system, and we will investigate the levels that individually and collectively either nurture or crush creative action. Most importantly, you will understand creativity from a unique perspective—as an energy that always exists as a potential but, under the right conditions, can be activated and amplified.

Section 2: How Creativity Powers All Public Sector Change

With a shared understanding of creativity, we examine how it is at the core of overcoming all community challenges and all public sector change. While there is much interest and investment in innovation, you will see that creativity is not only the origin of innovation, but also the capability that enables challenges to be overcome for successful implementation. You will also see how creativity is imperative to productivity improvements—a current and pressing economic issue in Australia.

Additionally, this section illustrates how creativity drives the flexibility, adaptability, and agility required for problem-solving and resilience. It also sits at the heart of strong relationships and collaborative governance, both of which are crucial to successfully delivering shared value.

We will also dive deeper into how creativity is enacted across an organisation or community, demonstrating it as a series of risk-and-reward decisions. What will be made clear is that while each person has a unique level of risk tolerance, the conditions under which decisions are made significantly shape people's perceptions of how risky it is to share and develop their ideas and can prevent progress.

Section 3: Why Your Creativity Matters Most

Bringing greater creativity to your organisation begins with you. You are creative, and so is your work. Additionally—and importantly—as a leader, you build the conditions that help others expand and express their creative potential. You do this by investing in their ability, motivating their effort, and providing opportunities to practice managing risk and build creative skills.

This section will detail the core components of creative conditions over which you have influence and identify practices that provide conducive team climates and organisational cultures. It will outline the abilities that you must foster as creative foundations and how you motivate creative action. It will also describe the behaviours and systems you put in place, which permit people to expand and express their creative potential.

Moreover, this section will address your powerful position as a creative role model. Your people look to you for how risks are reconciled, failures are treated, and how new problems are approached. It shows, therefore, that if your team is struggling with creativity and meaningful change, it could very well be the example you are setting that is the issue.

Section 4: A New Approach—The Creative Energy Equation

By the end of the book, you will understand the wealth of research available around creativity, and how it relates to your vital public sector work. However, while the research is rich, it can be overwhelming, fragmented, and how it can be applied on a daily basis is not necessarily obvious.

To make the research actionable, a simple, practical model is presented, called the Creative Energy Equation:

$$C = EMC^2$$

Creativity = Emotion × Meaning × Connection (self and others).

Emotion is the spark that activates creative potential, with the aim of this component to foster both confidence and courage. Confidence comes from ensuring a person can do their work well and has strong creative capability. Courage is achieved through being supported in sharing ideas, accepting the risks, and dealing with the difficult emotions that come with moving forward into the unknown.

Meaning is the compass that directs and sustains creative effort, and this element concentrates on developing a sense of purpose around the work a person is doing and alignment with the mission of the organisation in which they reside.

Connection is the amplification factor for creative energy, with self-connection driving authenticity upon which creativity rests, and connection with others multiplying its potential exponentially.

Using the Creative Energy Equation, you can make intuitive assessments anywhere, anytime, about what conditions within your own life, team or organisation are helping or hindering creativity. Reflection questions are also provided to help you identify and celebrate the areas in which you already excel and where greater attention is needed to nurture and unleash creative potential.

Creativity Is Not A Choice

I am sure, like so many of your peers, you joined the public service to make a positive difference for your communities. This is what makes working in government so rewarding and such an honour—every day you can bring about meaningful change and improve people's lives. I also have no doubt that you work hard every moment to deliver excellent outcomes for your customers, clients, citizens, and constituents, and your dedication, while not always acknowledged, is greatly appreciated.

My hope for this book is to provide you with the understanding that creativity is not optional—it is core to achieving excellent community outcomes. Moreover, I hope reading this book comes with the realisation that creativity is imperative for both your professional and personal lives. Creativity is central to human wellbeing, and when we recognise and nourish it for ourselves, we can be of great service to our loved ones, colleagues, and communities.

May this book be your permission to provide yourself with the space and time to honour your creative selves for the benefit of all. Because our communities demand change, and to achieve it in a sustainable way, we must change first.

Instead of sidelining and shunning creativity, let us recognise its central role in all our great work. Let us celebrate the creativity that already exists and take proactive action to spread and amplify it across our agencies. Let us become disciplined in developing it so that we can deliver what our people deserve—a world where wicked problems are solved, productivity drives prosperity, collaboration across sectors delivers incredible value, communities are cohesive and resilient, and there is both courageous action and optimism for the future.

Creativity is the energy that fuels all life. Let us use it to leave a positive legacy for those lives we touch every day.

1

WHAT IS CREATIVITY?

Each person reading this book brings with them a unique set of ideas about creativity, shaped by the lessons we learnt as children, the opinions of our peers, and our recent personal experiences. All these views are valuable, for they tell us not only where we have come from, but also what form our future will take. Because what we believe becomes our reality.

The purpose of this section is to challenge any limiting beliefs by presenting the full picture of what creativity is. The aim is to broaden your understanding of creativity as a concept and show the vast contexts in which it operates. We will see that creativity is centred around the notion of delivering something new and valuable but is also much bigger than this. Creativity is multidimensional, multi-layered and operates more like an energy than a discrete capability.

However, while the objective of this section is to present definitions and diagrams to develop a shared understanding, the content is provided with a proviso. Through my creative practice, I have come to realise that creativity always contains some magic that can never be fully explained. While here we will cover the theory, please know that creativity will always reserve some mystery that can only be understood through experience.

1   Creativity Is Novelty and Value

Creativity is the ability to develop a "novel and appropriate, useful, correct or valuable response to the task at hand" (Amabile, 1996, p.35)

While we may speak of creativity as something concrete, it is, in fact, an invisible entity. We cannot see creativity, only those things in which it is contained, be it ideas, products, services, behaviours, systems, or structures. But what makes any of these items creative, and when do we know creativity has occurred? What sets the ordinary apart from the outstanding?

Since Guildford's address to the American Psychological Association in 1950 where he pushed for dedicated research into creativity, numerous researchers have investigated every aspect. When it comes to a definition of what creativity is, the one above from Teresa Amabile is the most widely accepted and is adopted by academics and practitioners alike. There are three key components of this definition that need to be noted:

1. **Novelty**. To be creative, something must be new, not necessarily to the world, but at least to the context.

2. **Value**. The second element relates to impact. To be creative it must also be *"appropriate, useful, correct or valuable to the task at hand"* (Amabile, 1996, p.35).

3. **Response**. This element shows that creativity goes well beyond coming up with innovative ideas, products, policies and services. Creativity is also captured in our behaviours; how we act, adapt, and change.

The definition of creativity can be shown in shorthand as follows:

$$Creativity = Novelty + Value$$

Something is considered creative when it is both original in its context and judged to be useful or impactful for its intended purpose.

In turn, we can say that creativity is the ability to develop something new and valuable.

The Tension: When Novelty and Value Compete

The dual pillars of creativity as novelty and value sound relatively simple. The reality, however, is far more complex, as the two can, and often do, conflict, posing real leadership challenges.

For example, it has been shown that as ideas become more extreme in terms of novelty, the less consensus there will be on whether the idea is valuable. This inverse relationship between novelty and value judgements stems from newness bringing with it signals of risk. The newer the idea is, the less likely there will be a precedent, and with no prior experience, people start to feel fear. All they know is that the proposed future is wildly different, and this comes with discomfort.

Even if there is great positive potential, uncertainty triggers caution and reduces a person's willingness to invest in or support the idea. In other words, the very originality that makes an idea creative can make it harder to implement, as stakeholders are more likely to hesitate in the face of discomfort and division (Johnson & Proudfoot, 2024).

This downside of novelty means that leaders not only need to encourage the generation of new ideas but also manage the dynamic between originality and practicality to find the optimal blend for the situation at hand.

For public sector agencies, this means finding the sweet spot where ideas are new enough to make a difference, but not so radical that they are dismissed or resisted as too risky. The most successful leaders are those who can sense where that balance lies and guide their teams accordingly.

> The message here is when it comes to creativity, contextual sensitivity is key: sometimes novelty needs to take the lead (for example, when facing unprecedented challenges), while in other cases, acceptability must be prioritised to ensure at least a partial solution can be enacted.

To allow both novelty and value to have a voice, many organisations find a sequential approach helpful—focusing on generating novel ideas first, then shifting to evaluation and refinement to maximise value and ensure feasibility.

The Emerging Third Dimension – Emotion

Novelty and value have been the accepted components of creativity for decades. However, research is reshaping our understanding of how creativity works by highlighting a powerful third dimension—emotion.

This research is confirming what we have all experienced for ourselves: that the assessment of a new product, process, service, or suggestion is not a logical process, but an emotional one. How people feel about the idea—whether it excites, inspires, unsettles, or reassures—profoundly shapes their view of its worth (Lerner et al., 2015).

Positive feelings—such as excitement, hope, or a sense of possibility are more likely to lead to favourable judgements about a new idea, even if practical benefits are still uncertain. Conversely, as we have seen with movements into the great unknown, if an idea triggers discomfort, confusion, or anxiety, perceptions of value will decrease, even if there are clear objective merits supporting the solution.

We would like to consider ourselves sensible and rational human beings, nevertheless, the reality is that emotions are frequently used as a decision-making heuristic. We use feelings as a shortcut to determine if an idea is worth progressing.

While as we will see shortly, our emotions are based on beliefs, but we don't often delve behind the curtain of our feelings to test our assumptions and see if they hold true. Therefore, emotions become the default decision-maker when it comes to assessing creative approaches.

Figure 1 – Judgements of novelty and value are influenced by emotion

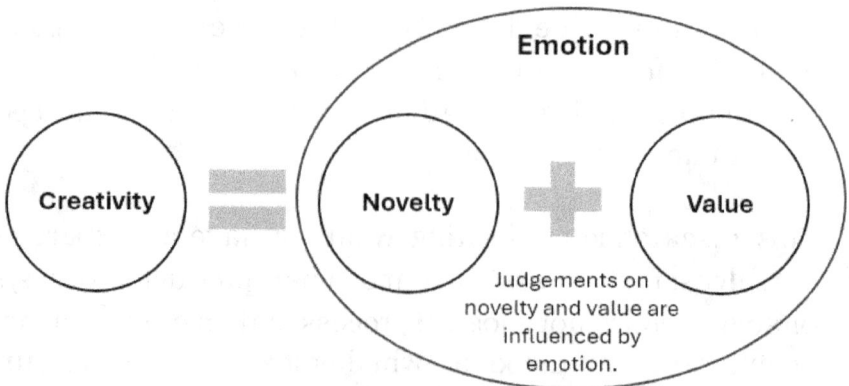

> The impact of emotions is a critical consideration for leaders and teams responsible for driving change – understanding the emotional landscape is just as important as the innovation itself.

We will investigate the emotion element of creativity further in Section 4 when we encounter the Creative Energy Equation. For now, though, there is one key message to take away – creativity is deeply intertwined with emotion, and it is the awareness and transformation of our own emotional state that is paramount to the creative process.

Working With This Definition

Understanding creativity as the combination of novelty and value (which is moderated by emotion) can be used to inform all stages of change projects including planning, problem-solving, capability and relationship building. For example, it assists with:

Strategic Thinking. Recognising that both novelty and value are essential enables more intentional and effective strategy development, allowing for explicit choices about how these characteristics will be combined. Additionally, recognising that emotions play a pivotal role in stakeholder assessments enables a more informed view of how and why stakeholders are making certain value judgements and better targeted engagement and communication activities.

Sharper Diagnosis. Using this definition of creativity supports a more thorough diagnosis of why some solutions work and others don't—was it too new to be deemed acceptable, or not novel enough to generate excitement? Perhaps the value offered was not big enough to encourage buy-in, or insufficient effort was made to understand the potential emotional reaction and points of resistance.

Building Team Capability. Knowing the three different components of creativity—novelty, value, and the influence of emotion—enables proactive development of your team's skills in all areas. Some people may be great at generating new ideas, others at evaluating their usefulness, and some may have a knack for empathising with others and managing the emotional judgements. Every single one of these elements is part of the creative process and recognising this makes creativity a part of everyone's job.

Engaging Stakeholders. Recognising that different groups may care more about novelty or about value enables effective development and decision-making. Some want fresh thinking; others want proven outcomes, and all will be influenced by how they feel about the proposed solution. Understanding that increased novelty also comes with greater division in stakeholder evaluations, you can plan and prepare more proactively to build consensus and support, and even work to boost the levels of risk tolerance over the longer term.

Additionally, by knowing that how stakeholders feel about a proposal will determine their decision, it brings greater importance to early and extensive stakeholder engagement. Intelligence can be gathered about what they believe about the idea or new approach, their assumptions, hopes, fears and needs, with the ultimate aim of helping people feel positive about the proposed change.

But Wait...

It would be wonderful if we could end there with our definition of creativity. It would be fantastic if we could just say that it is all about novelty and value, and that would be final. However, there is so much more to consider.

If you have ever been tasked with developing a new idea or have been involved in an innovation project, you would have realised that there are many complexities underlying these two characteristics.

For example, what exactly do we mean by "new" and how do we decide what level of novelty is needed?

Also, who gets to decide what is valuable, and how do we objectively assess and advertise it?

These fundamental questions will be addressed in the following chapters, helping us piece together the complete picture of creativity.

2 What Do We Mean by 'New'?

Novelty is a spectrum which recognises and celebrates every invention, whether incremental or immense.

Novelty is not a simple yes-or-no checkbox. Newness sits on a continuum between being barely distinct and dramatically different. Moreover, two separate viewers can make vastly varied assessments of where an idea sits on this scale. For example, a technological system may be groundbreaking to a small organisation. However, it can be considered business-as-usual to a large corporation that has made ongoing investments in digital transformation. So, the answer to the question, "Is this new?", is "It depends". It depends on who is looking, where they are standing, and when they sneak a peek.

Understanding the Levels of Novelty

The 4C Model of Creativity developed by James Kaufman and Ronald Beghetto (2009) shows a spectrum of novelty by focusing on who the idea or innovation is new to. As shown in the table on the following page, each level of creativity, from the small-scope mini-c creativity to the domain-shifting Big-C variety, makes a unique contribution, albeit to different extents.

One of the most significant contributions of this model is the validation it provides for mini-c, or individual-level creativity. A personal insight or innovation may seem insignificant, but this is where all innovation begins. Because something cannot be new to the team, agency, community or the world until it is first new to the inventor.

Personal insights always precede expansive change.

Table 1 – Levels of creativity (Kaufman and Beghetto)

C Level	New To	Description	Examples
Mini-c Creativity	An individual	A new and personally meaningful insight.	A frontline worker discovering a more efficient way to process applications, even if that method is already known elsewhere.
Little-c Creativity	The immediate environment	Incremental changes to existing, routine processes.	Amending a training protocol that improves team performance or improvements to communication processes that increase stakeholder engagement.
Medium-c Creativity*	The immediate environment	New but conventional processes in line with the current way of thinking.	Development of custom reporting dashboards that centralise and streamline decision-making.
Pro-c Creativity	Professional domains	Radically new processes and products that divert from the current way of thinking.	Policy innovations that are adopted across jurisdictions or the application of private sector models to public sector contexts.
Big-C Creativity	Entire fields or cultures	Innovations that change entire domains or societies, be it domestically or globally.	Transformational technologies that reshape public service delivery or trade relationships that reinvigorate entire nations.

* The Medium-c Creativity level is an addition to the typology made by Glenn Houtgraaf (2022) to support his analysis of creativity within the public sector. Further information is provided in following sections.

In the context of a government agency, a mini-c revelation by a frontline worker can be just as valuable for organisational improvement and customer satisfaction as a Big-C innovation that gains national attention. The key is recognising which level you are operating at and celebrating each one for the contribution they make.

Creativity – Bending or Breaking Conventions

We can also assess novelty not from who it is new to, but how much it shifts the current paradigm. Philosopher Margaret Boden's categorisation of creativity identifies three distinct types of creative processes, differing in the extent to which they work within existing rules and ideas about what is possible, or seek to disrupt and transform current conventions (Boden, 2004). These categories of creativity are:

1. Combinatorial creativity
2. Exploratory creativity
3. Transformational creativity

1. Combinatorial Creativity: Surprising Connections

Combinatorial creativity creates surprise by bringing together familiar elements in previously unthought-of ways. This type of creativity might seem deceptively simple, but it can produce genuinely shocking and valuable innovations. Consider how virtual technology merged with fitness to create immersive workout experiences, or how food fusion brought together culinary traditions that had never previously intersected. Augmented Reality running apps like "Zombies, Run!" demonstrate the power of this approach—they transformed mundane exercise into an engaging gaming experience by simply combining two existing concepts in a novel way.

2. *Exploratory Creativity: New Possibilities In Current Rules*

Exploratory creativity generates novelty by discovering fresh possibilities within current systems and rules. Rather than breaking boundaries, this type of creativity pushes against them, finding unexplored territory within established frameworks. Jazz improvisation provides a perfect metaphor: musicians follow established rules of music theory, chord progressions, and rhythm, yet within those constraints, they create something entirely new through experimentation with melodies, harmonies, and timing.

3. *Transformational Creativity: Rewriting the Rules*

Transformational creativity produces the most dramatic surprises by fundamentally breaking existing rules and creating something previously thought impossible or never before conceived. This is creativity that doesn't just surprise—it revolutionizes entire ways of thinking. Pablo Picasso and Georges Braque's development of Cubism exemplifies this type: they didn't just create new paintings, they shattered the fundamental rules of visual representation, presenting objects from multiple angles simultaneously and giving birth to entirely new ways of seeing and interpreting reality.

The Creative Value of Combination

It's crucial to understand that combinatorial creativity—simply bringing together existing element in new and valuable ways—represents genuine creative achievement. There's a persistent misconception that true creativity must involve creating something entirely from nothing, but Boden's research decisively refutes this notion.

The act of recognising which elements to combine, how to integrate them effectively, and when such combinations will create value requires significant creative insight and often produces innovations that are both surprising and transformative. The iPhone, for instance, was fundamentally a combination of existing technologies—phone, internet, camera, music player—but the creative vision lay in integrating them elegantly and into something that revolutionised how we interact with technology. As recognised by the Australian and New Zealand School of Government:

"There's a misconception that innovation has to be new, it could be 95% old and some new way of re-engineering it or applying it differently." (ANZSOG, 2023b).

The Creativity We See in The Public Sector

Recent research has confirmed that most of the creativity in the public sector (around 80%) is comprised of Little-c and Medium-c change (Houtgraaf, 2022). A longitudinal digital diary study analysed creative ideas and practices of 141 public servants working in Dutch public executive agencies. The research revealed the following breakdown of creativity being applied by the respondents:

1. 43% of ideas were classified as little-c magnitude, involving incremental adjustments and additions to existing products and processes.

2. 37% were medium-c magnitude, representing new but conventional approaches that align with current thinking patterns.

3. 20% were Pro-c magnitude, involving radically new processes and products that diverge from conventional approaches.

Houtgraaf and colleagues used these findings to develop a taxonomy of public sector creativity, comprising pragmatic and pioneering types (Houtgraaf et al., 2023), with the recognition that most occurring within the public sector is pragmatic.

- **Pragmatic creativity** is characterised by:
  - Incrementalism - small-scale adjustments to existing systems.
  - Reactivism - ideas generated in response to specific situations and problems.
  - Realism - evaluation based on usefulness and feasibility.
- **Pioneering creativity** involves:
  - Radicalism - fundamental, transformative change to existing systems.
  - Proactivism - anticipatory identification of future opportunities before demands arise.
  - Idealism - evaluation based on aspirational value and long-term vision.

The Australia Productivity Commission (2023b) uses the terms "incremental innovation" or "micro innovation" to describe the mostly smaller scale, pragmatic creativity found within the public sector and recognises them as the backbone of economic resilience. Rather than decrying these lower levels of creativity, it calls on public agencies to be more proactive in this area and become dedicated diffusers of best practices to improve productivity.

The OECD has also developed a categorisation of innovation which is outlined in the following table. From this we can describe most of the creativity seen in the public sector as either enhancement-oriented or adaptive (OECD, 2021a).

Table 2 - Innovation categories (OECD)

Category	Novelty Levels	Description
Enhancement-oriented	Mini-c to Medium-c creativity	Build on existing structures and governance arrangements while achieving improvement in efficiency or effectiveness.
Adaptive	Medium-c creativity	Testing and trying "new approaches in order to deliver a rapid response to emerging challenges or experimental approaches to known problems.
Mission-oriented	Medium-c to Pro-c creativity	Changes to deliver on longer-term visions and goals or systematic responses to wicked problems.
Anticipatory	Big-C creativity	Explores emergent issues that will shape future priorities and involves experimental policies and pilot programs.

It can be argued that the focus of the public sector on enhancement-oriented or adaptative activities, is both reasonable and appropriate. Our government agencies are recognised for playing a crucial role in delivering stable and reliable services while also adapting to the evolving needs of citizens. It is this type of creativity that provides the balance between stability and sustainability.

Nevertheless, given the pace of change in our modern world, planning and preparation are necessary for more distant horizons, and without it, governments risk irrelevance and sliding backwards in terms of service quality.

> Organisations that focus exclusively on low-novelty enhancement-oriented innovation may become efficient but lose their ability to continue to deliver on citizen needs and to remain relevant.

This situation seems to be the reality, with the most recent Responsive Government Survey (Global Government Forum, 2023) showing public servants are becoming less confident in their department or organisation's ability to respond to the changing needs of citizens and to improve services.

Action must be taken to anticipate change, and bigger leaps must be made if public agencies are to achieve longer-term visions. As the OECD suggests:

"Breakthrough innovation—creating new and more effective solutions ...is required to respond to the current set of demands and constraints faced by the public sector." (OECD, 2017c p.15)

However, given the uncertainty around more distant timeframes, greater levels of creativity will need to be applied, and the more we deviate from what is known, the riskier the process of change becomes. This is where creativity becomes a balance between risk and reward.

Risk and Reward Considerations

Higher levels of creativity have greater degrees of novelty, while also offering opportunities for more significant impact (value). However, with each successive step on the creativity ladder, there is a subsequent growth in risk. This is because it involves moving further away from the known and shifting into more radically new states.

Therefore, there are pros and cons for each point on the newness spectrum that must be evaluated in the context of risk appetite and strategic goals. A snapshot of these is provided in the following table.

Table 3 - The pros and cons of novelty

	Low Novelty	**High Novelty**
Pros	• Delivers quick wins and immediate improvements • Precursors to higher-novelty approaches • Build confidence, competence and reputation for more ambitious innovations • Suited to risk-averse cultures • Defined time boundary which is an advantage with limited government terms	• Delivers transformational change • High payoff potential • Ability for future-proofing outcomes • May be seen as best use of available change resources • Suited for risk-accepting cultures
Cons	• Limited transformational impact • May be seen as simply maintaining the status quo and breed scepticism around creative capacity • May receive criticism for poor use of change resources • Prevents building capability and confidence in implementing newer approaches creating stagnation	• More likely to result in division around perceptions of value • More susceptible to public criticism and scrutiny • High risk - uncertain return on investment • Requires intense change management resources • Difficult to gain bi-partisan approval and to maintain momentum over successive governments

Low-novelty, pragmatic and enhancement focused initiatives, are great for delivering fast results, addressing immediate needs for improvement and preparing teams for bigger leaps in the future. Teamed with a commitment to continual improvement, they have consistently delivered significant cumulative improvements in service delivery and citizen satisfaction over time.

High novelty, pioneering or anticipatory efforts can offer future-oriented rewards and place agencies and their communities ahead of the curve. However, they also come with higher risks, increased scrutiny, greater complexities in implementation, and uncertainty about outcomes. Given the greater likelihood of division around perceptions of value, there may be difficulty in gaining bipartisan support and sustaining the change initiatives over successive governments.

Each point of novelty has its pros and cons, which is why the OECD states that, *"Innovation should not simply be about implementing something new, but about achieving results for society."* (OECD, 2015, p.14). It goes further to suggest there are three critical aspects to consider, with novelty only being one:

1. Novelty: Novelty should be considered in context, and relevant to the specific setting where it is being introduced.

2. Impact: An equal focus must be on the value the initiative provides. Leaders do not need to create something radically new to deliver value for their communities.

3. Implementation: It is of no benefit just to talk about ideas. The imperative is to make meaningful change.

> Every agency needs a mix of approaches, and for this reason that the OECD recommends public sector agencies adopt a portfolio management approach to novelty (OECD, 2021a).

The Portfolio Approach to Novelty

Portfolio management is a strategic approach that involves selecting, prioritising, and overseeing a collection of projects, programs, or initiatives. We can use this approach to help us map and manage the different degrees of novelty being applied across organisational projects now, and plan for better resource allocation in the future.

By mapping the current approach to creativity across the organisation it allows a clear understanding the cumulative level of change occurring across all divisions and functions. It is possible to see the creative priorities, where there are synergies and gaps and where there may barriers to delivering a balanced approach.

The tool can also be used to plan a future portfolio, one that involves strategic decisions about resource allocation, and aligns with the organisational risk appetite.

> By consciously spreading creative projects across various novelty baskets, an agency can achieve both short-term wins and long-term legacies.

The following page provides one example of a portfolio map, showing different areas of organisational focus and the type of projects found at each level of novelty.

The New Questions

Understanding the different degrees of novelty and the benefits and limitations of each enables an enhanced level of intelligence, both in planning and executing improvement initiatives. It also calls you to get clear about the level of newness required to deliver on the desired outcomes.

Figure 2 - Example of an innovation portfolio map

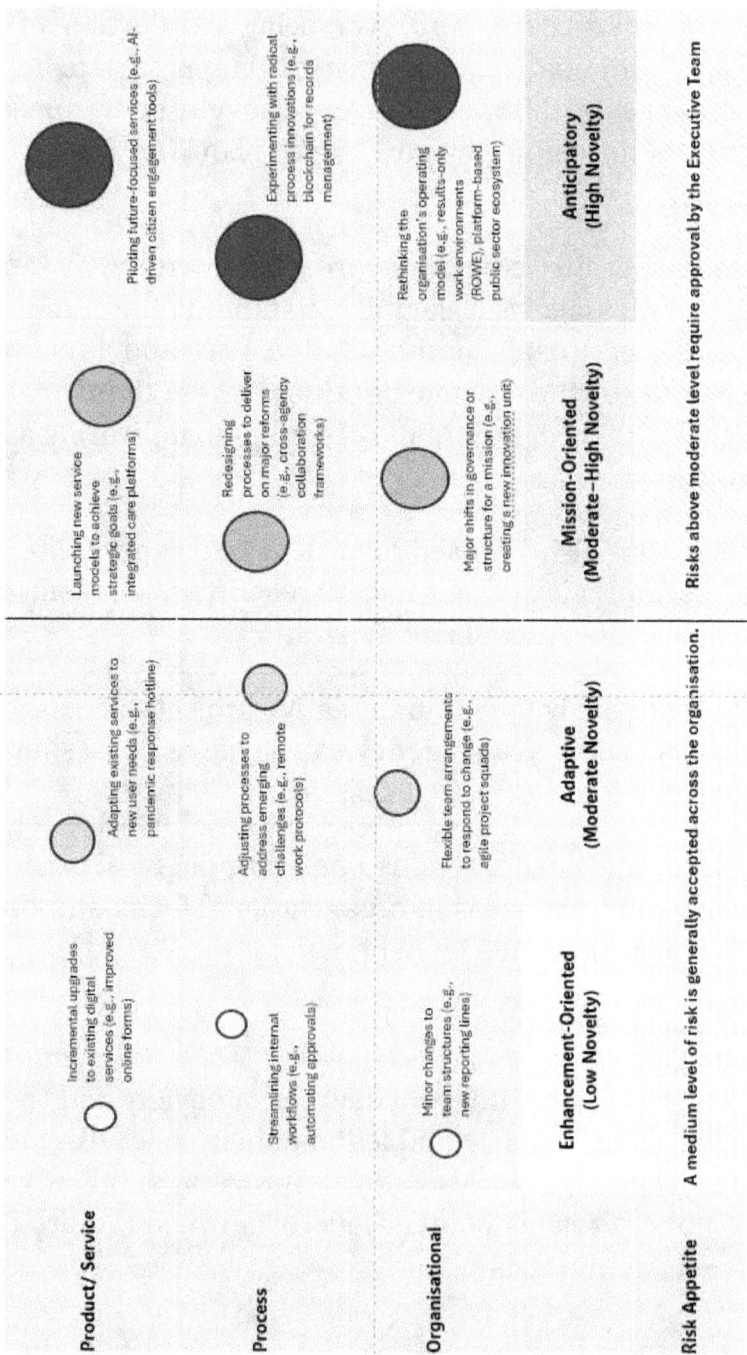

Product / Service

Incremental upgrades to existing digital services (e.g., improved online forms)

Adapting existing services to new user needs (e.g., pandemic response hotline)

Launching new service models to achieve strategic goals (e.g., integrated care platforms)

Piloting future-focused services (e.g., AI-driven citizen engagement tools)

Process

Streamlining internal workflows (e.g., automating approvals)

Adjusting processes to address emerging challenges (e.g., remote work protocols)

Redesigning processes to deliver on major reforms (e.g., cross-agency collaboration frameworks)

Experimenting with radical process innovations (e.g., blockchain for records management)

Organisational

Minor changes to team structures (e.g., new reporting lines)

Flexible team arrangements to respond to change (e.g., agile project squads)

Major shifts in governance or structure for a mission (e.g., creating a new innovation unit)

Rethinking the organisation's operating model (e.g., results-only work environments (ROWE), platform-based public sector ecosystem)

Enhancement-Oriented (Low Novelty)

Adaptive (Moderate Novelty)

Mission-Oriented (Moderate-High Novelty)

Anticipatory (High Novelty)

Risk Appetite — A medium level of risk is generally accepted across the organisation. Risks above moderate level require approval by the Executive Team

Clarity comes from asking the right questions, and here are some which may be beneficial to help you consider how the novelty aspect of creativity is playing out for you currently:

1. What are the goals of our current initiatives (to enhance, adapt, achieve our mission or anticipate future change)?

2. What level of novelty is required to achieve our strategy?

3. What is the risk tolerance of our stakeholders and communities?

4. Do we need to match novelty to the current risk tolerance, or should we be shifting the risk tolerance over time?

5. In which areas have our focus on enhancement-only led us to fall behind technological or social change?

6. Can we increase input from a diverse range of perspectives to identify new solutions outside our direct experience?

7. Can we develop an innovation portfolio to illustrate the current spread of novelty and the risk-reward balance?

8. How can we leverage the current lower levels of creativity to build confidence in more impactful initiatives?

The Next Question

In this chapter, we have concentrated on the first of the two characteristics of creativity, novelty. However, the question—"Is this new enough?"—is only the beginning. The next question revolves around value and asks, "Is this good enough?" As we will soon see, understanding the degree to which something is new is relatively simple compared to the subjective value assessments made by stakeholders.

Understanding what counts as new gives you the diagnostic tools to assess innovation potential and to plan for the inherent risks. Understanding who decides what is valuable and how they arrive at these assessments provides the political intelligence to make change happen. So, let's delve into the vital value concept.

3   What Do We Mean By 'Value'?

The notion of public value is multi-dimensional and multi-layered, requiring consideration of not only who benefits, but how deeply they benefit, and when those benefits will emerge.

As this book is being written, the complex issue of creative value is unfolding in real time. We are seeing many Artificial Intelligence (AI)-driven customer service systems being implemented, all designed to streamline customer and citizen interactions, improve efficiency and reduce costs. Those in charge of the projects advertise their success, citing reductions in call volumes, shorter time taken to resolve customer problems, and lower costs per call.

Frontline staff, however, are expressing their frustration, stating that they are now receiving more work from confused people who want to avoid the bots and have decided to come into service centres so that they can speak to a human. Customers and citizens are themselves divided—some appreciate the convenience of the automated AI approach. At the same time, many feel distanced, disrespected and disgruntled with the digital-first focus.

Meanwhile, behind closed doors, politicians and public servants are facing the pressure for their departments to keep up with technological advancements. Yet, they are also concerned about the radically different value judgments. Who is right? Who gets to decide? Moreover, how do we navigate these competing perspectives?

This scenario illustrates the multifaceted challenge of determining and delivering value in public sector environments, also known as public value.

What Is Public Value?

> Public value involves complex interactions between outcomes such as efficiency, equity, legitimacy, and even democratic accountability (Moore, 1995).

Public value is the value that government organisations create for society through the delivery of policies, services and actions. Unlike private sector contexts, where value can often be reduced to profit margins or industry share, public sector value does not rest on such simple market-based metrics. Instead, public value is measured by the extent to which services are delivered efficiently and effectively, collectively desired social outcomes are achieved and trust and legitimacy are established.

As it *"is consumed collectively by the citizenry rather than individually by clients or customers."* (ANZSOG, 2017), the question on public value is not simply whether something works—it is whether it works for whom, under what circumstances, and according to whose definition of success. It is not just about whether taxpayer dollars have been well spent, but whether the people who pay the taxes feel like they have been well served.

Public value is one of the fundamental pillars of our government institutions, and core to their continued legitimacy. However, the notion is also characterised by conceptual ambiguity, competing definitions and assessments, and methodological challenges in measurement, making it a notion that is *"much debated in a democratic society."* (ANZSOG, 2017).

Given both the importance and conflict around public value, it is a topic that has been comprehensively researched and documented by many reputable experts. Therefore, it must be noted that the purpose of this chapter is not to try and cover the field of public value in its vast detail, but to introduce the idea of value as a characteristic of creativity and provide an overview of some key frameworks for your consideration.

Moore's Strategic Triangle

The most famous model of public value is Professor Mark Moore's Strategic Triangle (Moore, 1995), illustrated below. It shows that achievement of public value is dependent upon whether the agency has:

- Legitimate authority and support for the change (known as the authorising environment).
- The ability to implement the idea and the skills to make success sustainable (known as operational capabilities).

Figure 3 - Moore's strategic triangle model

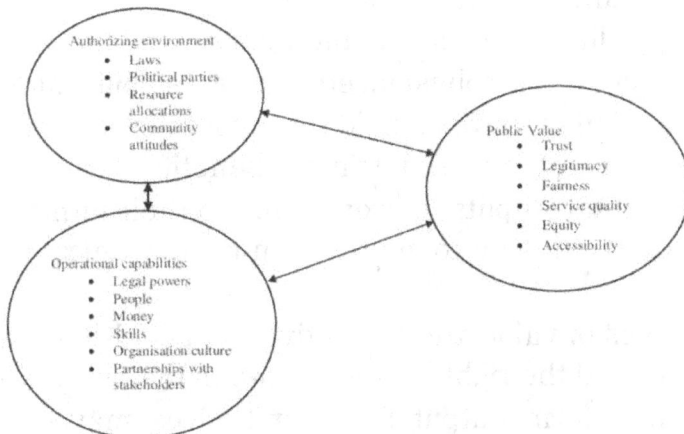

Moore's model makes it clear that public value goes well beyond service quality to encompass such things as: effectiveness, transparency, participation, integrity and lawfulness (Jørgensen & Bozeman, 2007). It shows us that public value extends beyond tangible indicators to encompass broad democratic and social considerations that may not be captured in traditional performance metrics.

Instrumental and Intrinsic Value

One useful typology for understanding the different types of public value identified by Moore is the instrumental/intrinsic distinction.

Instrumental value refers to the short-term, tangible, and measurable benefits gained from an activity or improvement initiative. They include benefits such as increased efficiency, cost savings, and enhanced customer satisfaction. They are named instrumental because while they are essential, they are also elementary, serving not as an end in themselves, but as a tool to achieve other outcomes (Thabit et al., 2025).

Intrinsic value is the longer-term outcome that results from the instrumental value, and which is core to success and sustainability. It includes intangible benefits such as trust, legitimacy, social cohesion, equity, accessibility and democratic participation, and which hold value for their own sake. Often, the importance of these intrinsic benefits far outweighs the instrumental outputs; however, due to their immaterial nature, they can be difficult to measure and communicate effectively.

Both types of value are imperative, with decisions needing to be made to find the right balance between the two. Because if there is a short-term output focus, initiatives may be targeted at improving efficiency and cost, but at the expense of customer capability and stakeholder trust. Some technology transformations fall into this category, where there is a rush to deliver new solutions without adequate consideration for the impacts on people's perceptions of credibility, care and integrity.

Likewise, agencies may place all their efforts into creating intrinsic value, working hard on building relationships and public participation, but without tangible improvements in services to show for it, they are then targets for claims of incompetence. Lengthy reform projects run the risk of falling into this trap, putting in the hard work of building foundations for change. However, if there is no evidence of effectiveness, the leaders will be accused of squandering taxpayers' money on a talkfest.

The reality is that we all want the grand ideals of truth, justice, wellbeing, and trust. However, we also want to be able to get help when, where, and how we want it, and not have governments waste our time.

Value Through The Eyes Of Stakeholders

Another way we can think about value is through the eyes of stakeholders (Amabile, 1996). Amabile's research shows that when assessing any new initiative, stakeholders will be weighing up the following elements of value:

- **Usefulness** addresses the fundamental question: *"Does the idea solve a real problem or deliver tangibly better outcomes?"* This dimension focuses on the instrumental benefits—measurable improvements in efficiency, effectiveness, or service quality that give the project both credibility and relevance.

- **Appropriateness** asks, *"Is this solution suitable for the context?"* It considers the initiative's coherence with the culture, environmental constraints, customer, client, or citizen expectations, as well as with other existing policies, strategies, or interventions.
- **Meaningfulness** considers, *"What's in it for me?"* This aspect recognises that people are looking for alignment with their values, personal goals, or sense of purpose. Rather than a logical indicator, this is more of an emotionally driven response that has a profound impact on their perception of value.

Assessing Value at Different Levels

Benefits may also vary depending on whether the individual, a group or the broader community is affected by the change. For example, housing reforms may negatively impact baby boomers who foresee decreasing property prices and investment returns. However, for the wider society, an increase in housing stock and affordability means that more people have access to this basic human right, improving health and wellbeing across the community. On this basis, we also need to consider value from the perspectives of the:

- **Individual**: personal benefits such as satisfaction for staff members or individual citizens. These benefits might include improved job satisfaction for an employee or enhanced convenience for a service user.
- **Collective**: encompasses group, team, or organisational benefits measured through improved performance, collaboration, and shared outcomes.
- **Public**: represents collective and societal interests served. It is value delivered beyond individual or specific group self-interest. It is consumed by and benefits the community as a whole.

Bringing It All Together - A Visual Value Summary

The value dimensions and levels presented previously do not operate in isolation; instead, they work interdependently to present a complete picture of value. We can see how these elements interact by mapping them on a matrix, an example of which is found in Figure 4.

This diagram shows the various dimensions of value (usefulness, appropriateness, and meaningfulness) against the levels at which the value is experienced (individual, collective, and public) and whether intrinsic or instrumental value is involved. By laying out these intersections, the matrix shows how an innovation might deliver value (or fall short) across multiple perspectives.

Mapping value delivered across all dimensions helps to identify the strengths of an initiative's value proposition, where changes are needed to balance the benefits and where investments must be made to improve meaningfulness, because as we will see in Section 3, this is a core factor in the motivation for change.

From this visual summary, it is also possible to envision a progression of value delivery, either across the dimensions, up the levels, or a diagonal movement that includes increases in both impact breadth and significance. By adjusting the project scope or enhancing change management, cultural, and communication activities, a project can escalate from a simple individual utility to a social impact.

> What is clear from this diagram is that lower-level value is foundational for higher-level impact, and small-scale change can feed into broader-scale success.

Figure 4 - A visual summary of value dimensions

Legend: ○ Instrumental value ○ Intrinsic value ● Both

	Individual	Collective	Public
Meaningfulness	**Personal fulfilment** Supports personal values, goals and growth aspirations, providing a sense of personal satisfaction and accomplishment.	**Shared purpose creation** Fosters a sense of shared mission among stakeholders by aligning group interests and encouraging collective ownership of objectives.	**Enhanced democratic legitimacy** Enhances democratic legitimacy by increasing transparency, inclusivity, and public trust in institutional processes and outcomes.
Appropriateness	**User experience fit** Ensures that the innovation matches users' expectations, needs, and everyday realities, offering intuitive and accessible user experiences.	**Team workflow compatibility** Integrates seamlessly with established team workflows and practices, supporting collaboration and minimizing disruption to existing processes.	**Policy alignment** Aligns with cultural expectations and policy frameworks, supporting institutional mandates while reinforcing legal and ethical standards.
Usefulness	**Personal efficiency/ effectiveness** Empowers individuals to be more productive, reducing effort for routine tasks or increasing effectiveness in higher-value activities.	**Team productivity boost** Strengthens team output, collaboration and achievement of goals more effectively and efficiently through better resource sharing.	**Service delivery improvement** Improves public service delivery by increasing reliability, accessibility, and quality of services provided to the broader community.

Planning Value Pathways

One useful tool to proactively plan value pathways is the service logic model, often employed in government performance frameworks. The service logic model illustrates how resources are transformed into desired outputs and outcomes. At each stage in the process, there is the potential for benefit to be created, with short-term and immediate actions contributing to overall long-term impact. The value pathway described in the service logic model follows this structure:

If inputs and activities produce outputs, this should lead to outcomes that will ultimately contribute to impacts.

The separate stages of the value pathway, along with the type of benefit being delivered in each, are presented in the following table.

It is important to note that the stages in the service logic model are not isolated or linear—each level is interdependent on the one beside it. For example, outcomes, such as employee engagement and customer satisfaction, become important inputs for future initiatives. Similarly, well-planned value at the input level can amplify the quality of outputs, outcomes, and impacts, creating a virtuous cycle of continuous improvement.

> The interconnectedness across stages means that value should be deliberately planned and managed at every step of the process. Ignoring the interdependencies risks creating isolated pockets of value that fail to realise their full potential or even negative outcomes that then feed into future cycles.

Table 4 - Value delivered through the service logic model

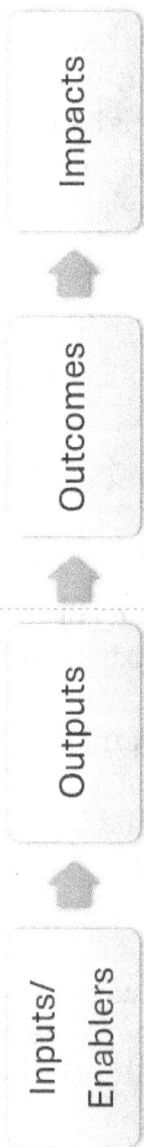

	Inputs/Enablers	Outputs	Outcomes	Impacts
Description	The financial, human, and material resources invested to deliver the activities, and which create the conditions for innovation to occur.	The direct, tangible products and services delivered as a result of the activity.	The short- to medium-term effects and changes resulting from the activity.	The long-term, systemic changes and transformations brought about by the activity encompassing lasting effects on organisational culture, leadership, environmental conditions, and broader societal benefits.
Value Type	Inputs/Enablers are fundamentally instrumental—they represent resources, capabilities, and investments that serve as means to achieve other goals. They include funding, human capital investments, and organisational capabilities that are valued for the products, processes and services they enable.	Outputs are predominantly instrumental, representing the direct, measurable products of activities—such as number of projects, people served, or costs born during the process. These outputs measure the efficiency of resource use and are a stepping stone to broader benefits.	Outcomes align more with intrinsic value as they capture meaningful changes in effectiveness measures such as service quality, user satisfaction, employee engagement, and organisational trust—benefits that have inherent worth beyond being means to other ends.	Impacts are where intrinsic value is most evident, encompassing long-term, systemic transformations in culture, identity, leadership, and purpose that are valuable in themselves—representing what organisations and societies become, not just what they achieve.

Proactively planned value pathways are incredibly powerful tools, ensuring that every investment, activity, and result contributes meaningfully to the overarching goals of tangible organisational performance and positive societal progress. They remind us that the path to impact is built incrementally but sustained through deliberate, coherent efforts at every layer of the value chain.

Distributed Public Value Creation

Before we move on from discussions on public value, it is important to mention the changes in how it is being delivered and the implications for public sector capabilities.

> The research recognises that the delivery of public value is increasingly becoming a shared responsibility of all societal sectors (Thabit et al., 2025). More public service initiatives are being implemented through multi-actor collaborative channels.

Collaborative governance—bringing public and private stakeholders together to plan and deliver public policy and services—is now the priority as governments realise that they cannot deliver the breadth or depth of value required in such a rapidly changing world. Increasingly, governments seek to build shared value networks with citizen, businesses, non-profits and other public agencies.

The result of this shift is that governments are also being called to enhance their capabilities in managing more complex social processes and distributed value creation. Specifically, with increasingly distributed value models, governments must rethink the input resources required and build the following competencies:

- **Multi-Actor Thinking**: Leaders must move beyond traditional government-centric approaches to embrace collaborative value creation involving *"citizens, businesses, and the third sector"* (Thabit et al., 2025). This expanded delivery model requires developing capabilities in stakeholder engagement, collaborative governance, and network management.

- **Strategic Governance Capabilities**: Rather than focusing solely on traditional management competencies, leaders need integrative leadership and strategic management capabilities that can effectively guide collaborative efforts and the shared delivery of public value.

- **Process-Outcome Integration**: Leaders must attend to both process-oriented and output-oriented value, recognising that *"the creation of public value crucially depends on the processes through which this materialises"* (Thabit et al., 2025). Not only do leaders need to consider what is to be delivered, but also who should be involved and the process characteristics that are important to achieve the overall objectives.

We will spend more time discussing collaborative governance in Chapter 30 when we consider the creative act of building connections. For now, though, it is important to recognise that more commonly, public value is not only being consumed, but created, collectively.

The Value Questions

As has become clear through this chapter, creativity's characteristic of value goes much deeper than output metrics and calls on you to consider how your decisions will serve diverse stakeholders, strengthen community trust, and deliver a lasting beneficial legacy.

The following questions may help guide your thinking about the value of your projects, ensuring your work is not only effective in the short term but also delivers meaningful, sustainable public value for the future.

- Whose voice is loudest when it comes to determining the value of an idea or initiative?
- How does this project benefit different stakeholders?
- Am I engaging a truly diverse range of voices in the planning and assessment of project value?
- Which instrumental benefits (like output statistics) am I prioritising and why?
- Are the intrinsic aspects of each initiative (such as trust, legitimacy, or inclusion) receiving enough attention?
- Are we realising the full potential of the intrinsic benefits from each of our projects? If not, what is preventing our projects from making a greater impact?
- Are we striking a balance between what can be measured now and what must be valued over the long term for lasting public benefit?
- How well do our evaluation tools and criteria allow us to understand both short-term achievements and enduring impacts?
- Are there opportunities for us to unlock new forms of value or to achieve it in different and more effective ways?

Value Requires Intelligent Investments

Through the last few chapters, we have seen that creativity is not just a light-hearted or whimsical pursuit (however, we must not dismiss the role of play in producing great ideas and delivering powerful inspiration). What we have seen is that creativity, at its core, is a rich combination of novelty and value, with emotion weaving through every aspect of its planning, delivery and assessment.

The complexity of both the novelty and value constructs means that striking the right balance between them takes incredible foresight, ingenuity, patience, and an ability to understand the connections between competing priorities. Moreover, when you think about the influence of emotions on value judgements it becomes clear a deep level of nous is required to balance conflicting views and guide stakeholders to support beneficial creative outcomes.

In this way, creativity is a mature discipline. It uses immense intellect and insight to deliver impact in ways that matter most to people and communities. Let us continue this theme to investigate the vast intelligence that lies behind creative endeavours.

4   Creativity Is Integrated Intelligence

"Creativity is intelligence having fun."
~ **Albert Einstein**

So far in this book, we have explored creativity as a complex interplay between novelty and value, examining how neither concept can be reduced to a single definition or discipline. We have seen that both dimensions require an expansive perspective, one that encompasses consideration of various perspectives, timelines, objectives, outputs and outcomes.

The ability to comprehend and balance these multiple dimensions requires incredible intellect. Therefore, we can see that creativity itself is not a single skill or narrow cognitive function but rather requires an integrated intelligence—a synthesis of our full intellectual, emotional, and social capacities.

The Vast Array Of Human Intelligence

To understand creativity as integrated intelligence, we must first recognise that intelligence itself is far from a singular notion. Howard Gardner's (1993) identified nine distinct types of intelligence, each representing different modes of thinking and understanding. His theory of multiple intelligences (MI) provides a robust framework for understanding the diverse ways humans process information and interact with their world.

What makes creativity so powerful is that it draws upon most, if not all, intelligences simultaneously and integrates them seamlessly, leading to a sense of wholeness and wellbeing.

Rather than relying on a single cognitive strength, creative work requires the orchestration and unification of the following intelligence toolkit.

Table 5 – Gardner's Nine Intelligences

Intelligence	Description
Linguistic	The ability to use language effectively for communication, including sophisticated skills in reading, writing, and speaking
Logical-mathematical	The capacity for deductive reasoning, problem-solving, and mathematical calculations.
Spatial	The ability to visualise and manipulate objects in three-dimensional space.
Bodily-kinaesthetic	The capacity to use one's physical body skilfully and handle objects with precision.
Musical	The ability to recognise, create, reproduce, and reflect on music, including sensitivity to rhythm, melody, and tone.
Interpersonal	The ability to understand and interact effectively with others.
Intrapersonal	Self-awareness and self-reflection, including the understanding of one's own emotions and motivations.
Naturalistic	The ability to recognise, categorise, and draw upon features of the natural environment.
Existential	The capacity to ponder deep questions about human existence, meaning, and purpose.

Far from being just an interesting theoretical model, research has confirmed that creativity does involve the integration of multiple intelligences into a unified cognitive process. Dawahdeh and

Mai's (2021) study demonstrates that engaging diverse intelligences activates and strengthens creative thinking abilities. People who draw on multiple intelligences during their thought processes (such as linguistic, logical, kinaesthetic, interpersonal, intrapersonal and natural intelligences) have more cognitive tools at their disposal to identify new and useful approaches.

This integrative nature of creativity is further supported by Scotney et al. (2019), who found that the majority (67%) of inspiration for creative activities came from outside the domain of the final creative product. Rather than relying on a single cognitive mode, creativity draws upon and synthesizes information from diverse areas of our lives, with creative outcomes emerging not from isolated expertise, but from the integration of diverse cognitive capabilities and life experiences.

The neurological research by Liu et al. (2024) also provides evidence that creativity involves the collaboration of multiple distributed brain networks. Using brain imaging, they found that creative thinking involves integration of such diverse brain systems as those for sensory information processing through to abstract, higher-level cognition.

The intellectual integration that occurs in creative activities explains why creativity feels so engaging and why creative solutions often possess a richness and sustainability that purely analytical approaches lack.

Creative approaches pull from a diverse range of perspectives, with each intelligence acting as a unique lens through which to look at problems. Combining the intelligences in different ways allows for a myriad of possible inspirations and solutions.

According to Dr. Gabor Maté (2003), the integration of mind, body, and emotions is fundamental to human wellbeing. Given that creativity inherently engages all three dimensions simultaneously, it serves as a mechanism for achieving this integration, making creativity not only personally satisfying, but also crucial for maintaining human health and wholeness.

While Gardner's model has been criticised for its lack of rigorous empirical validation, it has been applied in practical settings with exceptional results. Schools implementing MI approaches tailor learning to each student's intelligence strengths and find that those who struggled in traditional school environments experience significant improvements in engagement, motivation, academic achievement, and learning outcomes. Additionally, schools that invest effort in expanding the suite of dominant intelligences of their students also record higher overall academic success, well above those students with only a singular dominant intelligence (Yavich & Rotnitsky, 2020).

So, despite its technical limitations, the MI model is an effective tool in the real world. The following example provides another real-world example to show how creating a new policy approach draws upon numerous intelligences in order to address complex problems.

The Creative Process Of A Policy Analyst

Consider a senior policy analyst working on a multifaceted social policy challenge, such as developing a new approach to homelessness services. This professional does not simply apply their technical policy expertise or analytical capability in an isolated, two-dimensional manner. Instead, even without their awareness, they are engaging the entirety of their intelligence in an integrated, expansive, creative process.

Their linguistic intelligence enables them to craft effective research questions, gather and review evidence. It helps them develop consultation papers and policy documents that communicate complex ideas clearly to diverse stakeholders. They employ logical-mathematical intelligence to analyse data patterns, understand statistical relationships between causal factors and recorded effects, and construct evidence-based arguments for their advice. Spatial intelligence helps them map geographic patterns of need, visualise service delivery systems, and conceptualise how different program components would connect in practice.

The policy analyst's interpersonal intelligence enables an empathetic and human-centred approach, as well as effective stakeholder engagement. It aids them in understanding different perspectives, navigating political dynamics, and building coalitions for change. Their intrapersonal intelligence keeps them aware of and connected to their own values and purpose, ensuring the policy reflects a genuine commitment to public service and that their intrinsic motivation sustains them through the process.

Naturalistic intelligence might seem less relevant, but it plays a crucial role, as the analyst systematically observes environmental patterns affecting homeless individuals—such as the seasonal weather's impact on service demands and environmental risk factors like unsafe sleeping locations or areas lacking access to sanitation. They would recognise interconnected urban ecosystem patterns to propose holistic policy solutions addressing both immediate shelter needs and longer-term health considerations.

Meanwhile, existential intelligence is another essential component in their considerations, as they grapple with fundamental questions about human dignity, social responsibility, and the purpose of government intervention.

While musical intelligence (sensitivity to pitch, rhythm, melody, and musical patterns) may not seem directly relevant to policy development, the analyst might draw on this intelligence when evaluating programs that use music therapeutically (such as Sounds of Strength and the Music Kitchen) to understand how musical interventions work. Their recognition of how these programs increase socialisation, reduce isolation, and boost self-esteem reflects appreciation for music's psychological impact.

Similarly, bodily-kinaesthetic intelligence does not directly apply to policy analysis. Nevertheless, the analyst's body provides vital intelligence that is input to decisions. The gut and heart function as independent processing centres: the enteric nervous system processes information and provides intuitive signals ('gut feels'), while heart rate coherence enhances cognitive clarity and creativity (McCraty et al., 2004). Crucially, these pre-conscious somatic signals are not supplementary to decision-making, but integral to it. They provide the intuitive and emotional intelligence essential to holistic, nuanced and grounded policy development.

As this example illustrates, while the analyst was not even likely aware of the individual intelligences they were employing, it is through the effective use and coordination of all of them that they were able to develop policy recommendations that were not only technically sound but also emotionally resonant, politically viable, and socially meaningful. This is why I believe:

Creativity is an inspired form of integrated intelligence.

Fostering Diverse Intelligences

If organisations seek to enhance creativity, understanding that it emerges from the integration of multiple intelligences provides a powerful framework for designing practices that cultivate it. The following demonstrates how this knowledge can inform three critical areas in the public sector:

- Individual capability development
- Project team composition
- How we approach AI.

Individual capability development

As we have heard, the educational sector is well advanced in applying MI to achieve significant effects on student engagement and learning outcomes. The same approach can be taken in our workplaces to improve creative thinking and wellbeing.

Traditional training approaches tend to focus narrowly on single skills such as divergent thinking, communication techniques, or project management methods. Yet when we recognise that diverse intelligences are required to approach complex issues with integrity, we must similarly invest in fostering the full spectrum of human intelligence in our people.

Just as a policy challenge demands linguistic intelligence to communicate effectively, spatial intelligence to visualise solutions, interpersonal intelligence to understand stakeholder needs, and logical-mathematical intelligence to analyse data, our professional development can seek to cultivate multiple capacities rather than treating them as separate, optional competencies.

> A holistic approach to capability development ensures that when public sector teams face complex challenges, they can draw upon their full cognitive and emotional resources, creating the conditions for genuinely innovative and sustainable solutions that serve the public interest.

Project team composition

While we all understand that diversity delivers superior solutions, do we only focus on demographic differences, or do we also consider individual intelligence strengths in project team compositions?

While individual public servants can access all nine intelligences, they typically have stronger capabilities in some areas than others, creating natural cognitive specialisations that, when combined strategically, can produce teams with superior problem-solving and innovation capacity. Mixing intellectual preferences can lead to more thorough discussions, better-informed choices, and enhanced creativity, as different thinking styles approach challenges from multiple angles.

For example, a policy team addressing climate change would benefit from combining members with strong naturalistic intelligence (to understand environmental systems), logical-mathematical intelligence (to analyse data and models), linguistic intelligence (to communicate complex concepts), interpersonal intelligence (to engage stakeholders), and existential intelligence (to grapple with long-term meaning and purpose).

This diversity of approaches counters individual blind spots and excesses in thinking, creating what researchers call "cognitive team diversity" that enables teams to tackle complex problems more comprehensively and generate solutions that no single intelligence type could produce independently.

How we approach AI

Understanding creativity as integrated intelligence also has profound ramifications for how we view the contribution of AI in public sector projects. Currently, AI demonstrates capabilities primarily in four out of Gardner's nine intelligences (linguistic, logical-mathematical, musical, and spatial intelligence) while struggling significantly with the personal intelligences (interpersonal and intrapersonal), naturalistic intelligence, bodily-kinaesthetic intelligence, and existential intelligence. Therefore, AI lacks the lived experience, embodied awareness, and deep contextual understanding required for contextually relevant and emotionally resonant decision-making.

AI's limited intellectual capacity must therefore be carefully considered when planning to use AI as a project resource. Leaders must ensure that human intelligence fills the critical gaps in emotional understanding, cultural sensitivity, ethical reasoning, and the kind of intuitive, experiential wisdom that can only come from navigating complex social and environmental systems over a substantial period of time.

As we will see in the following section, an over-reliance on AI poses a real risk of learned helplessness in its human drivers and homogeneity in outputs, meaning that more than ever, investments in nurturing human creativity are crucial. It is time to truly celebrate the innate human intelligence that cannot be imitated.

Creativity Is Connection

In this chapter, we have seen how creativity is far more than one specific trait or skill, but a collection of and collaboration between many different intellects. We have witnessed through an example how undertaking a creative endeavour connects parts of ourselves that we may not be fully aware of.

In the following chapter, we will go further to see how creativity also acts as a connecting force far beyond ourselves, flowing between our colleagues, organisations and communities. We will discover that there are multiple layers of creativity that all influence and impact one another, and that need to work in unison for creativity to thrive. Creativity is not an isolated phenomenon, stemming simply from individual genius, but a connection between personal skills, team climates and entire cultures.

5 Creativity Is a Multi-Layered Phenomenon

Creativity is not just a product of individual genius, but a collaboration between personal confidence, team and organisational culture, and the surrounding social context.

In the previous chapters, we have learned that the components of creativity—novelty and value—are contextual, assessed differently depending on perspective and circumstance. Creativity is the same, not being a product of individual genius operating in isolation, but rather being shaped by personal capability, team dynamics, organisational culture, and the broader social environment.

> Creativity emerges (or does not) from the combination of personal skill and beliefs, leadership behaviour, organisational climate and societal characteristics. Creativity is, in essence, a social system—one that unfolds across and between multiple, interconnected layers.

The layers of the creativity system are shown in the following diagram. At the very heart of this system lies an individual's domain knowledge—the deep, personal, substantive expertise that provides the raw materials from which new ideas emerge. This domain core is essential because, as research consistently shows, people generate their most original ideas in areas where they hold deep expertise.

On top of domain knowledge rests creative skills, those cognitive processes and problem-solving techniques that enable deliver new and valuable results. Individual creative skills are important, but they are also bound by a person's creative self-belief, with creative confidence being the prime determinant of if and how these skills will be employed.

Figure 5 - The multiple layers of the creativity system

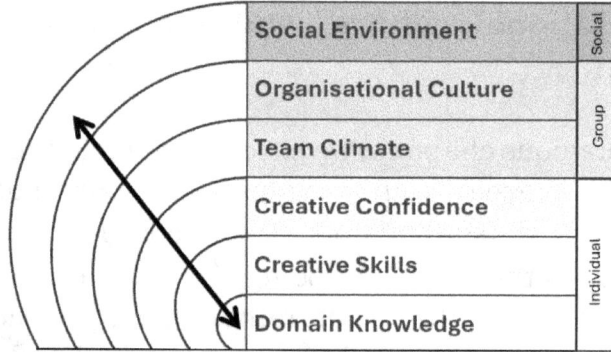

Domain Knowledge	• Expert knowledge specific to the professional field • Contextual understanding of field-specific problems, processes and solutions
Creative Skills	• Domain-specific creative techniques • Cognitive processes and problem-solving techniques
Creative Confidence	• Growth mindset: beliefs about whether creativity can be developed • Creative self-efficacy: confidence in one's own creative abilities • Intellectual risk-taking: willingness to engage in adaptive behaviours
Team Climate	• Supervisory encouragement and support • Peer collaboration and idea-sharing • Psychological safety for experimentation
Organisational Culture	• Values and norms around creativity • Risk tolerance and failure acceptance • Resource allocation for creative work
Social Environment	• Regulatory frameworks and constraints • Strength of cultural and creative sectors (CCS) • Cultural norms around creativity and innovation

Additionally, the influence of peers, managers, and the unspoken norms that comprise the team climate must be considered. Do they invite experimentation, or shut it down? Do they seek diverse views or solve problems in an insular fashion? Do they have a positive view of risk or prioritise predictability over improved performance?

Beyond the team, the outer layer of an organisation's culture sends powerful messages about what kinds of ideas are valued, who is allowed to innovate, and how risk is managed. It can either accommodate the anxiety that comes with the unknown or itself be an instigator of inhibitive fear.

Radiating outward still further, the broader social, political, and regulatory context, as well as community attitudes (as previously outlined in Moore's authorising environment), define the landscape in which public servants and institutions must operate and the boundaries of what is acceptable, all shaping what creative outcomes are actually adopted.

> Creative solutions can only go so far as the culture will allow. Therefore, part of the role of those seeking to effect social change is to shift the risk appetite within the communities they serve, so that they may be more amenable to alternative and valuable approaches.

Let us delve further into each layer of the creative system to understand how they interact to bring about change.

The Domain Knowledge Core

At the heart of the creativity model sits domain knowledge—the deep, substantive expertise and rich understanding of how a particular field operates. Through extensive experience, a person learns about the problems that typically arise, the solutions that have been tried before, and why certain approaches succeed or fail. This domain-specific expertise forms the essential raw material from which new ideas emerge, serving as the knowledge base that enables meaningful innovation (Amabile, 1996).

This knowledge base is crucial because creativity requires more than general thinking skills; it demands intimate familiarity with the constraints, opportunities, and evaluation criteria that define a particular professional domain. This dependency is why research consistently demonstrates that people generate their most original and valuable ideas within their areas of deep expertise (Baer, 2016).

In the public sector, where problems are often complex and solutions must navigate intricate regulatory and political landscapes, this domain knowledge becomes even more critical. It provides the contextual understanding necessary to generate ideas that are not just novel but also feasible, appropriate, and effective within the realities of public service delivery and stakeholder expectations.

Individual Creative Skill

Surrounding the domain knowledge core, we find the layer of individual creative skill. These are the practical techniques, cognitive processes, and disciplinary habits that enable individuals to transform their deep expertise into innovative solutions. Like domain knowledge, these skills are learnable.

Recent research suggests that training in brainstorming techniques, creative problem-solving, and systematic innovation approaches leads to observable improvements in an individual employee's ability to generate initiatives, enhance service delivery, and achieve cost savings (Alblooshi, 2024).

However, Baer's (2016) extensive research demonstrates that creativity skills are highly domain-specific and connected to their professional contexts. There are "vanishingly small" correlations between creative performance in different areas, and creativity skills have very limited transferability across domains or professional fields. Therefore, if we want to help people become more creative, we need to attend specifically to the domains in which we want to develop creativity, rather than assuming that general creative skills will transfer across fields.

For public sector professionals, this may include training in techniques such as divergent thinking for generating policy options, design thinking methodologies for improving customer service, lateral problem-solving approaches for addressing regulatory challenges, or systems thinking for complex inter-agency coordination.

Creative Confidence – The Self-Belief Layer

Suppose creative skills are the tools we use to change up our domain and do innovative work. In that case, creative self-beliefs are the operating system that determines whether we ever pick up those tools, how we use them, and how we respond when things go wrong. This layer encompasses the beliefs individuals hold about creativity itself, their own creative capacity, and their ability to manage risks as they arise. Rather than representing a single construct, creative confidence comprises three distinct but interconnected components:

1. **Growth creative mindset**: A growth creative mindset is the belief that creativity can be developed through attention, effort and practice. With a growth creative mindset, people are willing to engage in creative tasks because they are perceived as an opportunity to build new skills. They are also more persistence when initial attempts are unsuccessful because they see failure as a chance to learn, not as a personal judgement (Karwowski, 2014).

Holding a growth mindset about creativity is positively associated with better creative thinking performance because it enables people to engage in activities where they can practice creative skills, be open to receiving feedback, and take steps to improve (OECD, 2024). In contrast, a fixed creative mindset believes that you are either inherently creative or not, and that there is nothing you can do to change this characteristic. With a fixed creative mindset, people do not even try to develop creative skills or quit when challenges arise, thereby losing the opportunity to build creative capability.

2. **Creative self-efficacy**: Creative self-efficacy is the confidence a person has in their own creative abilities. Creative self-efficacy is a significant predictor of creative performance in organisational settings, with individuals who have higher creative self-efficacy found to generate more ideas, develop more novel solutions, and implement new and valuable approaches to tasks (Gong et al., 2009; Jaiswal & Dhar, 2017). They are also more likely to initiate creative projects, set challenging creative goals, persist through difficulties, and recover from setbacks (Pretz & Nelson, 2017).

3. **Intellectual risk-taking (IRT)** completes the triad by serving as the critical activator that translates confidence into action. Beghetto's (2019) research reveals that IRT—the willingness to engage in adaptive behaviours like sharing tentative ideas or attempting new approaches that place one at risk of mistakes—is essential for converting creative potential (self-efficacy) into creative behaviour. Action does not happen without the willingness to take risks.

These findings hold important implications for creativity training interventions. While investing in specific creative skills is beneficial, without equal support to build growth mindsets, creative self-efficacy through practical experience, and support for risk taking, these skills may deliver little tangible benefit.

Figure 6 - The three elements of creative confidence

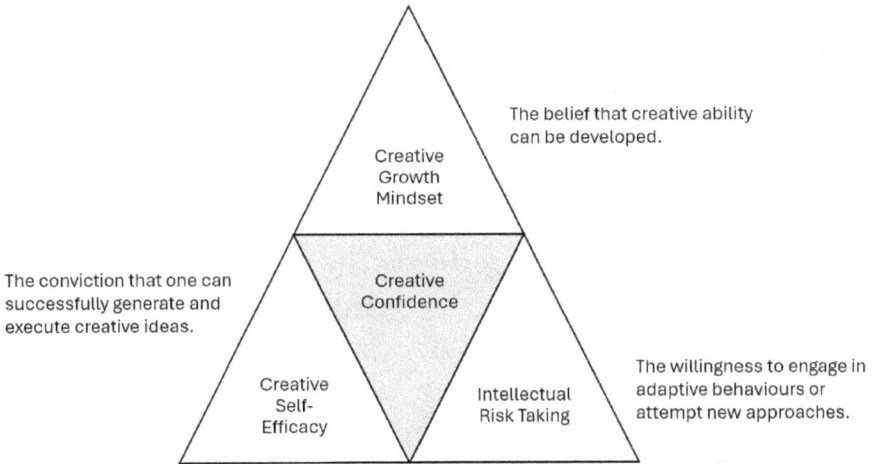

Team Climate – The Micro-Environment of Creativity

It is undeniable that creativity ultimately unfolds within social contexts. The team climate—the immediate work environment created by supervisors, peers, and local practices—can either amplify or suppress an individual's creative potential, regardless of their personal capabilities and level of confidence.

> Even highly skilled individuals with strong creative self-beliefs may produce little innovation in environments that lack support. At the same time, those with modest capabilities can flourish when planted in places where there are consistent safety and sponsorship.

The most comprehensive and empirically validated model for understanding team climate is the KEYS framework developed by Teresa Amabile and her colleagues (Amabile et al., 1996). Based on extensive research across organisational settings, this framework identifies six key dimensions of work environment that consistently predict creative outcomes, four of which are directly relevant to team climate:

1. **Encouragement of Creativity**. The degree to which employees feel supported and motivated by supervisors and peers to generate novel ideas, exemplified by constructive feedback, provision of meaningful challenges, psychological safety and recognition of creative effort.
2. **Autonomy/Freedom**. The extent to which individuals have independence in deciding how and when to conduct their work, such as flexible schedules, freedom to experiment with new approaches and processes, and discretion over task methods.
3. **Resources**. The availability of sufficient materials, time, information, and training required to pursue creative work, including access to relevant technology, an appropriate budget for projects, and educational workshops.
4. **Pressures.** The perceived level of time constraints, workload, and performance demands can either motivate or inhibit creativity. Creative engagement is limited when excessive workload demands leave no time or mental energy for experimentation, while moderate deadlines can spur focus.

The KEYS research shows that creativity emerges from a complex interaction of supportive and inhibiting factors rather than from any single environmental characteristic. Teams can have adequate resources and autonomy, for example, but still struggle with creativity if supervisory encouragement is lacking or if excessive workload pressures create stress that narrows cognitive focus.

Organisational Culture – Values, Rules, and Risk Norms

Organisational culture plays a vital role in shaping the creative capacity of individuals and teams through the shared values, rules, and norms that define what is possible, permissible, and rewarded. Organisational culture is encompassed by the remaining two components of Amabile's KEYS framework: organisational impediments and organisational encouragement. These stand out as critical forces that either suppress or catalyse creativity at scale.

1. **Organisational impediments** refer to structural or procedural obstacles that stifle creativity, even in the presence of capable people and good ideas. In the public sector context, these include rigid vertical reporting hierarchies, excessive bureaucracy, overly prescriptive protocols with limited discretionary authority for frontline workers and cultural norms that frame failure as unacceptable (Borins, 2001).

2. **Organisational encouragement** reflects the broader cultural support and institutional values that signal creativity is desirable, valued, and rewarded. Organisations that exhibit high levels of encouragement typically have leadership that champions innovation, formal mechanisms for recognising creative contributions, allocation of time to explore alternatives and structures that enable rather than constrain cross-functional collaboration.

In sum, organisational culture serves as both a barometer and a blueprint for creative action. Where obstacles persist, even motivated innovators may retreat. Where encouragement thrives, faint ideas can grow into bold, transformative solutions.

Social Environment – Systemic and Institutional Forces

Even the most visionary leadership and conducive organisational systems still cannot drive innovation in isolation. Every organisation operates within a social environment comprising cultural norms, political dynamics, regulatory frameworks, education systems, and public narratives. This outer layer of the creativity system—the systemic and institutional context—can powerfully shape what creative actions are possible, permissible, and sustainable.

These societal conditions can act as either institutional barriers or enablers. For example, social inhibitors may include:

- A general belief that creativity is solely the domain of the arts. This belief limits the acceptance of interventions to nurture it across all communities and to establish the characteristics required for meaningful change.

- Public narratives that prioritise risk aversion, accountability, and cost efficiency. These priorities create fear around innovation, particularly when failure in the public domain attracts significant scrutiny.

- Regulatory frameworks that overvalue compliance, standardisation, and procedural correctness. These frameworks stifle experimentation, even when innovation is rhetorically encouraged.

- Education systems that rely on standardised testing. Such systems' reduce creative capacity and stifle students' development of the confidence, curiosity, and interdisciplinary thinking required to navigate ambiguity and generate novel solutions (Sternberg, 2015).

Examples of social and institutional supports for creativity include:

- SME training to support innovation. For example, Australia's CSIRO "Innovate to Grow" program helps small and medium enterprises in the plastics and recycling industries develop practical skills in research and development, project design, and collaboration.

- Community-level celebration of individuals who take risks to make things better. Public recognition, such as awards, showcases, and positive storytelling, helps shift cultural norms, reduces the stigma of failure, and inspires others to pursue new solutions to shared problems.

- Targeted investments in the Cultural and Creative Sectors. Including direct funding for the arts, cultural festivals, creative hubs, and public workshops. These play a crucial role in opening opportunities for the broader community to participate in creative expression, share knowledge and disseminate creative skills.

- Cross-sector partnerships and networks. These are powerful enablers of creativity in Australia. For example, the Melbourne Innovation Districts partnership links local councils, the University of Melbourne, and RMIT, and pools participants' resources to create a vibrant ecosystem that supports experimentation in urban innovation and creative enterprise.

- Open access to knowledge and creative tools. For example, through investment in public libraries, digital learning hubs, and makerspaces. Networks like the Australian Makerspaces provide free or low-cost access to equipment, technology, and skills training. National platforms such as Trove (from the National Library of Australia) and government open data portals ensure that information is widely available for creative exploration and research.

These types of policy signals matter—they work individually and collectively to represent the broader "authorising environment" for public innovation that we have previously discussed (Moore, 1995), shaping not only what public servants can do but also what they feel permitted to do.

Creativity Flows Across Levels

As we have seen throughout this chapter, creativity does not originate from a single ingredient—neither individual genius, team chemistry, nor supportive leadership or societies alone. Instead, creativity emerges from a dynamic system that involves constant interaction between multiple layers: personal skills and confidence, team and organisational culture, and the broader social culture.

Also, as shown by the bi-directional flow lines on the diagram, creativity does not move in a straight line—it circulates, feeds back into neighbouring layers, amplifies, and sometimes hits barriers.

Each layer shapes and is shaped by the others. When multiple enablers align—such as supportive leadership, strong team dynamics, a psychologically safe climate, and a supportive organisational and societal culture—the creative system functions as a virtuous loop that multiplies potential.

In contrast, where misalignment occurs, friction and stagnation can result. If not acknowledged and addressed, this can constrain even the most creative and motivated contributors.

In this way, we can see creativity not just as a capability, but as an energy. Creativity flows within and across levels, either finding barriers or bridges along its course. We can witness it being blocked by fear and fatigue or amplified with care and courage.

Creativity acts like an energy in so many ways. It is felt as inspiration, observed as change, and measured in momentum. And so, in the next chapter, we focus on the flow of creativity, examining it not as a set of discrete components or capabilities, but as an energy that is eternal and ever-present.

6   Creativity Is An Energy

Creativity is an energy. It is the ability to do work, where the work is developing something new and valuable. It is also the capacity which brings about meaningful change.

Having explored creativity as a multi-layered phenomenon, we can see that creativity is not just a static skill or structural capacity within any one layer. It can be seen more holistically as a potential that is animated across layers and, when enabled by the right conditions, drives creative action. Creativity flows back and forth between individuals, teams, and institutions, generating innovation. In this way, it is possible to see creativity as an energy, a dynamic power that moves through people, organisations, and communities to create change.

The definition of energy is,

"the ability to do work or cause a change." (U.S. Department of Energy, 1992)

At every moment, we are experiencing some form of energy. We feel its influence in the heat of the sun and see its impact on weather systems. We use light energy to guide our everyday actions, just as plants use it to power the process of photosynthesis. Over days and decades, we see wind and wave energy shaping landscapes and shifting ecosystems. Chemical energy from food is converted into kinetic energy and heat, enabling us to think, move, and regulate our body temperature. The chemical energy stored in fuels—such as petrol, natural gas, or wood—is released to heat our homes and make our vehicles move. The heart uses electrical energy to coordinate muscle contraction and pump blood throughout our bodies. Electrical energy enlivens both our kitchen appliances and entire cities. Energy is the fundamental force behind every process in the universe, from the beating of our hearts to the formation of galaxies.

> Just like energy, creativity is the ability to do work, specifically the work of developing something new and valuable. And like energy, creativity can cause change. In fact, creativity has been the driving force behind every single development in human history, from the design of your chair to the significant advances in social justice.

Consider the development of the scientific method, the courageous civil rights movements, and innovations in sustainable energy. There are also new styles of fashion, art, music and theatre and their effects on modern culture. Also, consider inventions such as the printing press, personal computers, the internet, and social media. Every single one of these advancements, some of which we now take for granted, resulted from the application of creative energy.

Does Creativity Pass the Energy Test?

By definition alone, creativity passes the energy test. It is the ability to do work and make a change. However, thanks to the wonderful world of science, we have a more comprehensive understanding of energy's characteristics. It has been investigated in depth and experimented with endlessly, and we now have eleven criteria for what constitutes energy. These are shown in the following table, along with how creativity also exhibits these same characteristics.

Table 6 - How creativity meets the characteristics of energy

Characteristic of Energy	Description	How Creativity Aligns
Transformative	Energy drives change, altering states, materials, and conditions.	Creativity transforms ideas, materials, individuals and societies, leading to innovation and change.
Transferable	Energy moves between systems, objects, and environments.	Creativity spreads through partnerships, teams and communities through collaboration, influence, and inspiration.
Conserved (Cannot Be Created or Destroyed)	Energy changes form but always persists, following the principle of conservation.	Creativity does not disappear; it evolves, is adapted, and continues in different forms. Or it is blocked and builds up until something bursts.
Manifests in Multiple Forms	Energy exists in various states such as kinetic, potential, thermal, electrical, etc.	Creativity appears in many modes including artistic, scientific, problem-solving, collaboration and connection.
Requires Activation or a Source	Energy needs an initial force or trigger to be released.	Creativity requires a spark, such as curiosity, challenge or collaboration.
Can Be Stored and Released	Energy can exist in a dormant state and be activated when needed.	Creativity can be latent during certain periods of life but released when conditions allow.
Operates Within Systems	Energy functions as part of larger ecosystems, whether biological, mechanical, or cosmic.	Creativity operates in a system comprised of individual creators, teams, organisations, professions and societies.
Can Be Harnessed and Directed	Energy can be controlled, optimized, and focused for specific purposes.	Creativity can be focused through disciplined practice and utilised for specific projects.
Creates Ripple Effects	Energy radiates outward, influencing its surroundings and causing further interactions.	Creativity spreads, influencing people, industries, and entire historical eras.
Can Be Measured (Directly or Indirectly)	Energy is quantified in units like joules or watts, though some forms have indirect indicators of impact.	While not measured in physical units, creativity can be measured through inputs, processes, outputs and outcomes.
Has an Entropic Nature	Energy tends to spread out and dissipate unless actively contained or managed.	Creativity can fade if not nurtured and people slide into cultural conformity.

This table shows that creativity ticks all the boxes when it comes to meeting the characteristics of energy. Like energy, creativity is transformative, transferable, and conserved—it changes form, spreads between people and communities, and never truly disappears.

Even in the darkest times of human history, it has not been decimated but through arts, cultural movements and innovative communication has been used courageously to rally people's power, bring about hope, subvert the oppressors and restore peace.

Creativity also manifests in multiple forms, requires activation, can be stored and released, and as shown in the previous chapter, operates within larger systems, be it teams or national cultures.

Creativity can also be harnessed, directed, and measured through its impact, creating ripple effects that influence society. Think about innovation labs, think-tanks, roundtables, artistic communities and conferences. All these mechanisms work to activate creative energy, concentrate it to address a challenge, and, through collaboration, amplify the available energy and outcomes.

Without nurturing, creativity, it can be diluted and dissipated but never destroyed. We may, for whatever reason, choose to block its flow, but it will always continue to exist as a potential.

> Together, these parallels make a compelling case that creativity is not just like energy—**it is an energy** that shapes and sustains all human progress.

How Creative Energy Effects Change

To see how creativity works as an energy, let's consider a customer service unit tasked with improving service engagement and effectiveness. Through looking at the concepts of potential, activation, expression, entropy, amplification, and blockage, we can understand the mechanisms of creative change.

Potential: The Foundation

The staff in this customer service unit possess an existing store of creative potential—the latent capacity, capability, and willingness to make improvements and deliver better outcomes for their communities. This potential exists as stored energy, present but not yet mobilised. It represents what *could* happen if conditions allow it to be activated. This potential exists as deep experience about customer needs, knowledge about where existing processes fail, ideas about better ways to serve their customers and confidence that they could implement change.

Activation: The Spark

Creative potential transforms into progress when triggered by an activation mechanism. This spark could come in the form of a new leadership mandate, citizen needs that create urgency, an individual officer taking independent initiative, or cross-departmental collaboration that brings diverse perspectives together. In this case, activation occurs when new leadership arrives with a mandate to improve service quality and the willingness to support the team in delivering change.

The activation releases creative energy that becomes available to flow through the team, generating ideas, building momentum, and changing how services are delivered. Without activation, potential remains dormant. However, activation does not guarantee results—it must be sustained and directed through expression.

Expression: The Creative Flow

When creative energy is allowed to flow and be expressed, it becomes transformative. It does not merely produce new ideas; it fundamentally changes the people involved—shifting previously constrained mental models, increasing confidence in their ability to contribute to change, and deepening their connection to the purpose of public service.

In the customer service team, this appears as frontline staff who previously felt powerless now confidently suggesting process improvements, supervisors becoming collaborative problem-solvers rather than rule-enforcers, and the entire unit reimagining what citizen-centred service could look like.

This expression manifests through multiple intelligences working in integration:

- Logical and linguistic intelligences develop policies, plans, and problem-solving frameworks—the customer service team uses these to document new procedures and communicate changes clearly to citizens.
- Intrapersonal intelligence fosters connections through co-design and collaboration—team members engage deeply with each other and citizens to understand needs and co-create solutions.
- Spatial and naturalistic intelligences inform the redesign of service spaces and citizen interfaces—the team redesigns waiting areas, reorganises workflow, and creates more intuitive pathways for citizens to access services.
- Bodily-kinaesthetic intelligence emerges in physical service delivery processes and workflow innovations—

staff implement new greeting protocols, reorganise physical documentation systems, and develop smoother handover processes.

As discussed in previous chapters, the most effective responses integrate several diverse forms of creative energy rather than relying on any single approach.

Amplification: Exponential Expansion

Creative energy does not remain confined to its source. When expressed successfully, it amplifies across networks, transferring to colleagues and teams beyond the original group. When others see that positive change is possible, perceived risk decreases. The team's success provides permission for others to activate their own creative energy.

Enthusiasm and methods spread to other parts of the agency or to entirely new organisations—a process known as diffusion. The customer service team's visible improvements—faster resolution times, higher citizen satisfaction scores, reduced complaints— signal to other teams that change is achievable. These adjacent teams begin experimenting with similar approaches in their own contexts. The energy that drove initial experiments transfers to new contexts, creating momentum for broader change. However, this amplification depends on receivers' openness to overcoming fear and risk, and on the existence of organisational systems that support continued flow.

Blockage: When Energy Is Constrained

Creative potential and energy become slowed or blocked when activation mechanisms are absent or when activated energy encounters barriers. This occurs when:

- There is no leadership impetus, sense of urgency, or compelling purpose for change.
- The team's ideas encounter decision-makers unwilling to bear risks or commit resources.
- Organisational systems and cultures actively suppress creative expression.
- Communities or social groups reject or resist change.

For the customer service team, blockages might be: new leadership arriving with different priorities; higher-level decision makers rejecting the proposals as too risky, or budget constraints preventing implementation of planned changes. In this case, the team is advised there is no money for the improvements they were proposing, and they must focus their time instead on business-as-usual. The team's creative potential retreats but now accompanied by a healthy dose of cynicism about the possibility of meaningful change. The blocked energy dissipates into disappointment, disillusionment and likely, disengagement.

Entropy: The Natural Dissipation of Energy

Like physical energy systems, creative systems tend toward entropy—they gradually dissipate unless actively maintained. Initial enthusiasm for innovation naturally fades without reinforcement. Novel processes become routine. Cross-functional teams that sparked fresh thinking settle into predictable patterns and become comfortable.

Without ongoing attention, the customer service team risks this happening to them too. The danger is that they become institutionalised and suppress their creative spark. The excitement of co-design fades into compliance; citizens' genuine participation replaced by token consultation. New staff are trained not to question but maintain the status quo.

Entropic tendency is not failure—it is a natural characteristic of energy systems. The solution lies not in attempting to prevent entropy, but in caring consistently for these energy systems and building sustainable activation mechanisms that continuously renew creative energy. Effective interventions that can help maintain inspiration include:

- Regular rotation of team memberships to introduce fresh perspectives and expose them to different ways of working.
- Periodic exposure to external ideas and practices—site visits to other innovative services; attending conferences; engaging with research on emerging best practices.
- Ongoing professional development—training in design thinking, facilitation, systems thinking keeps creative tools and mindsets alive.
- Recognition systems celebrating creative contributions— acknowledging not just successful innovations but the effort and risk-taking involved.
- Leadership practices that consistently reinforce the value of creative contribution—leaders who model curiosity, ask "what if" questions, and visibly act on staff suggestions.

Implications for Public Sector Leadership

Understanding creativity as energy fundamentally shifts how public sector leaders approach cultivating creativity. Rather than solely focusing on building individual creative skills or implementing new processes, leaders must attend to all the conditions that activate and sustain the flow of creative energy.

This role entails leaders being willing to accept the following responsibilities, which will be discussed in further detail in Section 3.

1. **Nurturing potential**. Enhancing the domain and creative skills of their people and investing in building creative confidence.
2. **Activating creative energy**. Sparking the motivation for change and inspiring people to expend their effort on developing new and valuable solutions.
3. **Allowing creative flow**. Recognising and removing energy blocks—the bureaucratic obstacles, risk-averse policies, and cultural norms that impede the flow of creative energy.

> As described by the OECD the role of a leader is to ensure that the:
> *"Right people with the right skills and talents are working in the right ways to maximise creative energy."*
> *(OECD, 2017b, p.37)*

Leaders must think less like commanders and more like electrical engineers, designing systems that enable energy to flow where it is needed most and identifying what blocks its effectiveness. In this way, leaders are creators themselves—of the skills, structures and systems that spark and sustain creativity.

Creativity as Unlocking Potential

Viewing creativity as energy transforms it from a specialised capability into a universal power available to every person, agency, community and country. Like other forms of energy, creativity is always present—it may be dormant, blocked, or misdirected, but it never disappears entirely.

This view delivers a positive perspective for organisations currently struggling with innovation and provides a framework for activating and amplifying dormant creative potential. It is not that these individuals or institutions are not creative, but rather that there are constraints on potential, a lack of activating mechanisms and conditions corrupting its flow.

Seeing creativity as an energy provides the impetus for investing at all levels of the creative system, building potential through creative confidence and investigating all sections of the wiring to identify and remove blockages, including societal paradigms that may impede potential. In this way, boosting creativity becomes a holistic and expansive exercise, one that duly matches the universal nature of creativity itself.

Most importantly, the energy perspective connects individual creative acts to larger systems of change. When public servants harness their creative energy to serve citizen needs, they participate in a broader transformation process that extends far beyond their immediate work. They become part of a dynamic system that continuously adapts public institutions to meet evolving challenges and opportunities.

It is this greater sense of purpose and contribution to their communities that delivers the personal fulfilment and drive to continue their creative work and make meaningful change. Through tapping into their creative energy, and allowing it to flow, they can find an ever-present source of inspiration and motivation.

7 Creativity Is What You Believe It To Be

"Our beliefs are like unquestioned commands, telling us how things are, what's possible and impossible and what we can and cannot do. They shape every action, every thought and every feeling that we experience." ~ **Tony Robbins**

As we have seen in the section discussing creative self-belief, the ultimate influence on our relationship with creativity lies within our own minds. While the previous chapters have shown what researchers have determined creativity to be, in reality, creativity is whatever you believe it to be. This assertion might seem overly simplistic, but it reflects a profound psychological reality supported by decades of research in cognitive science, social psychology, and neuroscience.

> The beliefs we hold about creativity—its nature, our abilities, and its relevance to our work—shape our creative experiences more powerfully than any external condition.

The understanding that beliefs shape reality has ancient philosophical roots, with the first Hermetic principle of Mentalism, originating around the year 200 BCE, stating, *"All is Mind"*. This law asserts that through our thoughts, we actively create the world we experience. This ancient wisdom has found compelling validation in contemporary psychological research, which is now embedded within the Cognitive Behavioural Therapy (CBT) model shown on the following page.

Figure 7 - The Cognitive Behavioural Therapy (CBT) Model

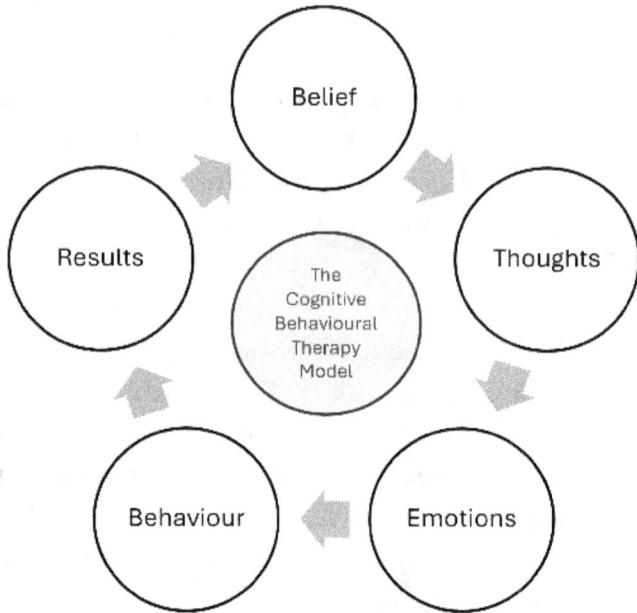

The CBT model provides a clear framework for how beliefs drive thoughts, emotions, and behaviours—ultimately determining our everyday experiences and outcomes (Beck, 1979). Within this framework, beliefs function as cognitive schemas that filter and interpret experience, creating self-reinforcing cycles that make our expectations increasingly likely to become manifest.

Crucially, a belief does not need to be factually accurate to influence behaviour—it only needs to be accepted as true. There is no better evidence for this than the placebo effect. Individuals who are given simple sugar pills but who genuinely believe they have received effective treatment show measurable improvements in conditions ranging from pain and fatigue to depression and even Parkinson's disease symptoms (Benedetti, 2009).

This is because, once internalised, beliefs operate as invisible forces that bend our perceptions, guide our attention, and shape our responses to challenges and opportunities. Our minds tend to avoid conflict, so we seek out information that supports our viewpoint and act on information that is consistent with what we already think to be true. The outcome then becomes predictable, but also assuring – see, we were right all along. By focusing our attention and action to support our beliefs, we have ensured that we walk away less challenged and conflicted and have preserved energy for other priorities.

If beliefs can lead to significant alterations in our physiological processes, then imagine the power they can exert over other psychological processes, such as creative thinking, risk tolerance, willingness to experiment, motivation, persistence and performance.

Leadership Beliefs Have Broad Impacts

As leaders, there are even greater ramifications, with the impact of our beliefs extending further and having broader consequences. Our beliefs shape the development and expression of others' creative potential in ways that can be either helpful or harmful. For example, the assumptions we make about others' creativity have a direct influence on who we assign to certain tasks, what we expect from them, and where training and development efforts are employed.

If you believe certain members of your staff are dull and do not have any creative potential, then this is exactly what that staff member will become. Because with this assumption about them in mind, you will either subconsciously or overtly decide not to waste development funds upon them or assign them to creative projects. In this way, they will not be provided the opportunity to learn new skills or to apply them in practice, missing out on experiences that will help them build creative confidence.

This belief about your staff member has become their career sentence. Yet, it is likely that you know nothing about how they spend their free time. They may have hobbies or community roles in which they have developed relevant and transferable skills. They may be creating new and valuable things all the time. Still, your one, uninformed belief about them has compromised the potential of this person, and of your team.

Additionally, your beliefs about the situation at hand also determine how you make decisions. If you are adamant that there is no scope for a creative solution, then you will not seek one. Wherever there is the assumption that this is just routine work with no time or ability for improvement, then that is exactly what it will become. The result? You will be surrounded by the mundane and then wonder why your people lack motivation or dynamism.

Similarly, suppose you believe that the "superiors" do not want to bear any risk or that you may suffer reputational damage from proposing something new. In that case, you will be less likely to use your creative energy, as you would be unwilling to expose yourself to the social and professional harm that could come from adverse feedback on your recommendations. Your belief that the higher-level leaders would not like creative solutions means that they never get the chance to consider them or practice courageously acting on them.

Challenging Your Beliefs

Therefore, if you seek to increase the creative capability within your own organisation, taking the time to reflect on your beliefs first becomes essential. Thus, here is an invitation for you to stop for a moment and consider the following:

- What do I believe creativity is?
- Who do I think is creative in my organisation—and why?
- Do I see myself as creative? What is shaping that belief?
- When problems arise, do I look for new ideas or default to known solutions and routine processes?
- How do my beliefs about creativity show up in how I lead and collaborate?
- What belief about creativity might I need to change to meet future challenges?
- What problems related to innovation or improvement is my organisation currently facing? How could my beliefs be contributing to these challenges?

The answers to these questions may be insightful but simply asking them is an important exercise in self-awareness, which we will see soon is a critical antecedent to your own creative capability.

Where Belief Becomes Impact

This chapter has explored how our understanding of creativity—shaped by our beliefs, mental models, and the frameworks we choose to apply—fundamentally influences our capacity to harness its power. Whether working in policy development, service delivery, regulatory oversight, or community engagement, public servants who believe in creativity—their own and others'—become part of the solution to the complex challenges facing democratic societies.

> The question is not whether you have creative potential, but whether you believe you do—and what you will do with that belief. Similarly, the question is not whether your agency can change to become more innovative, but whether you believe it can.

As we move forward, it becomes crucial to understand why creativity matters so profoundly in the public sector, not just as an abstract concept, but because of what it can deliver for the communities you serve.

In the next section, we will explore how creativity serves as the foundation for public sector effectiveness and relevance in an increasingly complex world—how it drives productivity, innovative problem-solving, fosters community resilience, and is at the heart of collaborative partnerships. We will delve into the inevitable destruction and risk that comes with all creative activity and explore the mechanism through which creativity is enacted — courage.

This understanding of how creativity drives public sector change is crucial, as it comes with the knowledge that creativity is central to all government work, and must be nurtured within every public sector agency. Creativity is not a nice-to-have. It is core to your organisation's ability to achieve excellent community outcomes and for you to make the contribution to the community that only you can.

2

HOW CREATIVITY POWERS ALL PUBLIC SECTOR CHANGE

We now know creativity's fundamental characteristics – novelty and value. In this section we will see, that even if it is not explicitly stated, this ability to come up with new and beneficial approaches is at the heart of achieving all public sector goals.

This section shows how creativity brings about change, looking at both its direct and indirect influences. We will see how it is the initiator of innovation and how it empowers productivity, two outcomes vital for national prosperity.

We will also come to understand how creativity powers change indirectly, through its positive influence on problem-solving, its contribution to building strong and positive relationships and through the way it fosters personal and community resilience.

Finally, we will also investigate two key mechanisms through which creativity delivers change, being through risk/reward decisions and through destruction. Both processes can be uncomfortable and may explain in part some of the hesitation around creative pursuits and the inability to achieve the intended objectives from innovation projects.

8   Creativity Is Central To All Change

If you are in the business of innovation, transformation, reshaping, or reform, then you are in the business of creativity.

If you have scanned the news headlines lately or tuned into a recent press conference, you may have heard about the large government investments being made in innovation, and the wide-ranging economic reform programs in progress. There may have been updates about a digital transformation project or an announcement about the reshaping occurring within a government or one of its departments. Between the headlines, there may be sporadic reports about initiatives described as an improvement, modernisation, revitalisation, renewal or realignment.

What is important to realise is that while the terms chosen may be slightly different, each of these words signals one type of activity—change.

In some cases, the change involves the introduction of something completely new, while in others it is about stripping away what is no longer needed or simply rearranging existing pieces to enhance efficiency. However, despite the type of change described, they are all bringing about a new state of being.

Moreover, regardless of the terminology used to describe the change, they all (hopefully) share the intention to improve people's lives in some tangible way.

We have already heard in the previous section that creativity is the process of delivering ideas, solutions, products, structures or services that are both novel (new) and valuable (useful or meaningful). Therefore, every single one of these projects, whether an organisation-wide transformation or a single team process improvement, is an act of creativity.

Creativity is the force that brings all these things to fruition. It is just the scope and scale of the creativity applied that differs.

Additionally, when we delve deeper into the definitions of some popular public sector terms, such as innovation, transformation, reshaping and reform, it becomes clear that they all have creativity at their core.

Innovation is defined as the introduction of new ideas, methods, products, or solutions that have a positive impact. With this definition, we can see that the aims of innovation are novelty and value, the core components of creativity.

Transformation is a complete change in the appearance or character of something, especially one that results in an improvement. In this way, transformation, indicates the delivery of a radically different and superior state, which signifies creativity is at play, this time at a large scale.

Reshaping is a change in the form or structure of something, especially to make it more suitable or efficient for its intended use. Again, reworking models, structures, or systems to make changes for the better, even if it is simply recombining existing parts in new ways – that is creative.

Reform involves making changes to an institution or practice to make it more suitable for the current context or future needs.

Reform is also aimed at finding new ways of doing things to enhance people's experiences and outcomes, and so at its core sits creativity.

So, if you are in the business of innovation, transformation, reshaping, or reform, you are also in the business of bringing forth new and valuable ideas.

And if you are in the business of bringing forth new and valuable ideas, you are in the business of creativity.

And if you are in the business of creativity, then you need to understand this essential input well, as well as how your creativity contributes to a project's success. Because each of these endeavours depends on much more than the maturity of project management, the adequacy of budgets, the elegance of policy frameworks, or the sophistication of technology.

Their success rests on the creative capacity to see problems differently, imagine better alternatives, respond and adapt to changing circumstances, and inspire the behavioural shifts necessary to deliver value to our communities. Creativity is the engine of all meaningful change; therefore, understanding it, its preconditions, and processes is essential for any agency serious about delivering the improved performance that citizens demand and deserve.

In this way, creativity is not just a trivial, childish notion, but a very serious precursor to government success and community prosperity.

"Creativity focused on public interest aims is a central task for our age." ~ *Landry & Caust (2017)*

9   Creativity Inspires Innovation

You cannot have innovation without creativity.

In 2019, Australia, along with over 40 other countries, signed the Declaration on Public Sector Innovation in which it made a concrete commitment to support, improve and expand public sector innovation. The definition of innovation used in the declaration is:

"Implementing something novel to the context in order to achieve impact." (OECD, 2019)

By now, you will be well-versed in spotting creativity—it is embedded within the definition of innovation, being the two characteristics of novelty and impact. Therefore, when we talk about innovation, we must recognise that creativity is its essential precursor, or as more succinctly stated,

"Creativity is the origin of innovation" (Houtgraaf et al., 2023).

Creativity constitutes the crucial front-end of innovation, representing the initial process of generating ideas and exploring the question, "What if?" Innovation takes one step further to consider the subsequent process of practical implementation and to ask the question, "What now?"

But creativity is also far more than just the front end of innovation. It is *"part of the essential lifeblood of innovation"* (OECD, 2017a), flowing through every stage. The implementation of the ideas will require continued creativity to overcome challenges. Creativity is also required for people to respond differently and adopt the new behaviours required to support the change.

However, it is not only a one-way relationship. Creativity also needs innovation, because ideas without implementation provide no practical support. While the development of ideas can bring much positive energy and joy to their developers, and the ideas can rally people behind new possibilities, they bring very little tangible benefit in themselves. Action needs to be taken to make them a new reality, and a commitment of resources is necessary to enact the creative vision.

> In this way, creativity and innovation exist in a symbiotic relationship, mutually enhancing each other. Creativity inspires and supports innovation, and successful innovation fosters new inspiration and creative confidence to take on even greater change. This relationship is shown below.

Figure 8 - The creativity/innovation relationship

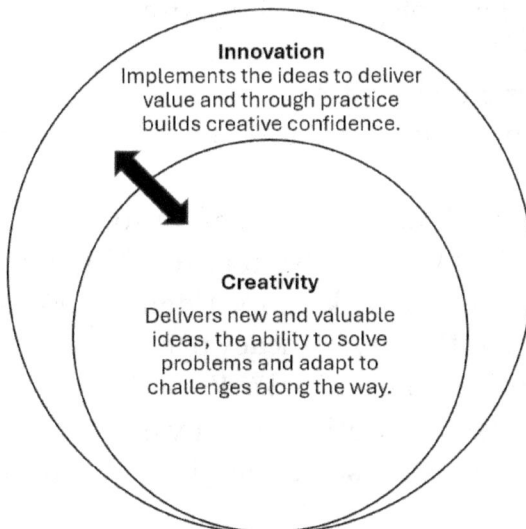

Innovation
Implements the ideas to deliver value and through practice builds creative confidence.

Creativity

Delivers new and valuable ideas, the ability to solve problems and adapt to challenges along the way.

The foundational relationship between creativity and innovation makes it imperative that, if leaders seek the latter, they make proactive investments in the former. If innovation is required, then building the creative potential and confidence of employees is a no-brainer, as it is an essential antecedent to their innovation success and will sustain them through the challenges ahead.

Creativity Through The Innovation Process

While creativity has been called the "fuzzy front end of innovation," it is far more than that. Creativity—the ability to develop novel and valuable responses—is required throughout the entire innovation process, just in different ways at each stage. It is estimated that 50% of innovation outcomes miss expectations, often because teams lack the creative capacity to solve complex, unpredictable problems that emerge during implementation, build necessary relationships, and embrace unfamiliar ways of working (Larson, 2023).

Innovation involves marching into the unknown. Problems constantly arise: budgets tighten, timelines slip, stakeholders disagree, technology underperforms, customers respond unexpectedly, and teams resist change. This is precisely why creativity is needed at every stage—not just during the initial brainstorming phase, but throughout the entire journey.

Creative confidence—the belief in one's ability to produce creative outcomes—is essential to this journey. Research by Mathisen and Brønnick (2009) demonstrates that individuals with high creative self-efficacy persist through difficulties and recover quickly from setbacks. Karimi et al. (2023) confirms that the same belief in creative capacity that enables idea generation also enables teams to solve complex problems during execution.

Creative confidence thus acts as a resilience factor, allowing teams to redefine problems, identify novel solutions as obstacles arise, and transform barriers into opportunities for even better outcomes.

Innovation is rarely linear. Because it breaks new ground and steps into the unknown, iterations, backward steps, and course corrections are normal. It is creativity—the capacity for novel and valuable responses—that enables more effective forward movement at each turn.

The following table illustrates how creativity manifests across each stage of the innovation process.

Table 7 – Creativity's role throughout the innovation process

Innovation Stage	How Creativity Contributes
1. Opportunity Identification	Divergent thinking to see problems others miss and market gaps from fresh perspectives.
2. Idea Generation	Generating and imagining multiple possibilities and producing original solutions to the opportunities identified.
3. Screening & Evaluation	Collecting diverse information to assess the value and feasibility of promising options.
4. Development & Prototyping	Problem-solving unexpected challenges. Adaptive behaviours to overcome challenges. Resilience: bouncing back from failures and setbacks.
5. Testing & Experimentation	Problem-solving unexpected results. Adaptive behaviours to overcome challenges. Resilience: persevering when experiments fail.
6. Implementation & Commercialisation	Problem-solving unexpected challenges. Adaptive behaviours to overcome challenges. Resilience: bouncing back from failures and setbacks. Building connections with customers and clients.
7. Scaling & Continuous Improvement	Adapting innovations for different contexts. Adopting new and valuable behaviours to address lessons learned. Continual development of new ideas to remain connected, inspirational and relevant.

Addressing Some Common Misconceptions

Just as we all have our own beliefs about what creativity is, we can also have individual ideas about innovation and the relationship between creativity and innovation. Getting clear about how they work together, though, is crucial; otherwise, we can target investments into the wrong areas or miss essential opportunities for improvement, collaboration, and effectiveness.

Here are some common confusions, along with clarifications on how things actually work.

"They're the same thing"
While creativity and innovation are often used interchangeably, conflating them can lead to confusion and hinder the development of core capabilities. Creativity is about generating new and valuable responses, be it ideas, behaviours, products or solutions. At the same time, innovation is the process of implementing these things to produce real-world change. Treating them as identical overlooks the distinct skills, approaches, and conditions each needs to flourish. It can lead teams to neglect the critical steps required for building confidence in creativity and then turning original thinking into action.

"Innovation is more important"
Innovation cannot exist without creativity. Creativity is both the origin and foundation of innovation. Creative thinking is the source of the novel concepts that fuel innovation efforts, making it the essential starting point. Without a healthy creative process, innovation stalls because there are no new ideas to implement. Additionally, without the ability for people to think creatively and address challenges in new and valuable ways, innovation will fail

to be implemented. So, investment in creativity is a prerequisite, not an optional extra.

"Creative people can't implement"

It is a misconception that creative individuals cannot also be effective implementers. Both creative and practical skills can be developed within individuals and teams through deliberate practice and supportive environments. Implementation itself often requires people to adopt new and valuable behaviours—making the act of putting ideas into practice a form of individual creativity that everyone can learn and embody.

"Innovation kills creativity"

Contrary to popular belief, adding structure through innovation processes can actually enhance creative output. Frameworks, constraints, and clear goals help direct creative energy and make ideas actionable, rather than stifling originality. Structure provides focus, encourages resourcefulness, and helps move creative ideas forward—making successful innovation a facilitator, not an adversary, of creativity.

Innovation Diffusion: Stalled By Low Creative Confidence?

The Productivity Commission has raised concerns about Australia's low rate of innovation diffusion—that is, the slow spread of new technologies, processes and best practices across both private and public sectors (Productivity Commission, 2023a). While a handful of organisations develop new-to-the-world innovations, the vast majority rely on adopting and adapting solutions that were developed elsewhere. Yet Australia continues to lag behind our international peers when it comes to implementing proven innovations at scale—a missed opportunity for boosting productivity and public value.

Given the significant size of the government, there is an understandable focus on increasing innovation diffusion in the public sector. Governments are responsible for nearly half the economy, with spending totalling nearly 40% of GDP and investments being made in critical areas like health, education, justice, and aged care. With this scale of operations, even modest gains in innovation diffusion can markedly enhance the quality of outcomes for Australians and help reduce pressures on public finances.

The benefits also extend beyond government itself, as improvements in public sector practice can foster a better environment for innovation across the whole economy. For these reasons, supporting innovation diffusion across the public sector has become a national priority.

But while reform efforts are now focused on removing regulatory barriers and building continuous learning cultures, what is not being addressed is the creative confidence required to support the innovation diffusion imperative.

You may wonder why public servants would need creative confidence when they are merely implementing innovations already developed. This is because taking on something new, even if it has been proven elsewhere, is still a creative act for the target audience.

At the very least it will require mini-c creativity as the individual gains personal insights and changes behaviours to align with the new system. If the changes effect whole teams or organisations, then the scale of novelty and risk increases, with the new systems reflecting a medium-c level of creativity.

Moreover, you cannot just impose an innovation upon an agency and expect them to accept established views about its value. Judgements about what's beneficial are shaped by context. Even if a new approach has been tried and tested elsewhere, it may be relatively radical for the target agency. Stagnant cultures, stifled by a fear of change, can distort perceptions of benefit and create resistance, even when new approaches clearly offer value.

So, simply, the adoption of any new practice or technology is a creative act. It requires people to take on new behaviours, which to be sustainable requires a positive assessment of value.

And therefore, creative confidence—at individual and organisational levels—is essential to engender the willingness to try the innovations that have worked for others.

In its papers addressing the diffusion problem, the Productivity Commission talks about a "growth mindset", which it defines as a continual focus on economic growth (Productivity Commission, 2025b). However, the real mindset that drives results is creative confidence: believing creativity is a skill to be developed and trusting that everyone can generate useful new solutions and adapt to change.

Empowering public servants and organisations to generate ideas, question long-held assumptions and experiment with new ways of working makes them more agile and open to learning from the best elsewhere. Building creative capability at all levels fosters not just adoption, but local adaptation and continuous improvement, helping innovative solutions take root in every context.

If government is serious about innovation diffusion across its agencies, it must also get serious about prioritising creative confidence. Creativity is the channel through which government can fast-track the uptake and spread of valuable innovations— lifting efficiency, service quality and outcomes for citizens.

Creativity Is The Companion of Successful Innovation

As seen throughout this chapter, creativity cannot be assumed in the innovation process, nor can it be seen as an optional extra. It is the origin, fuel, and ongoing companion of every successful innovation project, and therefore demands disciplined and dedicated attention.

Whether the challenge is to reinvent services, deliver policy reform, or create new public value, the quality and impact of those innovations will always be anchored in the creative capacity of people, teams and the communities that receive them.

This chapter has demonstrated that viewing creativity and innovation as separate, or prioritising one while neglecting the other, leads to missed opportunities, stalled initiatives, and underwhelming results. Creativity is what allows organisations to see problems differently, imagine superior alternatives, and respond with agility and optimism when projects evolve in unexpected directions.

Likewise, innovation is what transforms creative potential into reality—giving life and delivering value through practical action and offering invaluable learning that can translate into future inspiration.

Ultimately, to innovate and bring about much-needed change, the public sector must invest deeply and deliberately in building creative confidence, integrating creativity at every stage of the innovation   journey,   and   fostering   cultures   where experimentation, reflection, and collaboration are not only permitted but built into the fabric of the agency cultures. Only then can public sector organisations consistently deliver innovations that meet evolving community needs and drive lasting, positive change.

Creativity and innovation, working in partnership, are the keys to unlocking a better future for governments and the citizens they serve.

10 Creativity Delivers Productivity

Creativity enables individuals, organisations and nations to develop and deliver new approaches—which is the solution to the productivity problem.

Australia is facing a critical productivity problem. Recent data show that market-sector multifactor productivity rose by just 0.1 per cent between 2022–23 and 2023–24, while labour productivity grew by only 1.1 per cent over the same period—both well below the long-run averages that previously underpinned rising incomes and living standards (Productivity Commission, 2025a; Parliamentary Library, 2025). After a temporary boost during the pandemic, productivity gains have evaporated, leaving multifactor productivity—the measure of how efficiently we combine resources and ideas—nearly flat and trailing both national targets and international benchmarks.

The consequences are severe. Over the past four decades, more than 70 per cent of growth in real GDP per person has come from labour productivity, meaning a sustained slowdown directly threatens future wages, public services, and living standards (Parliamentary Library, 2025). Treasury modelling shows that if annual productivity growth falls from 1.5 per cent to 0.9 per cent, real income per person would be more than $10,000 lower in 40 years (Treasury, 2025). This erosion undermines our capacity to fund health, education, and infrastructure, and risks hardening into a long-term barrier to shared prosperity.

The scale of the challenge has forced an intensive response. Governments and key institutions have made productivity a central organising theme, triggering fine-grained inquiries across the economy: how to restore competition and market dynamism; how to lift human capital and management capability; how to accelerate digital technology diffusion and innovation adoption; how to reduce regulatory and planning friction; and how to redesign workplaces and institutions to support continuous adaptation, experimentation, and learning.

The message is clear—our sustained ability to make improvements in productivity over time will determine whether Australia can sustain rising incomes and strong public services, or whether we accept a future of stagnation. This crisis also serves as a stark reminder of our need to continually find better ways to work, create, and adapt.

The Solution To The Productivity Problem – Creative Confidence

Ultimately, and as recognised by the Productivity Commission, there are two fundamental requirements for growth:

1. The discovery of ideas
2. The application of the new ideas (Productivity Commission, 2025a).

> It sounds so simple, yet creativity is the fundamental solution to the productivity problem. Productivity growth is powered by creativity—the identification and implementation of new and valuable ways of working.

This assertion is not just theoretical; it is supported by compelling evidence that shows creative capacity serves as a fundamental driver of improved performance, efficiency, and value creation across all levels of the economy.

Creativity Powers Individual Performance

At the individual level, there is substantial evidence showing that creativity has a direct and positive effect on job performance by improving qualities such as independence, confidence, openness to risk, and adaptability (Duarte et al., 2021) – all factors that translate to the ability to develop and adopt new ways of working.

Most importantly, creativity is essential to wellbeing with an extensive global evidence base now showing this causal relationship. In a landmark review of over 3,000 studies, the World Health Organisation confirmed that engagement with the arts and creative activities plays a major role in preventing ill health, managing chronic conditions, and promoting wellbeing— delivering benefits that range from improved cardiovascular outcomes and cognitive function to reduced stress and enhanced immune response (Fancourt & Finn, 2019).

Wellbeing is a key driver of productivity, with recent experimental evidence suggesting that meaningful increases in employee wellbeing can improve productivity by around 10% (Krekel et al., 2019). In this way, for the good of the people and for economic growth, creativity is a no-brainer. It is the fundamental capacity that drives all other desired outcomes.

We will also see in the coming chapters that creative confidence is key to our ability to solve problems, build positive relationships, and harness the power of AI, all of which contribute to an improved capacity to turn inputs into outputs efficiently and, more importantly, to deliver valuable outcomes.

Creativity Powers Organisational Outcomes

It is well-established that organisations investing in creative cultures consistently outperform their less creative counterparts across multiple productivity metrics. Comprehensive research demonstrates that organisational creativity delivers measurable economic outcomes, including increased efficiency, higher quality output, lower costs, faster project completion times, and improved adaptability to unexpected challenges (Basadur et al., 2023).

Organisations with creative cultures also experience significant people outcomes that support improved individual productivity, such as higher job satisfaction, increased motivation and commitment, better teamwork, reduced turnover and absenteeism, and enhanced strategic thinking capabilities.

The evidence shows that these benefits are not just one-off outcomes, but compound over time, with creative organisations developing superior resource allocation capabilities and more effective decision-making processes that not only deliver but sustain productivity advantages.

Creativity Powers Productive Cultures

It may seem too obvious to state, but our collective national culture significantly influences our ability to innovate, adapt, and align with the productivity agenda. Innovation is fundamentally a psychological process that is shaped by social pressures (Kastelle, 2015). Cultural factors significantly influence a nation's capacity to translate creative potential into productivity.

Such factors include a cultural tolerance for uncertainty and a nation's ability to foster psychological safety. When social norms prioritise conformity and punish failure, individuals quickly learn that the safest course of action is to maintain the status quo, regardless of their creative talent. Conversely, cultures that normalise experimentation and frame risk-taking as a necessary part of learning create the psychological conditions where innovation can thrive. As Kastelle argues, we cannot simply mandate innovation; we must cultivate the social environment that supports the inherent vulnerability of creative work and sends signals that experimentation and intelligent failure are celebrated not criticised.

Complementing this cultural foundation, OECD research provides compelling evidence that cultural and creative sectors (CCS) function as direct drivers of productivity through four main spillover mechanisms: supply chain linkages that embed creative inputs throughout the economy, geographic proximity effects that generate innovation clusters, skills movement that transfers creative capabilities across sectors, and collaboration networks that facilitate knowledge exchange and co-innovation (OECD, 2021c).

Interestingly, research also confirms that highly educated people working in creative occupations are the most relevant component in explaining total factor productivity (Marrocu & Paci, 2012). Non-creative graduates had some impact on productivity, but only four times less than that of their creatively employed colleagues.

Therefore, if governments are committed to achieving productivity gains, investing in understanding cultural constraints at the national level and supporting employment in the CCS are two evidence-based initiatives that would generate economy-wide spillover effects.

Australia's Poor Innovation Productivity

There is much to celebrate regarding Australia's creative potential. Australian teenagers rank fourth globally in terms of creative and critical thinking skills (OECD, 2024), and we are recognised as an Innovation Leader by the Global Innovation Index (WIPO, 2024).

Over two-thirds of businesses also report they are innovation active, and 62% describe themselves as innovative, which sets a positive foundation for productivity. However, despite these promising inputs, the data shows that Australia produces far fewer innovation outputs relative to its level of innovation investments (WIPO, 2024). Fundamentally, our innovative productivity is poor.

The cultural contributors to this paradox cannot be underestimated. How a nation copes with uncertainty is paramount, and people need to feel supported in order to take creative risks, especially in challenging economic circumstances. Innovation is applied creativity, and with this comes uncertainty and fear. How cultures find the confidence to move through this to reap the creative and collective rewards is critical.

In Australia, risk aversion is identified as a substantial barrier to innovation (Australian Parliament, 2015). Results from Australia's Workplace Innovation Index indicate that around one quarter of businesses perceive the risk-averse nature of their staff as a threat to their innovation agenda (Ricoh, 2019).

Additionally, while nearly two-thirds believe they have innovation capability, 75% of Australian businesses do not consider it core to their business (Ricoh, 2019). The majority then view creativity as an optional extra, an add-on to their business success. This belief is a massive psychological barrier to effort and investment.

Taken together, these findings suggest that Australia does not suffer from a shortage of ideas or talent, but from a failure to consistently convert creative potential into productive innovation. Closing this gap will require more than new strategies and structures; it demands a deliberate investment in creative confidence—the belief, across workplaces and communities, that people are capable of generating and implementing new and valuable responses.

If Australia wants to lift its innovation productivity and turn existing potential into greater efficiency and effectiveness, it must build environments where experimentation is expected, intelligent risk-taking is supported, and creativity is treated as core business rather than a discretionary extra. Only by strengthening creative confidence at scale—across sectors, regions, and levels of government—can we unlock the innovation capacity needed to sustain future prosperity.

Creative Confidence Is Economic Infrastructure

The evidence is unequivocal: creativity is the powerhouse behind productivity, operating as both the source of new ideas and an essential capacity for implementing them effectively.

Creative confidence empowers individual workers to adapt, solve problems and experiment with more effective techniques. Creative confidence enables organisations to develop new approaches, align their teams to the new direction and achieve efficiency gains through innovation. Creative confidence also enables nations to approach risk positively, to be resilient in the face of challenges, and to support their communities in delivering meaningful change.

It is also clear that governments play a pivotal role in shaping the culture of creative confidence necessary for productivity growth. They do so by addressing risk aversion and cultural silos that prevent innovation, but also actively investing in creative confidence at individual, organisational, and social levels as essential economic infrastructure.

As we have seen, traditional approaches to productivity enhancement through tax reform, infrastructure, and technology adoption are essential to provide creative supports; however, productivity gains depend on people's willingness and ability to think differently, adapt continuously, and implement novel solutions in an increasingly complex world. In this way, creativity must be built into the national psyche.

The imperative to build creative confidence becomes even more urgent when we consider that the productivity challenges governments face are not simple technical problems with straightforward solutions, but rather complex, interconnected challenges that defy conventional approaches.

11 Creativity Produces Solutions To Wicked Problems

"Why is there so little interest in creative thinking? We shall not solve the problems of our age without it." ~ J.P. Guilford

Public sector leaders today face a range of complex challenges that defy conventional solutions and traditional bureaucratic approaches. These challenges—from climate change and population aging to digital disruption, housing affordability, and social inequality—represent what planning theorists Horst Rittel and Melvin Webber (1973) first identified as wicked problems.

Unlike the "tame" problems that characterised much of the past traditional public administration, wicked problems are distinguished by their fundamental characteristics: they have no definitive formulation, their solutions are not true or false but better or worse, there is no immediate test of solutions, every attempt at resolution has significant consequences, and each problem is essentially unique (Rittel & Webber, 1973).

These challenges continue despite decades of policy attention and substantial resource investment, creating persistent frustration for both public servants and the communities they serve. Most importantly, though, their lack of resolution means that people continue to suffer.

Strangled By Organised Irresponsibility

Wicked problems are just one symptom of what has become known as a VUCA environment—one characterised by volatility, uncertainty, complexity, and ambiguity. In these conditions, rapid and unpredictable change demands adaptive, experimental responses that sit uneasily with the traditional command-and-control instincts of public administration. The COVID-19 pandemic made this painfully clear, exposing limits in government's ability to anticipate, coordinate, and communicate, while simultaneously demonstrating the urgent need to innovate and learn in real time.

In such contexts, the public sector can easily slide into what Ulrich Beck (1995) calls organised irresponsibility. Here, risk-averse institutions respond to complexity by layering on more processes, committees, and sign-offs until decision-making becomes so over-engineered and diffused that it is almost impossible to identify who is responsible for outcomes. Beck likens this to "a laboratory with nobody responsible for the outcome of the experiment": policies are tested on citizens, but accountability for failure evaporates.

The consequences are profound. First, democratic legitimacy erodes. When citizens cannot see who is answerable for major failures or stalled reforms, trust in government declines and the basic promise of representative democracy—being able to "throw the rascals out" when things go wrong—loses credibility. Second, and less visibly, the system fails to build creative confidence through practice. By avoiding clear ownership of difficult, high-stakes problems, leaders and institutions miss the chance to exercise and strengthen their collective problem-solving capability. Over time, the creative "muscle" needed to grapple with complexity atrophies: if you do not use it, you lose it.

Paradoxically, the very risk aversion that drives organised irresponsibility ends up increasing systemic risk. By dispersing responsibility and suppressing experimentation, governments become less able to act decisively, learn from mistakes, or adapt as conditions change. Escaping this trap requires a different stance: recognising that, in a VUCA world, problem-solving itself is a creative act—one that depends on imagination, experimentation, and collaboration every bit as much as it does on analysis and control.

Problem-Solving As A Creative Process

I know I am risking your ire by repeating the definition of creativity. However, it is essential to remember that, at its core, it is about developing new and effective solutions, where 'effective' could be replaced with notions such as usability, value, or appropriateness. This definition accurately reflects what happens when we solve problems.

> When public servants develop solutions to policy challenges, they are fundamentally engaged in creative work: they must generate approaches that are both new to their context and effective in addressing the specific problem they face.

Even if there are recognised approaches documented in policies and procedures, if the process results in some insight for an individual, then it ticks the boxes for both novelty and value and can be categorised as mini-c creativity. This recognition makes it clear that creative problem-solving is the purview of all public servants, not just those working in innovation or reform roles.

Creative Problem-Solving Behaviours

Developing new and valuable solutions to problems of any type requires several unique behaviours, all stemming from the creative confidence of those involved. These include:

Collecting diverse stakeholder information: seeking input from multiple sources to broaden perspectives and enable problems to be defined and framed in ways that open new possibilities for action. In the public sector context, this means engaging with diverse communities, interest groups, industries, and subject matter experts to build a richer, more nuanced understanding of policy challenges and encourage the cross-pollination of ideas across sectors and disciplines.

Accepting disruptive information: welcoming unexpected, contradictory, or challenging data rather than staying within the safety of conventional assumptions and known trends. This openness to surprises can disrupt established policy thinking and lead to creative breakthroughs, while promoting the adaptability necessary for rapid adjustment when new information challenges established beliefs.

Empathy and perspective-taking: actively considering the feelings, needs, and viewpoints of different stakeholder groups, leading to more human-centred and innovative policy solutions. This approach fosters collaboration by building trust and encouraging input from a broader range of contributors, resulting in more comprehensive and thoughtful responses to public challenges.

Balancing divergent and convergent thinking: flowing between different modes of thinking enables the generation of a wide variety of policy options without immediate judgment, encouraging originality and breadth of consideration. Convergent thinking then critically evaluates and refines these options to ensure solutions are practical, relevant, and effective for the specific policy context.

Deferring judgment and fostering supportive environments: suspending criticism early in problem-solving processes so that ideas can be generated and creative thinking can flourish. Delaying critical analysis of ideas encourages a "yes, and" mindset that seeks to build on others' ideas rather than immediately identifying obstacles, creating evaluation-free zones that increase engagement and the likelihood of innovative policy outcomes.

Flexibility and adaptability: seeing the bigger picture and devising flexible implementation strategies, anticipating obstacles, and adapting solutions to real-world complexity. Maintaining an open mind about how the idea may be implemented ensures ongoing relevance and resilience, while providing the ability to pivot and ensure continued effectiveness in dynamic policy environments.

In totality, these behaviours contribute to an atmosphere of expansiveness, where doors are opened for diverse input, there is space for connections to be made, and where participants are supported to share and bring their optimism to the table. They foster an emotional climate that is conducive to people bringing their best selves to the process, which is exactly what is required for wicked problems.

The Evidence For Creative Problem-Solving Effectiveness

Those individuals, teams and communities that use creative problem-solving approaches gain significant advantages, with studies showing that they significantly boost both the quality and originality of solutions produced. Moreover, the more creative processes are practised, the more reliable these positive outcomes become (Mumford et al., 1996).

Furthermore, research demonstrates that even partial application of creative approaches produces superior outcomes. Even if public sector leaders only invest creative effort in problem framing while using traditional approaches for other stages of problem-solving, they are still more likely to generate effective and novel solutions than those who rely entirely on conventional methods (Mumford et al., 1991). This finding has significant implications for public sector practice, suggesting that even small investments in creative problem-solving can still produce meaningful improvements in effectiveness.

These results are also observed in specific complex team settings, with research in the healthcare setting finding that teams using creative approaches were able to construct an ecological view of care processes that reflected a more comprehensive understanding of relationships and led to superior clinical outcomes (Brewster et al., 2021). The research demonstrated that creativity occurred at both stages of problem-solving—uncovering non-obvious problems and finding novel solutions—with measurable impacts on healthcare performance.

Creative problem solving is also directly relevant to the public service and its wicked challenges. The United Nations Development Program undertook a comprehensive analysis of design thinking applications in government, which are interventions aimed at stimulating creativity. They found that such creative approaches deliver measurable benefits to public decision-making, including:
- Comprehensive problem perspectives
- Reduced duplication of effort and policy inconsistencies
- Enhanced synergies and better-addressed trade-offs
- Integrated solutions with stronger reality checks at earlier stages

- Reduced risks of unintended consequences
- Higher chances of delivering complete and resilient solutions (UNDP, 2019).

Most relevantly for the world in which we find ourselves, it was found that design thinking delivers its most promising results when applied to wicked problems that have no off-the-shelf solutions.

Creative Confidence as the Foundation for Wicked Problem Solutions

The capacity to effectively address wicked problems depends fundamentally on creative confidence—the belief in one's ability to generate creative solutions and the willingness to engage in creative problem-solving processes despite uncertainty and risk (Kelley & Kelley, 2012). As Kelly Cederberg (2018, p.1) observes,

"If we don't have confidence in our ability to think creatively, we may never come up with the novel solutions to problems that our society and our professions face."

This confidence operates at multiple interconnected levels within government systems, creating the psychological and organisational foundations necessary for sustained creative problem-solving.

When governments successfully model creative confidence— taking intelligent risks, learning from failures, and adapting approaches based on evidence—they build public trust in innovative governance approaches, which in turn provides political support for continued creative approaches to complex challenges (UNDP, 2019).

Conversely, when creative approaches are systematically discouraged or penalised, both individual and organisational creative confidence erodes, reducing the government's capacity to address wicked problems effectively.

There is a fundamental truth that public sector leaders can no longer ignore: in a VUCA world characterised by volatile, uncertain, complex, and ambiguous challenges, creativity is not an optional luxury but an essential capability. To neglect the development of creative potential can be seen as short-sighted and even careless. As Landry and Caust (2017, p. 6) state succinctly:

> *"The inability to tap the creative agility of the bureaucracy to solve problems is wasteful."*

Traditional bureaucratic methods are no longer fit for purpose and fail to address the interconnected, multifaceted challenges that now dominate the policy landscape. The alternative to inevitable organised irresponsibility is proactive organised creativity: deliberately building the individual skills, organisational cultures, and systemic supports necessary for sustained creative problem-solving across government.

Yet the implications of creativity extend far beyond government offices and policy development processes. While public sector leaders grapple with complex problems at the institutional level, communities across the nation face their own challenges that require creative responses: adapting to the impacts of climate change, navigating economic disruptions, maintaining social cohesion amid demographic shifts, and building local resilience in the face of global uncertainties.

12   Creativity Nurtures Resilience

Creative confidence is not merely a capability—it is the foundational capacity that enables resilience across all levels of society, from the individual navigating personal challenges to governments managing systemic change.

Resilience is the capacity to anticipate, absorb, adapt to, and transform in response to disruptions and disturbances. It has emerged as a critical capability for individuals, organisations, and communities navigating the VUCA world and the plethora of complex problems we discussed in the previous chapter.

While traditional approaches to resilience often focus on risk management, resource stockpiling, continuity management or structural reinforcement, creativity is at the core of adaptive capacity, providing the cognitive, social, and cultural flexibility necessary for persistence and sustained prosperity across all levels and spheres of society.

> Creativity is the ability to develop new and valuable responses to changed circumstances—precisely what resilience demands. Resilience, the capacity to adapt successfully to new situations, is impossible without creativity. Resilience is creativity in action.

Creative Capability Is An Individual Asset

At the individual level, creativity represents far more than artistic expression or innovative thinking—it is a fundamental psychological resource that supports adaptive coping with stress, uncertainty, and change. Rather than being a "nice to have" trait, creativity underpins how people think, feel, and act when facing disruption.

Cognitively, creative confidence enables individuals to consider multiple perspectives, question assumptions, and generate alternative approaches to problems. These are the skills needed for effective stress management and adaptive coping during times of crises (Kashdan & Rottenberg, 2010). This mental agility helps people avoid the cognitive rigidity that so often accompanies stress, such as black-and-white thinking or a sense of being trapped. Instead, creativity supports psychological flexibility—the capacity to reframe situations, see options where others see dead-ends, and adjust plans as circumstances change.

These cognitive benefits are closely intertwined with emotional ones. Studies show that engagement in creative activities triggers what Barbara Fredrickson terms the "broaden-and-build" response: creative engagement tends to generate positive emotions, which in turn broaden people's thought–action repertoires and help build enduring psychological resources such as resilience, optimism, and social connection (Fredrickson, 2001). Over time, this creates an upward spiral—creative activity lifts mood and expands thinking, which strengthens coping resources, making it easier to keep creating and adapting during future challenges.

Neuroscience helps explain why creativity is so powerful for both thinking and feeling. Neuroimaging studies show that during creative activity the brain's default mode network (linked to imagination and internal reflection) and executive control networks (linked to focus and regulation) coordinate more closely than usual (Beaty et al., 2016). This unusual cooperation between systems that often operate in tension is associated with enhanced cognitive flexibility and improved emotional regulation. With regular creative engagement, these patterns can literally "re-wire" the brain—strengthening connections between regions and improving the ability to shift fluidly between focused and more expansive modes of thinking.

These cognitive and emotional shifts then show up behaviourally. People who engage their creativity more often are better able to experiment with different coping strategies, seek support, re-prioritise, and try new ways of responding rather than getting stuck or defaulting to avoidance or distraction responses. In this way, creative confidence does not simply help individuals feel better in the moment; it builds a durable capacity to respond constructively under pressure, making resilience a creative practice.

Creative Culture Is An Organisational Advantage

Many organisations already understand that creative confidence is a strategic imperative for institutional resilience and adaptability and make dedicated investments to improve it. Through supporting enhanced creative skill in their people, they enable rapid sense-making, flexible decision-making processes, and the experimental mindsets necessary for adaptive learning (Amabile & Kramer, 2011). These organisations then gain the benefits of a superior capacity to anticipate challenges, adapt to disruptions, and emerge from crises stronger than before.

As organisational culture scholar Edgar Schein observed, it is the active cultivation of environments where curiosity, experimentation, and open-mindedness are cultural norms that acts as the foundation for resilient organisations to be formed (Schein & Schein, 2017).

These creative cultures also have tangible performance impacts. Boston Consulting Group has found that companies ranking in the top quartile for innovation capability were 2.6 times more likely to experience above-average growth rates and demonstrated superior resilience during economic downturns (Ringel et al., 2019). These organisations do not merely respond to change—they proactively drive transformation by encouraging employees to suggest process improvements, pilot experimental approaches, and collaborate across traditional departmental boundaries.

Studies of organisational behaviour during crisis periods provide particularly compelling evidence. Research examining corporate responses to the COVID-19 pandemic found that organisations with established creative cultures adapted more rapidly to remote work requirements, developed innovative service delivery methods, and maintained employee engagement more effectively than organisations with more rigid, bureaucratic cultures (Kniffin et al., 2021). The creative problem-solving capabilities that these organisations had developed during stable periods became critical adaptive resources during a crisis.

Creativity Is The Key To Institutional Resilience

The public sector presents unique challenges and opportunities in terms of resilience. Governments and agencies must provide their citizens and customers with a sense of security and stability while simultaneously adapting to evolving community needs, technological advancements, and crises.

However, these two states, security and creativity are not mutually exclusive. We have seen from neuroscience that creativity enables cooperation across diverse cognitive networks, meaning that those public sector organisations that develop creative capabilities in their people are better placed to balance these competing demands and to navigate their conflicts. Their people can weigh the pros and cons of novelty and value and use creative problem-solving to find the most effective and sustainable solution. As a result, they show superior ability in policy adaptation, service delivery innovation, and crisis response effectiveness (Torfing & Ansell, 2017).

The COVID-19 pandemic provided a natural experiment in public sector resilience, with research finding that those jurisdictions with established creative problem-solving cultures responded more quickly to pandemic requirements. They implemented novel policy solutions, redesigned service delivery systems, and maintained community engagement more effectively than jurisdictions with more performance-centric and control-focused approaches (Kattel & Mazzucato, 2020).

> Creativity inherently involves stepping into the unknown. So, when the unknown then arrives, those with creative confidence are already primed to respond positively.

Creativity Is A Social Resilience Resource

At the community level, creativity functions as both a catalyst for social cohesion and a mechanism for collective problem-solving, crafting the social capital necessary for effective community resilience. This is why communities with active creative sectors and strong creative engagement demonstrate a superior capacity to adapt to challenges, maintain social cohesion during disruptions, and serve as a driver of resilience and recovery (OECD, 2021c). Those with creative confidence are fundamentally better able to deal with change—to adopt new beliefs and behaviours to respond to whatever challenges come their way. They are well practiced at being adaptable.

The Creative, Community, Wellbeing and Resilience Hub in New South Wales provides a great example of the role creativity can play in community resilience. Established by the Blackheath Area Neighbourhood Centre in response to the devastating 2019-2020 bushfires, subsequent natural disasters, and the COVID-19 pandemic, the Hub delivered 217 workshops and events, attended by over 2,500 people during an 18-month period (NSW Government, 2023). The program integrated:

- Creative activities such as art therapy, animation, writing, and Indigenous crafts.
- Practical skills, including community gardening, bushfire preparedness.
- Wellbeing sessions, for example, psychoeducation and support groups.

Evaluations of the services found that participants reported increased confidence in coping with emergencies, stronger social connections, a greater sense of community belonging, and measurably improved wellbeing.

Most significantly, the creative components of the program appeared to enhance the effectiveness of practical resilience training by increasing engagement, improving retention of emergency preparedness information, and building the social networks necessary for effective collective response (NSW Government, 2023).

Resilience Requires Creative Confidence

The Oliver Wyman report *A Resilient Australian Public Sector* (2024) recognises that the contemporary operating environment requires public sector organisations to develop significant resilience capabilities, as they must *"better predict, prepare for, quickly respond to, recover from, and adapt to multiple events and risks that may threaten national security, economic conditions, and the safety and wellbeing of Australians".*

The report emphasises that building this resilience is not possible through ad-hoc approaches but requires the systematic identification and development of core capabilities for navigating uncertainty and change. It is my firm belief that creative confidence is the core capability underlying resilience across all levels of society.

From the psychological flexibility that enables individuals to deal with uncertainty, through the organisational cultures that support institutional learning, to the social characteristics that enable communities to connect and adapt, creativity provides the cognitive, social, and cultural foundations for transformation in the face of tumult.

This understanding also significantly reframes resilience from simply being a defensive capacity focused on returning to previous states toward a proactive capacity focused on pre-emptive change. In this view, resilience rests upon creative capabilities—not as additional components of community skill-building frameworks, but as the core competency around which all other sustainability strategies are to be organised.

13   Creativity Enables Collaboration

There is a reason we use the term "building relationships"; it is because establishing a connection with another person is essentially a creative process.

In an era of rapid change and complex challenges, public sector leadership must be more responsive and relevant than ever. Addressing issues that cross boundaries—such as climate resilience, social inclusion, and digital transformation—requires a shift from traditional command-and-control approaches to more collaborative, community-driven solutions.

The old machinery of government—built on hierarchies, fixed mandates, and predictable processes—was never designed for the volatility, uncertainty, complexity, and ambiguity (VUCA) of today's world. To stay effective and deliver meaningful community outcomes, collaboration must move from being a nice-to-have to an operational imperative—an essential way to harness diverse perspectives, build trust, and co-create solutions that truly meet the needs of citizens.

As ANZSOG's comprehensive research makes clear:

"The most pressing problems that remain are the ones that cross agency boundaries" (ANZSOG, 2022).

Coordination across departments is now viewed as essential to core government business, representing a fundamental shift from traditional siloed approaches toward integrated models. But here is the critical point: collaboration is not simply a project management technique; it is a creative act. And without creative confidence, it fails.

Collaboration As A Creative Act

The term "building relationships" is instructive as to the nature of forming any relationship. We do not "install" or "procure" them—we build them. This is because every authentic connection between people is a creative process: it involves imagining another's perspective, experimenting with communication styles, and navigating the uncertainty of trust.

> Modern governance operates through multi-actor collaborative channels, making personal connections indispensable. As Beyers (2024) notes:
>
> *"Personal relationships are thus a crucial component in collaborative governance for sustainable transformation."*

When a public servant partners with a community group, a non-profit, or another agency, they are not executing a pre-scripted playbook. They are, in real time, co-creating a shared language, a common purpose, and a mutual commitment to action. This is why creativity—not process manuals—underpins effective collaboration.

The Creative Capabilities Collaboration Demands

Effective collaboration requires:

"A willingness to work in an innovative, creative and flexible way" (DemocracyCo, 2016).

Breaking this down even further, we can see that collaboration engages three specific skills that call on a person's creativity.

First, empathy: the ability to step beyond one's own experience and construct a mental model of another's world. This is not passive understanding; it is an imaginative leap. Therefore, those people with high creative capacity can generate a richer, more nuanced emotional maps of others, which is the foundation of forming a deep connection and trust (Anderson et al., 2023).

Second, communication: translating between different worldviews, value systems, and professional jargons requires improvisational skill—finding the metaphor that lands, adjusting tone in response to feedback, telling a story that resonates. This is creative work, not administrative routine (Sawyer, 2017).

Third, conflict management. As Professor Michelle LeBaron observes:

> *"While all leaders encounter conflict, those who can access their own creativity are the ones best equipped to handle it" (ANZSOG, 2018).*

Her research demonstrates that leaders who develop their creativity are better able to manage conflict, work with differences, and inspire coworkers to imagine a wide range of possible outcomes.

Each of these capabilities—empathy, communication, and conflict resolution—depends on the willingness to enter the unknown, to experiment, and to risk vulnerability.

When Creative Confidence Is Absent

The consequences of lacking creative confidence are stark, resulting in what has been evidenced in the public sector already—resistance to new approaches and construction of barriers to collaboration (Public Sector Network, 2025). In its absence, public sector actors default to what DemocracyCo (2016) warns against—rigid, procedural engagement that is more about self-protection that productive results.

When leaders cannot imagine alternative futures, they cannot build the psychological safety that encourages stakeholders to invest their full selves in service of shared goals. They cannot generate the trust that reduces transaction costs in multi-party agreements. They cannot model collaborative behaviours that cascade through organisational cultures. Instead, partnerships become exercises in managed defensiveness: polite, procedural, and ultimately hollow.

All Community Outcomes Are Relationship Outcomes

All community outcomes are relationship outcomes. Whether addressing homelessness, improving educational achievement, responding to climate change, or building economic resilience, success depends on coordinating action across multiple stakeholders with different priorities, resources, and constraints.

Every one of these relationships requires the capacity to envision what does not yet exist, to communicate across difference, to navigate conflict constructively, and to sustain partnerships over time. In short, relationships require creativity.

This is why creative confidence is not a soft skill but essential economic infrastructure. It is the enabling capacity that allows public sector leaders to form the networks, access the diverse expertise, and build the legitimacy necessary to deliver complex public value. It enables leaders to:

- Generate trust that enables faster decision-making and reduces transaction costs in multi-party collaborations.

- Create psychological safety that encourages stakeholder innovation and risk-taking in the service of shared goals.
- Build networks that provide access to diverse resources and expertise necessary for addressing complex challenges.
- Develop reputations that attract high-quality collaborative partners and enhance organisational influence.
- Model collaborative behaviours that cascade throughout organisational cultures, improving overall system capacity for collaborative, relationship-based governance.

Without it, even the best-designed policies and most generous resources will fail to achieve their intended impact.

With it, leaders can turn the latent potential within their communities into productive, resilient, relevant and adaptive governance.

Fostering this confidence across the public sector, from frontline staff to senior executives, is the single most important investment government can make to ensure that collaboration delivers the community outcomes citizens expect and deserve.

14   Creativity Ensures AI Effectiveness

AI's transformative potential depends upon the creative confidence of its human partners; without it, the harms of learned helplessness and homogenisation are inevitable.

There is one collaboration that is becoming increasingly predominant in all public service offices, and that is the partnership between people and AI systems. Public servants are employing AI to augment their human capabilities, generating advice, answers, best-practice approaches, and all manner of documents almost instantly.

AI's potential is profound, not only for undertaking routine work but also for the research and analysis necessary to inform innovation and reform projects.

However, while each day AI is becoming increasingly sophisticated, we are also gaining a deeper understanding of the factors that drive successful human-AI creative collaboration.

> What is becoming clear is that a core driver of effective human-AI partnerships is not how advanced the tool is, but the level of creative confidence of the humans who wield it.

It is an individual's confidence in their creative abilities that serves as the determining factor in whether AI partnerships can propel an organisation or a nation forward, or drive it into destructive dependence.

AI's Contribution To Creativity

While AI has been available at a wide scale for only a relatively short time, we are already seeing some really exciting results in its contribution to creativity. Experimental research demonstrates that generative AI can significantly boost creative performance across multiple dimensions.

Comprehensive experiments have been conducted to track the outcomes of creative writing, finding that access to AI-generated story ideas increased novelty by 5.4% and usefulness by 3.7% (Doshi & Hauser, 2024). When writers could choose from multiple AI suggestions, improvements reached 8.1% in novelty and 9.0% in usefulness, representing tangible creative enhancement rather than mere efficiency gains.

The democratising effect proves most dramatic for individuals struggling with baseline creativity. Research reveals that individuals scoring low on divergent thinking tests showed creativity gains of 10.7% and usefulness improvements of 11.5% when using AI-assisted tools (Doshi & Hauser, 2024). These results suggest AI tools can serve as artificial scaffolding for imaginative capabilities.

AI demonstrates particular strength in promoting divergent thinking by suggesting associations among remote concepts, enabling users to explore novel combinations they might never have considered on their own. Educational applications show that AI stimulates creativity by introducing new ideas and problem-solving techniques while providing personalised feedback that can boost creative confidence.

The added benefit AI presents is its contribution to productivity. AI-powered tools speed up and, in some cases, fully complete mundane tasks such as data entry, research, and administrative functions. This frees cognitive resources for higher-order thinking, potentially enabling its human partners to concentrate effort instead on critical improvement initiatives.

Nevertheless, as the research shows, AI is no magic-pill for productivity, nor is it a replacement (yet) for the breadth of human intelligence.

AI Is Not So Intelligent After All

Despite the use of the term 'intelligence' in its name, AI's creative partnership potential is actually limited by a lack of intelligence. As outlined in Chapter 4, Gardner's framework of multiple intelligences shows that creativity draws upon most, if not all, of the nine forms of intelligence: linguistic, logical-mathematical, spatial, bodily-kinaesthetic, musical, interpersonal, intrapersonal, naturalistic, and existential.

Current AI systems demonstrate impressive capabilities in only four of these intelligences.

1. AI excels in linguistic intelligence through advanced natural language processing and large language models, achieving sophisticated understanding, generation, and translation of human language.
2. In logical-mathematical intelligence, AI rapidly analyses data, recognises patterns, and solves complex problems using structured reasoning and advanced algorithms.
3. Spatial intelligence has advanced significantly through geospatial AI processing, which interprets complex spatial relationships across both space and time dimensions.
4. AI shows musical intelligence in recognising, analysing, and creating musical patterns.

However, AI remains severely limited in the remaining five intelligences:

1. In bodily-kinaesthetic intelligence, AI lacks the embodied experience, detailed sensory data and true understanding of physical coordination that humans possess.

2. Interpersonal intelligence proves particularly problematic: though AI can facilitate social interactions, it lacks genuine empathy and struggles with a nuanced understanding of human relationships.

3. Intrapersonal intelligence poses an even greater limitation, as AI lacks authentic self-awareness and a genuine understanding of the emotions and motivations that give experiences deep meaning.

4. Naturalistic intelligence allows AI to process environmental data effectively, but without embedded ecological understanding.

5. Most critically, existential intelligence—the capacity to ponder deep questions about human existence and meaning—remains far beyond AI's scope, despite these contemplations serving as primary inspirations for art and innovation.

These limitations have prompted significant organisational reversals in AI implementation. Klarna, the Swedish fintech company, aggressively replaced customer service staff with AI agents in 2023 but reversed course within a year, acknowledging that service quality suffered and that human empathy and nuance remain irreplaceable. CEO Sebastian Siemiatkowski admitted that focusing on cost-cutting through automation led to diminished customer experience, prompting the company to rehire human agents and develop human-centric service models.

Klarna's experience is not unique, with Gartner's 2025 research predicting that by 2027, 50% of businesses planning major customer service job cuts due to AI will reverse course (CX Today, 2025). Replacing humans has been confirmed to be ineffective, with customers expressing severe dissatisfaction with technological alternatives and stating that they are willing to wait longer for human help. As stated by Kathy Ross, Senior Director Analyst at Gartner,

"While AI offers significant potential to transform customer service, it is not a panacea. The human touch remains irreplaceable in many interactions" (CX Today, 2025).

This example illustrates that creativity extends well beyond artistic expression to encompass the unique and valuable ways humans form relationships and provide services—domains that require integrated intelligence, which AI cannot yet replicate.

Creative Confidence Determines AI Partnership Success

Emerging research also reveals the effectiveness of human-AI partnerships depends critically on a factor often overlooked in technological discussions: the creative confidence of the human partner. Creative confidence has emerged as the key predictor of whether AI partnerships generate inspirational innovative outcomes or merely descend into sophisticated dependency.

McGuire et al. (2024) conducted comprehensive research demonstrating that individuals with high creative confidence scores produce significantly more innovative outcomes when collaborating with AI systems. The study found that confident creators effectively leverage AI's strengths while compensating for its limitations through their own capabilities. In contrast, individuals lacking confidence in their creativity saw minimal benefit from AI partnership and were often relegated to less value-adding roles, such as sub-editing, rather than primary creation.

This research reveals a fundamental prerequisite for effective AI collaboration: humans must first believe in their ability to be creative. The technological sophistication of AI systems becomes irrelevant if human partners lack confidence in their own creative capacity. Those with high creative self-efficacy approach AI as a tool to amplify their existing capabilities, using machine-generated inputs as springboards for emotionally resonant works that only humans can fully realise. They maintain creative agency while leveraging the computational strengths of AI.

Conversely, individuals with low creative self-efficacy tend to over-delegate creative responsibility to AI systems, resulting in outputs that lack the human insight, emotional resonance, and contextual understanding necessary for truly innovative solutions. They become dependent on AI-generated suggestions rather than using them as inspiration for further creative development, ultimately producing work that reflects AI's limitations rather than human potential.

The implications of the research results are compelling and serious: organisations seeking to harness AI's creative potential cannot simply "skill up" on AI technologies. An equal or greater investment must be made in developing the creative confidence of the individuals who will operate these systems.

> The power of human-AI partnership ultimately rests on the creativity of the people involved, not the sophistication of the technology.

The Risk of AI-Induced Atrophy

The ability of AI to assist people to be more creative is clear, but evidence is also showing that an over-reliance on AI systems may systematically erode the human creative capacities essential for long-term innovative capability. Research by Gerlich (2025) revealed a significant negative correlation between frequent use of AI tools and critical thinking abilities. The study revealed that cognitive offloading—delegating cognitive tasks to AI rather than engaging in deep analytical reasoning—was strongly correlated with AI tool usage and inversely related to critical thinking performance.

Most alarmingly, these cognitive deficits persisted even when participants attempted work without AI assistance, indicating lasting impairment rather than temporary reliance. Younger participants aged 17-25 showed the highest dependence on AI tools and correspondingly lower critical thinking scores, suggesting that digital natives who have grown up with AI-integrated technologies may be particularly vulnerable to what researchers term "learned helplessness" in creative domains.

The mechanism underlying this dependency involves the gradual atrophy of neural pathways supporting spontaneous ideation. When individuals consistently delegate creative challenges to AI systems, the mental muscles required for imaginative struggle weaken over time. Rather than developing tolerance for ambiguity and building creative resilience through productive struggle, users become habituated to surrendering creative agency at the first sign of difficulty.

This outcome creates a concerning feedback loop: as AI systems become more sophisticated and accessible, individuals with already-compromised creative confidence increasingly rely on machine-generated solutions, further weakening their creative self-efficacy and reducing their capacity for independent creative work. The result is a generation trained to assume their own resourcefulness is, at best, a backup to algorithmic assistance.

The homogenisation effects of widespread AI adoption are also becoming clear. While individual users may experience enhanced creativity, as more people turn to AI for creative input, the collective pool of ideas grows increasingly similar rather than diverse (Doshi & Hauser, 2024). AI systems, trained on existing human outputs and optimised for engagement rather than radical innovation, tend to channel creative exploration into familiar territories, inadvertently contributing to what researchers term "model collapse"—the progressive narrowing of the creative possibility space as machines train on their own algorithmic outputs.

The Creativity Investment Imperative

> The research evidence creates a clear imperative for strategic investment in human creative capacity at individual, organisational, and national levels. To fully benefit from AI's creative potential, we must first strengthen precisely the human capabilities that AI adoption risks eroding.

For individuals, this means deliberately cultivating creative self-efficacy through regular engagement in creative challenges that cannot be easily delegated to AI. People need to practice becoming comfortable with ambiguity, tolerating failure, and gaining confidence in generating novel solutions. Individuals must learn to approach AI as a collaborative tool that amplifies existing creative capabilities rather than a replacement for creative thinking. To achieve this, disciplined boundaries around

AI usage are necessary, ensuring that human creative muscles continue to receive the exercise required for healthy development.

For organisations, the implications demand fundamental rethinking of AI implementation strategies. Rather than simply deploying AI tools to increase efficiency or reduce costs, organisations must simultaneously invest in building creative confidence throughout their workforce. This investment includes training programs that develop creative confidence, organisational cultures that reward creative risk-taking and learning from failure, and performance systems that recognise the value of human insight and emotional intelligence alongside AI-generated outputs.

Organisations must also recognise that the most innovative outcomes emerge from human-AI collaboration where humans provide vision, context, meaning, and emotional resonance, and AI contributes computational power, pattern recognition, and rapid iteration capabilities. Human creative expertise must be developed and rewarded, rather than simply replacing human judgment with algorithmic efficiency.

At the national level, the implications are even more profound. Countries seeking to maintain innovative capacity and competitive advantage in an AI-dominated world must invest systematically in creative education and cultural development. Educational systems must prioritise creative thinking skills alongside technical competencies, cultural policies must support creative engagement across the population, and economic strategies must recognise creative capacity as essential infrastructure for national resilience and adaptability.

In Australia, we face an innovation paradox. We have teens who rank fourth globally for creative thinking. However, we have adults who fear risk, do not recognise the role creativity plays in economic success, and struggle to translate their creative potential into innovative outputs. This contrast highlights the importance of maintaining creative confidence at scale across all age groups and industries.

Nations that focus solely on technological advancements at the expense of human creativity risk having their populations' creative self-efficacy eroded by algorithmic systems. The consequences of this are dire —the loss of the adaptive capacity necessary for addressing wicked problems and maintaining democratic vitality over the long-term.

15   Creativity Flows Where Reward > Risk

The uncertainty inherent in creativity means it is a courageous act, requiring the perceived rewards to outweigh the personal risks.

The two characteristics of creativity—novelty and value—establish a fascinating dichotomy. On the one hand, bringing something new into being means moving into the unknown, which inherently involves risk, with the degree of risk to be born related to the extent of novelty of the solution. On the other hand, there is the notion of value, which implies that our actions will have a positive effect, bringing something useful, appropriate, or beneficial into being and delivering some reward to ourselves or our communities.

Humans are naturally risk-averse creatures, making the thought of risk almost guaranteed to bring a sense of discomfort. However, at the same time, we desire to be of service and have the need to contribute to making the world a better place. These two sides of the creativity story bring about a tension between avoiding the risk of the new and approaching the reward of the benefits to be achieved.

Figure 9 - The creative tension

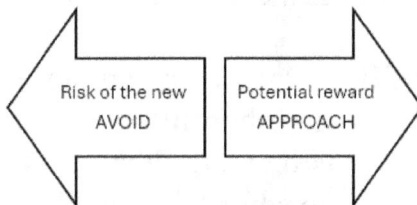

Risk of the new
AVOID

Potential reward
APPROACH

Creative potential is realised when the rewards are deemed greater than the perceived risks, and it is suppressed when the anticipated threats outweigh the believed benefits. This evaluation occurs constantly, and at every level of our organisations, with every person, every day deciding to act or not to act based on their evaluation of risk and reward.

The Risks Of The New

The thing that makes risks sound so risky is that they carry the potential for some loss. When we think about the risk of bushfires, our minds automatically consider the harm that may occur to all forms of life, livelihoods and possessions. When we discuss the risk of fraud in the workplace, conversations centre around the loss of financial assets and reputation. And when we begin contemplating a creative task, the thought process is similar, as we immediately evaluate what we could lose if we proceed. Some of the things that have been shown to spring forth in terms of what people believe they may need to forgo include:

Professional Reputation and Social Standing. Sharing creative work can result in rejection, criticism, or confrontation with authority. If ideas are presented that challenge current norms or leadership preferences, then professional growth may be compromised, and the person may be ostracised from social circles and future opportunities. These events impact our sense of belonging, which is a core human need.

Mental Stability. Proposing something new comes with vulnerability and an inherent anxiety about other people's judgments. It is challenging to separate criticism of an idea from criticism of the person who shares it. Thus, creative pursuits can often come with stress and anxiety.

Emotional Comfort. In addition to the loss of mental comfort, engaging in creative pursuits also risks the loss of emotional stability. Criticism, rejection, and failure can evoke deep feelings of shame or inadequacy, negatively impacting our sense of belonging and self-worth.

Physical Comfort. The social and reputational risks involved can lead to concerns about job loss, lower income, and the inability to meet other core needs, such as housing and food. Additionally, implementing an innovation requires effort, both physical and mental, which will potentially reduce the current level of comfort. If people are already financially vulnerable or overworked, then any perceived loss of further comfort would be a key consideration.

Unless the situation is urgent and we must act immediately, when a new idea arises, we have time to consider the consequences of investigating and implementing it. It is in this space that we consider the things we could lose by moving forward, and it is the notion of loss that evokes the feeling of fear.

When we sense fear, the natural reaction is to hold back and to avoid the threat. Overcoming this fear and taking action despite the risk is a courageous act.

It is essential to note that this risk evaluation is not a sign of weakness, and considering the negative consequences of creative action is not a fault. For most of human history, loss of access to food, shelter, safety, or social bonds could mean genuine harm— or death. Therefore, it makes sense that our brains evolved to prioritise threat-detection, steering us away from uncertainty and potential loss. We are instinctively wired to fear loss and to protect ourselves and those we care for from harm.

Risk Perception Versus Tolerance

A distinction must be made between how risky we perceive an action to be and our confidence in our ability to manage the risks effectively.

Risk perception refers to how risky we believe an activity or decision to be—our subjective evaluation of the potential hazards or negative consequences involved. In other words, risk perception is about *what we see* or feel as dangerous in a given situation.

Risk tolerance is our willingness or capacity to take on that risk regardless of how high or low we perceive it to be. It reflects our innate or developed comfort with uncertainty and our belief in our ability to manage or overcome potential obstacles.

Someone might perceive a significant risk but, possessing a high risk tolerance, can still choose to proceed if they value the potential reward. While risk perception may incline us toward caution or avoidance, our individual risk tolerance—shaped by personality, competence, and prior successes—can encourage us to embrace the challenge when we believe the benefits outweigh the risks.

Evaluating The Rewards

While humans have evolved to be naturally cautious about potential losses, we are equally wired to seek more for ourselves and others—to move towards activities that promise benefits for us and our communities.

As Abraham Maslow recognised, once our basic needs are secured, we are driven by higher aspirations toward self-esteem and self-actualisation, which he described as *"the desire to become everything one is capable of becoming"*—the pursuit of realising one's full potential through personal growth, creativity, and meaningful achievement (Maslow, 1943).

This drive toward self-actualisation is fundamentally creative in nature, involving the expression of our authentic selves and the contribution of our unique gifts to the world around us. We all possess an intrinsic desire to make a meaningful contribution to our communities, and this motivation often propels us toward creative action, despite the risks involved.

When contemplating a creative endeavour, just as we instinctively evaluate potential losses, we also assess the possible gains that could result from moving forward. The potential benefits that can balance the risks and motivate creative action span multiple domains and include:

Personal growth and self-fulfilment. Creative pursuits offer opportunities for skill development, mastery, and authentic self-expression that contribute to our sense of competence and personal identity.

Self-esteem and satisfaction. The satisfaction of creating something new and valuable can generate profound feelings of accomplishment and purpose, and the associated achievements can lead to an increased sense of self-esteem.

Professional advancement and recognition. Successfully implementing creative solutions can lead to professional and social recognition, promotion, increased influence, and expanded networks, providing long-term career benefits.

Social impact and community contribution. Many individuals are motivated by the potential to solve problems that matter to others, to improve systems and services that affect their communities, and to leave a positive legacy through their work.

The evaluation of these potential benefits—whether conscious or unconscious—plays a critical role in our willingness to embrace creative challenges. When the perceived value of potential outcomes exceeds the perceived risks, we find the courage to move forward into uncertainty, driven by the hope that our creative efforts will generate meaningful change for ourselves and others.

Inputs Into The Risk/Reward Assessment

When evaluating whether to pursue a creative endeavour, we draw upon a complex array of factors both within ourselves and within our external environment to assess the potential risks and rewards involved.

These individual and organisational influences shape our perceptions and ultimately determine whether we feel confident enough to move forward with new ideas or choose to remain within familiar boundaries. Some of the diverse inputs used to determine the risk/reward ratio for any action are shown in the following table.

This multifaceted evaluation process highlights that unleashing creative potential and building creative confidence requires both internal work to overcome limiting beliefs and develop supportive mindsets, as well as external leadership action to create organisational conditions that encourage rather than inhibit creative risk-taking.

Table 8 - The inputs into the risk/reward assessment

Individual Factors	Organisational Factors
Knowledge and expertise – Depth of understanding in relevant field.	Psychological safety - Freedom to express ideas without fear.
Growth mindset – Belief that new skills can be developed with effort.	Leadership Support - Manager encouragement and modelling.
Creative self-efficacy - Belief in one's ability to generate valuable ideas.	Risk tolerance culture - Organisational attitude toward uncertainty.
Cognitive style - tolerance for ambiguity.	Reward and recognition systems - How creative efforts are valued.
Motivation level - Intrinsic drive to create, solve problems, make impact.	Resource availability - Time, funding, tools, and support for creative projects.
Social and intellectual risk appetite - Willingness to challenge norms.	Hierarchical structure - Degree of bureaucracy and autonomy.
Fear of failure - Anxiety about negative outcomes.	Collaboration climate – Support for diverse perspectives.
Emotional resilience - Ability to bounce back from setbacks.	Learning orientation - Treatment of mistakes as learning opportunities.
Values and beliefs - Personal commitment to growth.	Performance evaluation criteria - Whether innovation is acknowledged.
Personality traits - Openness to experience and risk tolerance.	Communication norms - Openness of dialogue, support for dissenting views.
Past creative experiences - Previous successes or failures with creative endeavours.	

While individuals must cultivate their own creative courage and capabilities, leaders bear significant responsibility for shaping the environmental factors that influence how people perceive and evaluate the risks and rewards of creative action. The interplay between these individual and organisational factors ultimately determines whether creative ideas emerge, develop, and flourish within any given context.

However, it must also be noted that there are feedback mechanisms at play that increase the responsibility of both individuals and organisational leadership for creative confidence. Individuals, whether they are conscious of it or not, do have a significant influence on the team climate and organisational culture, and so have the opportunity through their own actions to effect change.

Similarly, leaders can help individuals build greater capability and confidence by establishing supportive organisational cultures and practices. If the aim is to build more creative people and more innovative agencies, then attention needs to be placed on both individual capacity and organisational coherence.

The Problem – We Prioritise Loss Over Gain

Research in behavioural psychology has consistently demonstrated that humans exhibit a powerful cognitive bias known as loss aversion—the tendency to weigh potential losses approximately twice as heavily as equivalent gains when making decisions (Kahneman & Tversky, 1979).

This fundamental asymmetry in how we process risks and rewards means that the psychological pain of losing something is felt far more intensely than the pleasure derived from gaining the same thing, creating what researchers describe as a "losses loom larger than gains" phenomenon that shapes virtually all human decision-making. The following diagram illustrates the default decision-making mechanism in effect when we encounter new ideas.

Figure 10- We prioritise loss over gain

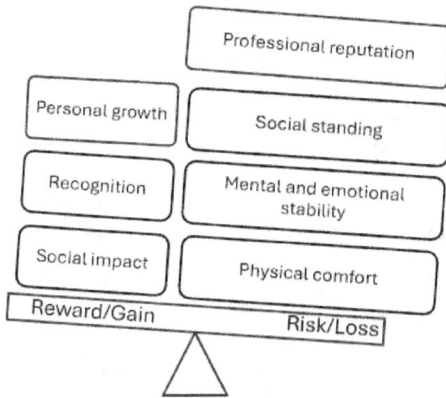

The implications for creative pursuits are profound: when individuals contemplate new ideas or innovative approaches, they instinctively focus more heavily on what they might lose— professional reputation, comfort, resources, or social standing— than on the potential benefits they could gain—growth, fulfilment, advancement and contribution—even when those benefits significantly outweigh the risks.

This cognitive bias, combined with the negativity bias (our tendency to give greater weight to negative information), creates a psychological environment where the fear of failure or loss leads to the premature dismissal of new ideas and undermines our willingness to pursue creative opportunities. In this way, the most significant barriers to innovation exist not in the external world, but within our own mental processing systems.

For individuals and organisations seeking to increase innovation and creative confidence, these psychological realities demand deliberate countermeasures. At the individual level, building creative confidence requires conscious strategies to reframe risk-reward evaluations—actively highlighting potential gains, practising pre-mortems that normalise potential setbacks, and developing resilience skills that reduce the perceived magnitude of losses.

Organisations must go further to balance the scales, systematically designing environments that reduce the actual and perceived costs of creative risk-taking while amplifying the visibility and value of potential rewards. To build a better balance means creating psychological safety where creative failures are treated as learning opportunities rather than career-limiting events, implementing reward systems that explicitly recognise creative attempts regardless of outcome, and providing leaders with tools to help teams overcome their natural bias toward loss avoidance.

Without these intentional interventions, loss aversion will continue to act as an invisible barrier to innovation, causing both individuals and organisations to systematically underinvest in creative potential and miss opportunities for breakthrough thinking and transformative change.

Change Occurs Through A Chain

In Section 1, we discussed the concept of creativity as an energy that flows between individuals and institutions, driving change. Now we can build on this, seeing change as a progression through an electrical circuit, with each person acting as a gate. Creativity can only flow as far as the circuits are aligned and the gates will allow.

Consider an innovation that must pass through the hierarchical levels of government, starting with the originating officer who must decide to share the idea, and then flowing through their manager, director, executive director, deputy director-general, director-general, minister, cabinet, and, if legislative change is required, potentially both chambers of parliament before reaching the community for implementation.

Viewed very simply, there are 11 gates where a risk/reward decision must be made for the idea to progress. This basic example does not include all of the various stakeholders—unions, industry groups, media, advocacy organisations, and community representatives—who play a key role in presenting ideas, supporting change and providing input to shape the enacting systems.

Each person along the chain makes their own risk and reward assessments about the idea. Where a person decides the rewards outweigh the risks, or that they have sufficient skill to manage them, then their response can be either to:

1. Accept the idea and perhaps provide assistance to move it forward.

2. Adopt and amplify the original idea, adding their energy to it and making it more meaningful.

In contrast, where a person believes that the risks outweigh the rewards, or that they have insufficient ability to manage the risks, then their response is likely to be either:

1. Introduce resistance that can dilute the idea, impede/delay its flow along the chain or prevent the required resources for its implementation.

2. Stop the progress of the idea altogether.

Two very simple representations of how this process works in practice are shown in the following diagrams. These diagrams are basic examples only; the reality is far more complicated. For example, it is recognised that ideas can come from any point in the chain. Leaders can instigate changes that are resisted or impeded by staff due to their own risk concerns, or amplified and acted upon due to their belief in the benefits.

Additionally, ideas may not be stopped in full but may be modified or diluted along the way to align with the decision-maker's risk and reward appetite.

Figure 11- Risk/reward decision chains

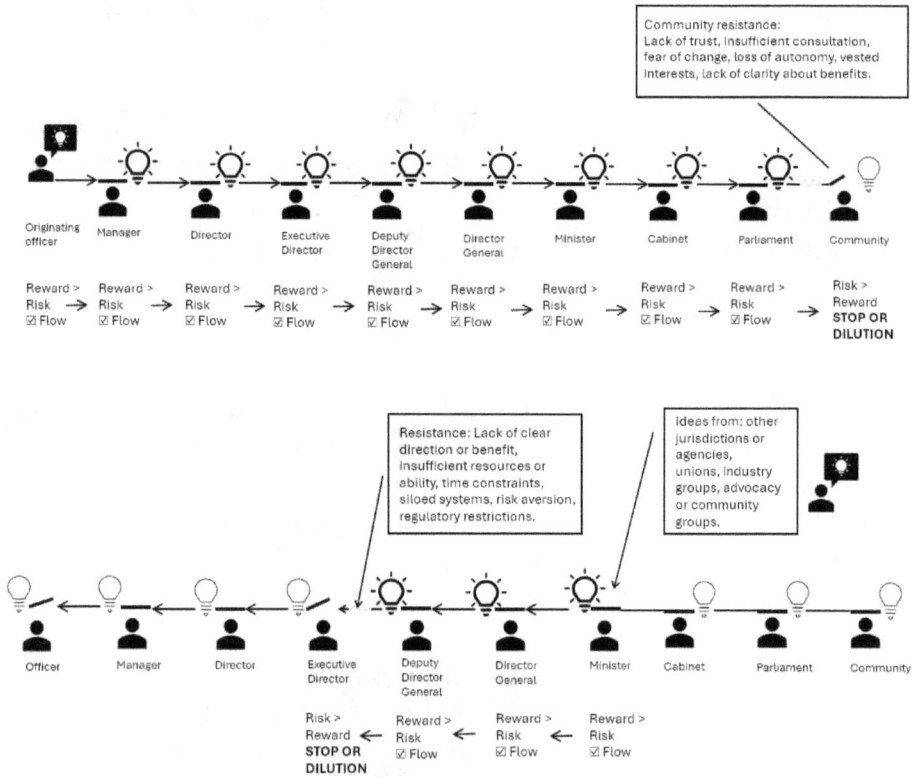

If any single decision-maker in this chain perceives the risks as too high, the rewards as insufficient, or faces overwhelming resistance from their stakeholder networks, they can effectively halt the entire innovation, regardless of how promising it is to other levels. This reality means that even the most brilliant creative ideas can be stopped not by a single "no," but by the compounding effect of individual risk assessments, stakeholder pressures, and institutional resistance.

> Of course, those in power can put pressure on others in the chain to accept a level of risk over their preference, and act despite a lack of confidence and fear of loss. It is unlikely however that any changes made under these conditions will be completely successful or sustainable.

Once any urgency has died down and pressure is removed, it is likely that people will return to the status quo and previously comfortable behaviours. It takes a great deal of work, both in shifting conditions and in communications to change the risk/reward balance for those all along the change chain.

In this way, each person's loss aversion, creative confidence, and external influences create either a pathway for innovation or an insurmountable barrier to change.

"The need for creativity is rising in all spheres of life. Public sector leaders agree it is a critical attribute for future leaders and staff at every level. Yet their instincts favour risk management, risk aversion and compliance. The culture is hard to shift." (Landry & Caust, 2017 p. 7)

This interdependence is why, when it comes to building creative confidence, it is insufficient to simply target public service officers for training interventions. As we saw in the systems model in Section 1, creativity is a social phenomenon; therefore, we must treat it as such, investing in building capability across all levels of an organisation and across all layers of society. For creativity to flow, there must be minimal resistance in the circuit, and each of the gatekeepers must be confident in their own creative abilities or at least convinced to act despite a lack of them.

16   Creativity Thrives On Coherence

When coherence exists within and across social layers, risk perception diminishes, creative confidence grows, and innovation becomes a natural expression of aligned purpose.

In Section 1 of this book, we explored creativity as a multi-layered construct—encompassing individual abilities, team dynamics, organisational culture, and broader social conditions. Building on this foundation, this chapter delves deeper into a critical understanding: creativity flourishes not just when each layer is strong individually, but when all layers are aligned and mutually reinforcing.

This alignment—what research increasingly identifies as coherence—represents the fundamental condition for creative confidence to develop and for creativity to flow freely through individuals, teams, institutions, communities and nations.

We have also examined how creative pursuits involve complex risk/reward evaluations, where individuals assess potential losses against potential gains before engaging in creative action. What emerges from the latest research is that incoherence—misalignment between layers—dramatically increases risk perception and undermines creative confidence.

When personal values clash with organisational expectations, when team dynamics contradict stated innovation goals, or when external pressures conflict with internal motivations, the perceived risks of creative action skyrocket. Conversely, when coherence exists within and across social layers, risk perception diminishes, creative confidence grows, and innovation becomes a natural expression of aligned purpose.

Professional Coherence: The Foundation For Risk-Taking

Research by Marie-Helene Massie and her colleagues (2022) has revealed how professional coherence—the alignment between personal values, identity, and organisational context—directly enables risk-taking and creative behaviours. In her longitudinal study of teachers enrolled in a professional master's program, Massie found that educators who experienced greater coherence between their sense of self and their professional environment were significantly more likely to engage in creative behaviours that benefited both themselves and their students.

The study utilised Korthagen's (2004) onion model of professional development, which examines six interconnected layers: environment, behaviour, competencies, beliefs, identity, and mission. Teachers who achieved coherence across these layers—aligning their core qualities, positive mission, and beliefs with their teaching practices—demonstrated remarkable creative confidence. They were willing to take what Beghetto (2019) describes as "beautiful risks", a term which describes creative risks that are intentionally undertaken with the hope of making a meaningful, positive contribution to others, even when success is uncertain and potential costs are present.

Unlike "good" risks, which primarily weigh personal benefits against costs, or "bad" risks, where costs outweigh potential gains, a "beautiful risk" is defined by its positive intent—to benefit not just oneself, but students, colleagues, organisations, or the larger community—while also thoughtfully addressing possible hazards and maximising potential benefits.

Beghetto emphasises that embracing beautiful risks requires courage, planning, and reflection, as it involves stepping into the uncertainty and vulnerability necessary for genuine creativity and innovation to flourish.

Beautiful risks are enabled when there is coherence both across layers (mission aligned with behaviour, identity consistent with competencies) and within layers (clear, internally consistent beliefs and values). When misalignment existed—for example, when teachers' personal missions conflicted with institutional expectations or their beliefs about learning contradicted mandated practices—creative risk-taking declined dramatically.

The implications extend far beyond education. Professional coherence is a prerequisite for creative confidence across all domains, reducing the psychological barriers that typically inhibit innovative action. When individuals experience alignment between who they are, what they value, and how they work, the perceived risks of creativity diminish while the perceived rewards—personal fulfilment, professional growth, positive impact—become more salient and motivating.

Coherence Explains Autonomy's Criticality

The importance of professional coherence also helps explain why autonomy has emerged as a critical factor in creative contexts, especially in workplace environments where there is a goal for people to take more creative risks. When individuals have autonomy—genuine freedom to choose how they approach their work, allocate their time, and make decisions about their methods—they can create the alignment between their personal values and their preferred ways of working that professional coherence requires.

This is why autonomy-supportive environments have been found to foster intrinsic motivation, enhance creative performance, and reduce the psychological barriers that typically inhibit innovative action (Gürbüz et al., 2024; Zhang et al., 2022).

> Autonomy allows people to work in ways that feel meaningful and authentic to them, creating the internal coherence that transforms creative risk-taking from a threatening prospect into a natural expression of personal purpose and professional identity.

The need for personal integrity is why organisations seeking to build creative confidence must move beyond simply encouraging creativity to systematically providing the autonomy that enables individuals to align their work with their values, ultimately creating the coherence that makes creative confidence possible.

Collective Creativity Through Organisational Coherence

While individual coherence is essential, creativity rarely operates in isolation. Research by Cirella (2021) on collective creativity reveals that optimal creative outcomes emerge when organisational variables achieve coherence with team-level dynamics and individual capabilities. Through extensive case studies, Cirella identified five critical organisational variables that support collective creativity:

Structured Processes: Clear, deliberate processes provide a balanced framework that channels diverse ideas into productive, goal-oriented creative efforts, helping teams manage ambiguity and maintain creative momentum.

Work-Related Team Diversity: Bringing together individuals with varied backgrounds, roles, and perspectives stimulates broader idea generation and enables creative problem-solving through exposure to different viewpoints and expertise.

Boundary Openness: Encouraging open knowledge flows and collaboration beyond traditional team or departmental boundaries breaks down silos and invites fresh, external input to enrich creative progress.

Adequate Resources: Ensuring that teams have sufficient time, funding, tools, and management support removes practical barriers, allowing members to develop and implement creative solutions without unnecessary constraints.

Relevant Technology Support: Providing up-to-date and accessible technological tools and platforms enables creative teams to efficiently capture, develop, and share ideas, as well as experiment and iterate throughout the innovation process.

The key insight from this research is that these variables must work coherently together—they cannot be implemented piecemeal. A structured creative process is ineffective without adequate resources; team diversity becomes counterproductive without boundary openness that allows for knowledge flow; technology support is meaningless without teams capable of utilising it effectively. When coherence exists across these organisational dimensions,

"Teams and groups [can develop] their (collective) creativity in ways that multiply individual creative contributions." (Cirella, 2021)

Importantly, this organisational coherence must also align with the characteristics and needs of the creative teams themselves. The research shows that collective creativity flourishes when there is coherence between organisational design choices and team composition, as well as coherence within each domain.

Teams need both internal alignment (shared purpose, complementary skills, effective communication) and external alignment (organisational structures that support rather than constrain creative work). Internally, coherence is fostered when all members are united by a clear, meaningful purpose and understand how their unique strengths and expertise contribute to shared goals.

Effective communication and mutual trust are the bedrock of this internal alignment, enabling team members to collaborate openly, resolve conflicts constructively, and adapt flexibly to changing demands.

Externally, coherence is reinforced when organisational systems, resource flows, and leadership practices create an environment where teams are empowered to make decisions, experiment, and learn together without unnecessary bureaucratic barriers.

When both the inner workings of the team and the external context are harmoniously aligned, teams experience greater psychological safety, resilience under pressure, a willingness to take risks, and the collective creative capacity needed to produce outstanding innovative outcomes.

When organisational coherence is absent—when stated innovation goals clash with decisions around risk, when resource allocation contradicts creative priorities, or when technology systems impede rather than enable collaboration—resistance becomes embedded in the system, and teams experience increased friction.

Due to increased risk perception, this results in a reduction in creative output. The misalignment creates additional sources of risk and uncertainty that team members must navigate, diverting energy from creative work and diminishing overall creative confidence.

Creative Systems Theory: Coherence for Sustained Innovation

The most comprehensive perspective on creative coherence comes from Creative Systems Theory (CST), which views creativity as emerging from the dynamic alignment of multiple interconnected systems. CST posits that meaningful innovation requires

"The systemic alignment of individual capacities, social context, and environmental conditions to produce change that is both novel and meaningful." (Creative Systems Theory, 2022)

According to CST, creativity operates through what can be understood as "circular causality"—where individual capabilities influence social contexts, which shape environmental conditions, which in turn affect individual development, creating continuous feedback loops of creative potential (Csikszentmihalyi, 1988).

Figure 12- The circular causality in the creative system

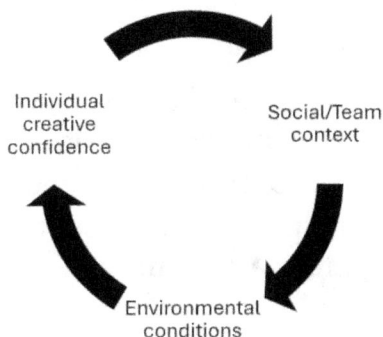

This systemic perspective reveals that sustainable creativity depends not on optimising any single component, but on achieving coherence across the entire creative ecosystem.

CST identifies coherence as operating at multiple levels simultaneously:

- Individual-Social Coherence: Personal creative capabilities must align with social opportunities for expression and recognition.

- Social-Environmental Coherence: Team and organisational creative processes must fit within broader cultural and market contexts.

- Individual-Environmental Coherence: Personal creative vision must connect with real-world needs and opportunities.

- Temporal Coherence: Creative efforts must be sustained over time through consistent alignment and mutual reinforcement.

When systemic coherence exists, creativity becomes self-reinforcing. Individual creative confidence grows through successful creative experiences, which enhances team creative capacity, which creates organisational innovative capability, which generates environmental opportunities for further creative expression.

Conversely, when systemic incoherence exists—when individual aspirations conflict with social norms, when organisational innovation rhetoric contradicts resource allocation or risk tolerance, when environmental pressures undermine long-term creative development—the entire creative system becomes fragmented, feels more risky and less capable of sustained innovation.

Building Coherence: Strategies for Creative Alignment

The research on professional coherence, collective creativity, and creative systems suggests several key strategies for building and maintaining creative coherence:

Individual Level Coherence: People benefit from engaging in reflective practice to identify and align their core values, beliefs, capabilities, and aspirations. Alignment involves honest self-assessment, clarifying what matters to them most, and undertaking a deliberate effort to create work environments that support the authentic expression of one's creative identity (Massie et al., 2022).

Team Level Coherence: Creative teams require structured processes for developing a shared purpose, establishing complementary roles, and establishing communication patterns that support both individual creative expression and collective creative achievement. Alignment at the team level requires attention to both task coherence (aligned goals and methods) and relational coherence (trust, psychological safety, mutual respect) (Cirella, 2021).

Organisational Level Coherence: Organisations must be clear about their innovation objectives and risk tolerance, and systematically align their formal structures, resource allocation, reward systems, and cultural norms with these guidelines. Achieving coherence means ensuring that performance management, promotion criteria, resource allocation, and leadership behaviours all consistently support rather than undermine creative risk-taking (Cirella, 2021).

Systemic Level Coherence: Leaders and organisations must actively scan their external environment to identify opportunities for creative contribution and align internal creative capabilities with external creative needs. Systemic coherence also involves strategic thinking about how:

- Organisational creative strengths can address real-world challenges and opportunities.
- Organisations can partner with other agencies, community groups, institutions, or organisations to develop creative skills and enhance better alignment with the societies they serve.

Coherence as the Catalyst for Creative Flow

When coherence exists across and within creative layers, something remarkable happens: creativity begins to flow naturally rather than requiring forced effort. Creative confidence emerges organically from the alignment between personal values and professional environments, between individual capabilities and team needs, between organisational aspirations and social realities. Risk-taking becomes beautiful rather than frightening because it occurs within a context of mutual support and shared purpose, and it allows individuals, organisations and communities to achieve their fullest potential.

The research consistently shows that this coherent creativity produces superior outcomes—not just more creative ideas, but more implementable innovations that create genuine value for individuals, organisations, and communities. Professional development accelerates, team performance improves, organisational innovation capacity grows, and societal benefit increases when creative systems achieve coherence (Massie et al., 2022; Cirella, 2021).

Leadership Builds The Bridges

As this exploration of creative coherence reveals, the alignment necessary for creativity to flourish rarely emerges spontaneously. It requires intentional cultivation, systematic attention, and ongoing maintenance. Most critically, it requires leadership that understands coherence as the foundation of creative capability and commits to building alignment across all layers of their organisation and communities.

The next section of this book examines the role of leaders in creativity, and more specifically, why your creativity matters most. We will see that fundamentally, your own creativity must be a priority, because it is through your inspiration and influence that the creative potential in others is materialised.

You serve as the architect and engineer of creative coherence within your organisations and across your communities. Through your decisions, you shape the conditions that either support or crush creative confidence, and you either build or destroy the bridges between layers that foster consistency and shared purpose. You are the enabler of creativity, and in the next section, we will explore how you can effectively exercise this role to achieve maximum impact and support meaningful change.

17   Creation Requires Destruction

"The old must always make way for the new, and one thing must be built out of the ruins of another." ~ *Lucretius*

In the previous chapter, we discussed the losses people perceive when faced with a creative challenge; from initiating and implementing new ideas. Now we come to the cold, hard truth: in order to enact creativity and bring about change, you will need to let something go.

You will need to accept some of the risks previously identified and sanction some form of destruction. This inevitability is explained by the ancient Hermetic principle of polarity, also known as the natural law of opposites, which teaches us about the profound and true nature of existence:

"Everything is dual; everything has poles; everything has its pair of opposites".

This wisdom reveals the fundamental reality that we cannot know hot without cold, light without dark, peace without war, or joy without sorrow. It also illuminates a fundamental aspect of creativity: we cannot create without simultaneously destroying something, whether it be tangible structures and systems or intangible beliefs, behaviours, and identities.

Change, therefore, not only depends on our ability to be creative, but also on our ability to be destructive.

The Concept Of Creative Destruction

There is no better place to begin exploring the inseparable partnership between creation and destruction than the field of economics. It was the Austrian economist Joseph Schumpeter who succinctly described the paradoxical relationship when he coined the phrase "creative destruction" (McCraw, 2007).

In his landmark 1942 work, Schumpeter described how capitalism is propelled not by gentle progress but by relentless cycles of upheaval. Every new technology, product, business or banking model disrupts and often dismantles what came before. The automobile replaced the horse and carriage; streaming services rendered video rental stores obsolete, and automatic tellers have destroyed long-held assumptions about customer service. Schumpeter argued that these erosions are not unfortunate byproducts, but the very engine of economic growth and renewal.

What makes this logic so powerful—and so often overlooked—is that it exposes a difficult truth: to reap the rewards of creativity and achieve the desired change, you have to disrupt and destroy what already exists.

Progress demands that familiar systems and comfortable routines be swept aside to make room for the new. Whether in markets, organisations, or our own lives, true creativity requires the removal of what came before. Sometimes this letting go is a little, sometimes it is a lot, but recognising and embracing this polarity is not just an economic lesson—it is a fundamental principle for growth and renewal in any sphere.

Creative destruction is just as vital in science and social movements as it is in economics. In science, progress often means dismantling established theories and methods to make way for new, more robust explanations. Recent approaches, such as "creative destruction replication," actively pit competing theories against one another, utilising rigorous testing and open science practices to prune outdated ideas and replace them with frameworks that better explain the world. This process ensures that scientific knowledge evolves, even if it means relinquishing once-cherished concepts.

Our societies, too, are engines of creative destruction. They challenge and ultimately dismantle entrenched social norms, laws, and institutions. Think of the civil rights movement, women's suffrage, or LGBTQ+ rights campaigns. These movements dismantled dogmatic beliefs rooted in inequality and systems that restricted participation, replacing them with new rules and a renewed respect for the dignity and equality of all human life.

The destruction phase was not necessarily peaceful, with many imposing resistance on the dismantling process, resulting in verbal and physical conflict. History shows that the transformation may not be a smooth process. However, it is through this cycle of destruction and creation that societies adapt and progress.

What We Destroy to Create

To make way for the new, the old must be dissolved, demolished or destroyed. But what is the "old" we need to let go of to move forward with creative opportunities? Most obviously, these can be the old systems and structures that no longer serve an organisation or community. However, a deeper layer of destruction occurs beneath the surface, involving the dismantling of existing beliefs, habits, and identities that are no longer relevant or inhibit the implementation of the idea.

It can be considered that creative destruction unfolds across three distinct layers: the most visible layer involves discarding the things that we can see—outdated tools, technologies and equipment that has outlived their usefulness. Beneath this surface, creativity requires the dismantling of less tangible things such as behaviours and unspoken rules, including ingrained habits, routines and expected behaviours. These act as the unwritten norms that quietly reinforce the status quo.

Most profoundly, true transformation demands letting go of deeply held beliefs, emotional attachments, and aspects of personal or collective identity that may not support movement to the new state. These levels of destruction are shown on the following diagram.

Figure 13- The layers of creative destruction

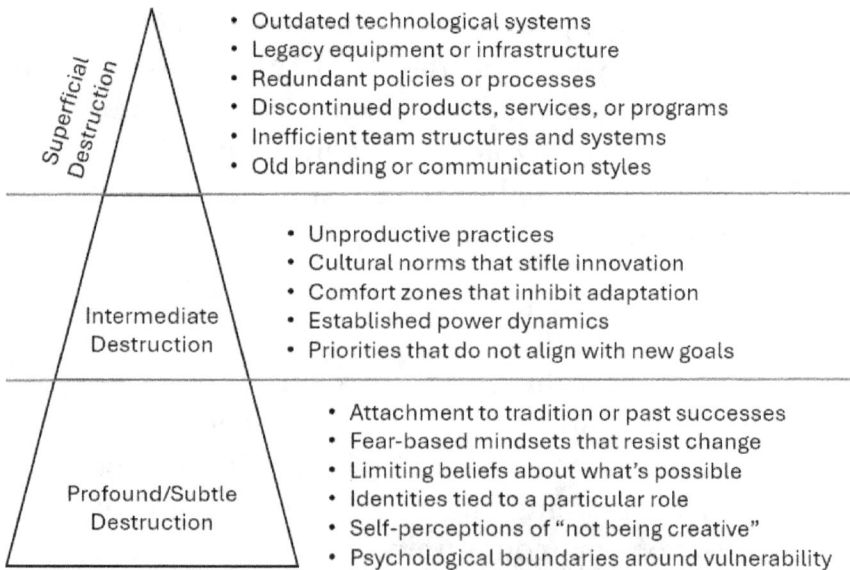

Superficial Destruction
- Outdated technological systems
- Legacy equipment or infrastructure
- Redundant policies or processes
- Discontinued products, services, or programs
- Inefficient team structures and systems
- Old branding or communication styles

Intermediate Destruction
- Unproductive practices
- Cultural norms that stifle innovation
- Comfort zones that inhibit adaptation
- Established power dynamics
- Priorities that do not align with new goals

Profound/Subtle Destruction
- Attachment to tradition or past successes
- Fear-based mindsets that resist change
- Limiting beliefs about what's possible
- Identities tied to a particular role
- Self-perceptions of "not being creative"
- Psychological boundaries around vulnerability

If we focus exclusively on superficial changes—removing legacy systems or processes—without addressing the deeper, more subtle layers of destruction beneath, even the most promising ideas will struggle to take root and flourish.

> Only by engaging with the destruction of assumptions, attachments, and identities that lie below the waterline can creators and organisations fully unlock creative confidence and realise the value of bold change.

True and sustained innovation requires not just technical upgrades but deliberate work to challenge mindsets, overcome personal limitations, and redefine what is possible, both collectively and individually.

Getting Comfortable With Creative Destruction

Developing comfort with creative destruction requires a dual approach that addresses both individual capability-building and organisational responsibility for reliable and relevant support.

On the personal side, individuals must cultivate a growth mindset through deliberate practice—embracing challenges as learning opportunities, developing psychological detachment skills through mindfulness, and building resilience through mastery experiences that strengthen their capacity to navigate uncertainty and let go of familiar patterns.

However, organisations bear equal responsibility for creating the psychological safety necessary to support the often-difficult emotional processes that accompany creative destruction, including grief over lost systems, roles, or ways of working that may have defined a deeply held professional identity.

It may not often be considered, but unresolved grief from organisational change can be a significant barrier to creativity and performance (McKinsey & Company, 2020), making it essential for leaders to acknowledge feelings of loss, hold rituals that honour what is being left behind, and provide structured support for employees experiencing the natural resistance that emerges when fundamental changes threaten basic human needs for control, certainty, identity, and belonging.

By combining individual growth mindset development with organisational commitment to psychological safety and grief support, organisations can create the coherence necessary for creative destruction to become a source of inspiration rather than debilitating fear—enabling people to confidently let go of the old to make space for meaningful innovation.

Creative Destruction And Coherence

The relationship between creation and destruction is fundamental to the innovation process. However, it is also just one of the necessary alignments for creative flow. We have seen in the previous chapters that there are individual and organisational components that play a role in creative risk evaluations, and that creativity only flows through organisations when there is continuity across the risk/reward assessments of multiple decision-making layers.

For creativity to be enacted and creative confidence to be built, there must be coherence between creation and destruction, as well as between our inner willingness to challenge ourselves and the external conditions that support transformation. Only when these elements are in sync can innovation take root and the foundations be established for ongoing creative action.

WHY YOUR CREATIVITY MATTERS MOST

In the previous section, we established that creativity powers all public sector change. We now turn our focus to one crucial insight: leaders are creators. Creativity is not just something you do on the weekends when you play with clay, landscape your garden, or develop a great new recipe. Every day, as a leader, you are constantly building, forming, and shaping systems, structures, capabilities and opportunities for growth.

This section explores why the creativity of leaders is foundational to the success of their organisations and the establishment of innovative cultures. Leaders occupy a unique vantage point: they see across boundaries, set the vision, coordinate resources, and craft coherence. They also nurture individual ability and motivation and create opportunities that allow people to achieve their fullest potential.

Perhaps most importantly, you cannot bring out creativity in others unless you actively cultivate it in yourself. When you invest in your own creative growth, you model what meaningful change looks like. This section will inspire you to recognise and celebrate the creativity you already exercise, and to nurture your own creative abilities with intention and awareness, for the benefit of yourself and the communities you serve.

18   You Are Creative

When you take a step back and see how many new and valuable things you bring forth each day, you will begin to appreciate just how creative you actually are.

When I meet people and tell them I work in the field of creativity, there is one response I hear frequently.

"I am not creative."

These words of self-criticism are shared usually in a nonchalant way and yet convey some crucial information. They demonstrate that this person believes creativity is an admirable characteristic. Yet, they also believe it is one in which they are deficient.

Through an upbringing that conflates creativity with art, and in a career that may have denigrated it as a distraction from "serious" work, they have come to a point where they believe they no longer possess it.

They bring into the conversation many myths about creativity – what it is, who has it and why they are not creative. They come bearing internalised comparisons with those they see as creative superiors, along with all the criticism they have received in the past when trying creative hobbies or contemplating alternative careers.

This chapter counters the claim that you or anyone else you know is not creative and dispels this malicious myth. Everyone is creative, and it is simply someone's beliefs that hold them back from embracing this gift. Here are some counterclaims that may help you shift your thinking and bring your best self to the table.

You Were Born Creative

You are born of creativity—you are the living result of a process that began with the meeting of two unique strands of DNA, blending genes in patterns that have never existed before. From the moment of conception, you became a stunning act of nature's invention, a combination of elements that culminated in your individuality.

> There has never been, and will never be, another person identical to you, and so merely through your existence, you embody the very criteria that define creativity: something new and something valuable.

The inherent nature of your creativity is confirmed by the fact that at age five you would have been classified a creative genius (Land & Jarman, 1992)—spontaneously imagining, inventing, and problem-solving with authenticity and undiluted creativity. Your beginning on this earth tells a different story than the myths you manifest now. While it may have been denied or closeted away for decades, creativity is an innate, foundational truth of your existence. No one arrives in this world without it.

Creativity Is Ingrained In Your Body

Creativity is also woven into every element of your body and is present in every process that keeps you alive. Neuroscience and psychology demonstrate that creative cognition is a universal human capacity; imagination is ingrained in our brains from the earliest stages of development. Moreover, in response to everything you experience, your brain is constantly forging new connections, reorganising and reshaping itself—a phenomenon known as neuroplasticity. Your brain recreates itself continuously based on where you choose to place your attention and effort, forging pathways for the habits you practice.

Beyond the brain, your body is right at this moment, manufacturing millions of new cells, revitalising tissues and adapting to changing environments. Every heartbeat, every breath, and every act of healing is an act of invention at the cellular level, showing that your body is constantly crafting new structures and chemistry in real time.

This creativity extends through our senses to the way we interact with the world. Using sight, sound, touch, taste, and smell, your body gathers endless information, and through your innate intelligence, you interpret it and express yourself in ways that only you can. You are constantly producing new and valuable responses to the stimulus you receive.

Creativity ≠ Art

One of the most prevalent myths about creativity is that it is synonymous with art. This misconception has gained traction over the years due to a narrowed educational and cultural focus. Creativity, in its purest form, is simply the development of something new and valuable—a process that exists everywhere, not only just in a studio or on a stage.

Creativity is present in the building of human connection, where two individuals, each with their own perspectives and experiences, come together to form something completely new— a relationship that has never existed before.

Creativity is also core to the resolution of everyday problems, where new and valuable approaches are found to fix a conundrum and forge a path forward. Even when a person has an insight that changes their view of the world or the way they work, creativity is there too.

> Creativity unfolds in countless ways in boardrooms and offices every day—manifesting in things we may take for granted: an improved workflow, a new policy or process, an informative conversation, a new collaboration or the way we navigate a challenging situation.

The truth is, most creativity is not captured in art, but these everyday forms are just as valuable. Every inventive act—whether developing a new technology or work practice, moderating a workplace conflict or simply adapting your behaviour to a small office change—demonstrates creativity in action. To limit our understanding of creativity to the realm of artistic pursuits is to miss its pervasive, transformative presence in every facet of human life.

Creativity Includes Individual Insight

Creativity is often imagined as the territory of Big-C creativity—groundbreaking inventions, disruptive technologies, bold new expressions that shape the world and earn recognition, fame, acclaim and awards. Yet, this view overlooks the process by which creative outputs are generated.

Every invention begins with individual insight, and a personal realisation precedes every profound change.

The concept of mini-c creativity validates the idea that every personal discovery is an act of creation. Every time you learn something new, you are recombining your consciousness, reshaping your systems of thinking and moving forward in a new form.

This is creativity at its most intimate—a fresh idea or realisation that is new and valuable to the person who experiences it, regardless of whether it ever shapes culture or is seen by others.

These moments of mini-c creativity do not have to be shared; they are significant simply because they exist and have created change within you.

Because new knowledge is not something passively received; it is actively formed through the interplay of experience, curiosity, and reflection and through a process of adding to and deleting information previously held. The process of creating meaning and forging new ways of thinking happens continually—sometimes quietly, sometimes dramatically—and it is this daily act of internal creation that generates new potential.

When creativity is understood as individual insight, it becomes clear just how much creativity flows through your life every single day. Recognising mini-c moments, embracing them, and valuing personal insight allows us to reframe creativity, from being a rare talent to a natural rhythm in the human experience.

Creativity Is Less About Courses and More About Courage

Many people think creativity comes with certificates attached – through degrees in art, courses in craft or with resumes listing agile development or design thinking accreditations. Supporting this myth is the plethora of programs urging us to invest in building creative skills, as if the key to creativity lies in mastering a specific technique or curriculum. Then there are the cranial stimulation products, selling creative advantage at a very profitable price.

While these courses, certificates and tools can certainly make a difference, the reality is that the results do not always translate into other aspects of life. The most fundamental skill for creativity is not found in formal instruction, but in self-confidence—understanding what is truly meaningful to us, knowing our values, our unique perspectives and strengths, and then taking action and learning through the process of practice.

Being in touch with our emotions and expectations, and finding ways to transform them into expansiveness, is essential. Creativity depends on being conscious of how we make connections—both with ideas and with people—and being open to perspectives different from our own. It comes from an understanding of who we are, what we have to offer, and the courage to express it, even if that means doing things differently or challenging the status quo. Creativity means moving into the unknown, and while others can serve as valuable guides, the only way you get better at it is by doing it.

Of course, due to the inherent risk in creativity, it does not happen without courage, and for courage to emerge, a person needs to be aware of all the fears and beliefs that hold them back. Yes, it is possible to invest in training and skill-building, but it is creative confidence must be built from deep individual intelligence. That confidence, that willingness to show up and create, comes from a deep personal relationship—knowing oneself, valuing one's insights, and daring to bring them forward.

You Are Creating Your Life Every Day

Here is the ultimate truth: If you believe you are creative, you will be. If you do not believe you are creative, you will not be. It is a truth acclaimed in ancient wisdom and proven in modern psychology; your reality reflects your beliefs.

> Your inner narrative is the critical barrier to creativity—not your ability or knowledge, but the beliefs you hold about your creative power, others, and the world around you.

Limiting beliefs like "I am not creative" become self-fulfilling prophecies. If you do not trust your creative energy, you will reject opportunities to practice creative skills and taking risks, you will dismiss ideas before they have a chance to grow, and the self-sabotaging notion that "I'm not creative" grows stronger with time.

On the other hand, embracing a growth mindset means that you are more likely to engage in creative exercises and practice skills, such as fostering curiosity and stretching beyond your comfort zone. With practice comes confidence—the belief in your own creative potential—and this fuels your willingness to try new things, embrace challenges, and persist through setbacks. Every time you choose to think differently or open up to new ways of seeing, you are actively shaping your experience and building a belief in your creative capacity. Through action, you alter your reality.

What is wonderful is that the fact that your beliefs shape reality is further evidence that you are creative, whether you believe it or not. Every moment, your thoughts and the actions that arise from them are shaping your personal and professional lives in ways seen and unseen. Every second, through your choices, you are constructing your life. This is the ultimate creative act and confirms that, yes, you are, without a doubt, creative.

19 Your Work Is Creative

There is no doubt that you are creative, and your work is too. You are engaged in what can be considered one of the most inherently creative professions—leadership.

If you were to keep a diary of all the decisions you made and actions you took during the day, it would be easy to see that the vast majority of your time is spent on non-routine, or heuristic, tasks.

Unlike routine (algorithmic) work, leadership does not come with any clear procedures, and it demands a high degree of personal judgement and empathetic problem-solving. You need to develop new and valuable responses to random problems, which we now know represent creativity in action.

> The daily work of leadership involves continual creative adaptation, using past experiences and imaginative futures to respond to urgent and uncertain circumstances. This is why, when we look under the hood of a leadership brain, we can see it using the same processes employed by artists and inventors.

As a leader, you are also the creator of the organisational structures, systems and culture that enable creative confidence in others. You are responsible for building the environments that allow people to be their best.

Leadership is, and always has been, creative work. Let's delve into why.

Leadership Is Inherently Heuristic Work

A heuristic is a mental shortcut or rule of thumb that people use to simplify decision-making and problem-solving in multifaceted situations where time, information, or resources are limited. When it is impossible to evaluate all information and every option systematically, these approaches allow us to reach good enough solutions efficiently.

While termed as a shortcut, heuristic processes are still comprehensive and reasoned. They use both intuitive and rational approaches (Gigerenzer, 2023), combining past experiences with imagination about future states, and then continually adapting the best guess to match the complexity of the environment.

Heuristic work is inherently creative because it requires generating new solutions and making adaptive judgments in situations without predetermined procedures. In this way, it demands the same imaginative and innovative thinking processes that characterise all forms of creativity.

Heuristic work is also the lifeblood of leaders who are consistently faced with ill-defined problems, many of which may have never been encountered before, and which are characterised by ambiguity, "complexity, conflict, and change" (Mumford et al., 2000). In these situations, the imperative is not only to solve the problem but also to first identify the core problem and determine what information is needed to assist.

Because there are no rule books or step-by-step guides for many of the problems you face, you are involved in not only heuristic work, but also creative work.

Neurological Evidence for Leadership Creativity

Given the creative nature of the work leaders do, it is no surprise that neuroscience reveals the cognitive processes they use daily are virtually identical to those employed by artists and inventors. They use the same neural networks driving creativity across all domains.

Three specific brain networks have been identified to work together during creative thinking: the Default Mode Network (DMN), which generates novel ideas and possibilities; the Executive Control Network (ECN), which evaluates and refines those ideas; and the Salience Network, which coordinates between them (Beaty et al., 2018; Kaufman & Gregoire, 2015).

What makes highly creative individuals unique is their ability to activate both the DMN and ECN simultaneously—something that normally does not happen, since these networks typically work in opposition to each other (Beaty et al., 2018; Jung et al., 2013).

When leaders are faced with ambiguous situations where there are no clear procedures to follow, then they must make decisions that combine information and intuition and engage both the DMN and ECN in the same way that artists do. The DMN generates multiple possibilities by drawing connections between disparate experiences and information. At the same time, the ECN simultaneously evaluates which options are most viable given the constraints and goals at hand (Beaty et al., 2018). The salience network then determines which creative insights deserve immediate attention and action, given the context that the person faces.

This process is fundamentally the same whether you are a leader designing a new organisational structure, a composer constructing a symphony, or an inventor developing the next best light bulb. All three require the brain to synthesise existing knowledge in novel ways, imagine possibilities that do not yet exist, and adapt solutions in real-time based on emerging information (Jung et al., 2013; Kaufman & Gregoire, 2015). Leaders, like artists, must constantly generate original responses to unique challenges, drawing from their full reservoir of experience to create something new.

The neurological evidence is clear: leadership work does not just require creativity—it is creativity, activating the identical brain processes that drive human innovation across all domains.

The Creative Mechanisms of Daily Leadership

The most compelling evidence for leadership as creative work comes from examining the specific tasks leaders perform daily. Each core leadership function demands the same processes that define creative work no matter where it is found: generating novel and valuable ideas, adapting to changing circumstances, and synthesising diverse elements into coherent wholes.

Vision Setting: Creating Futures

Visionary leadership is fundamentally an act of creative imagination. Leaders must reconcile and combine complex, often contradictory information about market trends, organisational capabilities, and stakeholder needs to construct a compelling future narrative. They must paint a picture of the new future that represents the values and desires of the teams and communities that they serve, and then communicate this in a way that creates emotional resonance. In doing so, they also play a vital role as a connector, linking present circumstances with imagined future states and showing how the employee's daily work contributes to making a meaningful difference.

Problem Solving: Creating Solutions to Complex Challenges

One of the primary jobs of a leader is problem-solving. As we have seen in the previous section, the development of new and valuable responses to challenges is a creative process. Because when plans unravel—whether due to resource shortages, shifting stakeholder expectations, or technical snags—leaders face a choice: double down on failed routines or pivot creatively and try something new. For those who meet the moment with bravery, they move into creative mode, inviting diverse perspectives, asking thought-provoking questions ("What could we do, not just what should we do?"), and rapidly test unconventional solutions. In this way, creative problem-solving and the willingness to experiment not only provide a way forward but also contribute to organisational resilience and creative confidence.

Team Building: Creating Human Synergy

Forming synergies among diverse personalities represents one of leadership's most creative challenges. To do this, and to establish effective teams, leaders must dynamically manage three components simultaneously, being "teamwork, taskwork, and affect" (Wróbel & Mikkelsen, 2021). Like conductors orchestrating complex musical arrangements, leaders must blend different personalities, skills, and perspectives into a harmonious and productive whole. They must harness the power of positive emotional states to bond and lift the team, while balancing the need for structure and process with the flexibility to adapt to evolving team and environmental dynamics. In this way, creating a positive team climate requires the same agility that characterises jazz musicians or improvisation actors.

Communication: Creative Translation Across Contexts

Leadership communication demands both storytelling capacity

and constant creative adaptation. To be effective, leaders must craft their messaging to engage people on an emotional level. They must both impact their audience through positive affect and influence team members to take action. This emotional work of leaders mirrors that of writers and performers who must craft narratives that connect with varied audiences while maintaining authenticity and impact.

The complexity arises when messages must be relayed to different audiences, requiring leaders to shape and recombine narratives in new ways for various audiences, contexts, and purposes. For example, the messaging to the front-line workers is different from how the vision will be sold to a minister and their advisors. It is this continual adaptation, sometimes required on an ad-hoc basis, that adds to the creative nature of leadership communication.

Why Leaders Underestimate Their Creativity

Despite overwhelming evidence that leadership requires constant creativity, it is not a characteristic discussed or celebrated overtly in public sector offices. Many leaders either fail to recognise or dramatically downplay their creative skills.

Research provides some explanation for this phenomenon, uncovering subconscious prejudice against creative expression that reduces the perception of leadership potential. Mueller, Goncalo, and Kamdar (2011) found that there is substantial bias against leaders who display creative behaviours, even in workplaces that explicitly claimed to value creativity. Their studies showed that "creative people" were seen as competent and personable, but were judged less fit for leadership, and were less likely to be promoted over their purely useful peers.

This bias stems from the stereotype of leaders as people who reduce uncertainty and promote stability. In contrast, creativity is associated with unproven solutions and rocking the boat. The stereotypes and systematic biases mean that creative employees are gradually filtered out as they move up the corporate ladder, either exiting the organisation or being relegated to roles where they cannot fully utilise their valuable creative potential.

This bias also creates powerful incentives for leaders to mask their creative thinking behind analytical frameworks and rational processes, presenting themselves as purely logical, data-driven decision-makers. This cultural emphasis on rationality results in the fixed mindsets that are the antithesis of creative confidence and are a major barrier to individual and organisational growth. It also prevents investing in learning and development opportunities that will help them enhance their capabilities, benefiting both themselves and their agencies.

> The irony is that today's volatile governance environment requires exactly the kind of creative intelligence that pure data analysis cannot provide.

As CEO Jon Kirchner noted,

"When the world feels volatile, it's tempting to double down on what's familiar: performance metrics, hard data, and a proven business playbook. But this instinct often comes at the cost of the skill leaders need most right now: thinking creatively in the face of the unknown" (Kirchner, 2025).

Sadly, leaders have learned through organisational experience that displaying creative behaviours can be professionally detrimental. That is why it is vital to make it clear that creativity is essential for effective leadership and to celebrate it in all of its forms.

Your Creative Leadership Legacy

In conclusion, the evidence from multiple disciplines—neuroscience, psychology, organisational behaviour, and leadership research—converges on an undeniable truth: leadership is fundamentally creative work. Every day, you engage in heuristic tasks that demand the same cognitive processes used by artists and inventors, activating identical brain networks to generate novel solutions, adapt to uncertainty, and synthesise complex information into coherent action.

Whether you are setting vision, solving problems, building teams, or communicating across diverse contexts, you are creating something new and valuable that did not exist before. While organisational biases may pressure you to hide this creativity behind analytical frameworks, the volatile and complex challenges facing today's leaders require exactly the kind of creative intelligence that routine procedures and pure data analysis cannot provide.

Recognising your work as inherently creative is not just an interesting intellectual exercise—it is essential for unleashing your full leadership potential and modelling the innovative thinking your organisation desperately needs.

Yet your creative capacity as a leader extends beyond your own problem-solving and decision-making. The most profound creative act of leadership lies in your ability to cultivate and unleash the creative potential of others, building environments where teams can think boldly and develop the creative confidence needed to tackle tomorrow's challenges.

20   You Create The Conditions

"Great leaders of innovation don't fit the conventional mould of 'good' leadership. Instead, they create the context in which others are both willing and able to innovate." ~ Linda A. Hill, Harvard Business School

In boardrooms and offices across the public sector, there is frequent discussion about the need for staff to be more innovative and to address the risk aversion that is hindering productivity. Leaders focus their discussions on recruiting creative talent, building innovation programs, reducing organisational red tape, and embedding expectations in performance agreements. Yet the most crucial factor in boosting creativity in organisations remains largely unspoken: leadership.

What is not acknowledged or addressed as much as it should be is the leader's role as the architect of creative conditions. It is leaders, like you, who lay the foundations upon which creative abilities are built and the framework that supports their expression. Moreover, you are also the engineer of the environment, ensuring that all parts of your team, division, or agency—all the cogs in your organisational machine—are working harmoniously to foster coherence. You are also the electrician for the broader creative system, ensuring the wiring and connections between boundaries are healthy and do not hamper creative flow.

It is a fact that organisational conditions—which you create—are the strongest predictors of confidence and performance (Amabile, 1998). However, they are often overlooked or underestimated due to the belief that creativity is the sole responsibility of an individual. We have seen, however, how creativity is contextual and how people's perceptions of risk determine their decisions to act creatively. Your role, then, is to design an environment where the risks of action are reduced and the rewards become powerful motivators. It is your responsibility to create the conditions that allow creative confidence to flourish.

Whether you are conscious of this or not, you do this every day by making deliberate decisions that develop ability, foster motivation, and provide opportunities for creative practice and to build confidence. Indirectly, your behaviour significantly influences what people believe is permissible and serves as a role model for their own risk-reward evaluations. Moreover, your unique vantage point enables you to connect ideas and people, aligning words and actions to increase your capacity to innovate.

Therefore, if you seek to bring about meaningful change, it is one of your most important responsibilities, if not the most important, to build the individual, team and organisational conditions that enable the development and expression of creative confidence in others. Here is how the decisions you make every day shape the ability, motivation and opportunity to build creative confidence in your organisation.

The AMO Framework For Creative Conditions

Understanding how you shape the environment for creativity is critical, and one of the most robust models to guide this is the Ability-Motivation-Opportunity (AMO) framework. Developed to explain the fundamental drivers of high performance (Marin-Garcia & Tomas, 2016), this framework reveals the truth about human performance: people perform at their best when they possess the necessary abilities, feel motivated to excel, and work in environments that provide opportunities for contribution.

What makes this framework particularly powerful for understanding creativity is its multiplicative nature, expressed as:

Performance (P) = Ability(A) x Motivation(M) x Opportunity(O).

Ability refers to the skills, knowledge, and cognitive capacity that enable individuals and teams to generate and implement new ideas. Ability answers the question: "*Can people act creatively?*"

Motivation centres on fostering intrinsic and extrinsic drivers that energise and sustain creative effort. Through motivation, we can answer the question, "*Do they want to act creatively?*"

Opportunity involves the structural and cultural conditions that allow support for positive risk/reward assessments. The opportunity components of the organisation help answer the question, "*Will people act creatively?*"

Unlike an additive model, where strengths in one area can compensate for deficiencies in another, the multiplicative nature means that a weakness in any single component dramatically undermines overall creative performance. Consider the implications: an employee with exceptional creative abilities and high motivation will achieve little if they lack opportunities to apply their talents. Conversely, providing opportunities without building abilities or fostering motivation yields equally disappointing results.

The multiplicative effect also creates significant benefits for anyone seeking to boost creativity, because it allows for synergistic ripple-like effects where improvements in one area amplify gains in the others. When you invest in building creative abilities, for instance, you simultaneously boost motivation as people gain confidence in their capabilities. Additionally, enhanced skills create new opportunities for broader participation in creative activities.

The OECD Observatory of Public Sector Innovation explicitly adopts the AMO model to guide its approach to fostering innovative capacity in government organisations. In its paper *"HR and Leadership Strategies for Building Innovative Public Sector Organisations"* (OECD, 2017), the OECD recognises that ability, motivation, and opportunity structures are essential for public sector innovation to flourish.

> As suggested by their framework, government agencies must systematically invest in practices that improve both domain-specific and creative skills, provide intrinsic incentives to invest creative effort, and build environments that transform abilities and motivation into real creative outcomes.

The following table presents a summary of the AMO components, and the next chapters will explore each dimension in greater detail.

Table 9 – The AMO model for creative confidence

	Ability	**Motivation**	**Opportunity**
Question it asks	*Can people act creatively?*	*Do they want to act creatively?*	*Will people act creatively?*
Elements	1. Domain-specific skills 2. Creative growth mindset 3. Creative self-efficacy 4. Intellectual risk-taking 5. Creativity skills	• Autonomy • Mastery • Purpose	• Structural components of the organisation • Cultural norms

Ability: Building Creative Capacity

Creative ability in the public sector is multifaceted, relying on five interconnected foundations.

1. Deep domain-specific skills form the essential groundwork. Public servants must possess solid expertise in their policy or service area or leadership specialty, as expertise is the source material from which creative ideas are drawn.

2. A creative growth mindset is crucial. Leaders can nurture the belief that creativity is a skill anyone can develop through effort and learning, rather than a fixed personal trait.

3. Creative self-efficacy—the confidence people have in their own creative potential—grows through experience, practice, and being given meaningful opportunities to contribute.

4. Intellectual risk taking—the willingness to bear discomfort in order to share ideas and deliver something of value—is essential for creative action.

5. Creativity-relevant skills—such as the capacity for divergent thinking, reframing problems, and experimenting with new approaches—enable individuals to apply their expertise in novel and useful ways within their domain.

These abilities are mutually reinforcing. Domain and creative skills equip people to tackle new problems; a growth mindset and self-efficacy prime them to move forward, intellectual risk-taking pushes them to act, persist through setbacks, and build creative confidence. Together, they answer the fundamental question: *"Can people act creatively? "*

Nurturing Intrinsic Motivation

As we discussed in the previous chapter, creative work is non-routine work and it is risky; there is no instruction manual, and challenges are complex or ambiguous. People must feel compelled to work through the discomfort, and through motivation, we can answer the question, "*Do they want to act creatively?*"

In such environments, it is intrinsic motivation, a sense that the work is inherently important, that compels people to act, and it is achieved through autonomy, mastery, and purpose (Pink, 2018).

Autonomy is achieved when leaders provide the freedom and control to choose how, when, and what work is done, allowing for personal initiative, alignment with individual preferences, and a sense of ownership over the work.

Mastery is supported by leaders who provide opportunities for continual improvement and the development of expertise in skills that individuals find meaningful. This element reflects the ability component discussed previously and has elements of both domain-specific skills and creative confidence.

Purpose is the sense that one's work contributes to a meaningful goal or vision and is aided by clear and constant communication from leadership about the benefits that the desired change delivers for the organisation and the communities it serves.

While extrinsic rewards (bonuses, promotions, or recognition) and punishments may seem like an attractive motivational tool, research shows that they must be employed with care, as they can unintentionally undermine intrinsic motivation. Being paid to do work that people already find purposeful cheapens the experience and can diminish creativity and engagement. Instead, to maintain motivation, the leader's role is to blend relevant recognition with opportunities for meaningful work.

Opportunity: Creating Permission for Practice

Creativity, like every other skill, is a practice. It can only flourish when individuals are given real space and permission to experiment, share ideas, take thoughtful risks and learn. Opportunity in this context is twofold: it hinges on both:

- Structural supports—such as time, resources, and decision-making authority.

- Cultural norms that define how safe it is to contribute ideas, try new approaches, and even fail.

When it comes to nurturing creativity, organisational design matters. Structures that empower teams with autonomy, flexibility, and access to resources determine the extent of creative space. Additionally, processes and procedures, especially for tasks such as approvals, procurement, or resource allocation, can either enforce rigidity or allow for local adaptation, subsequently stifling or supporting creative problem-solving.

Leaders have a profound influence by signalling through words and actions whether risk-taking and learning from failure are valued or punished. When leaders respond to mistakes as learning opportunities and encourage open discussion about what went wrong, they foster psychological safety—a prerequisite for innovative thinking and collaboration. Alternatively, by shying away from meaningful work due to fear of the consequences, they also show others that cowardice is condoned.

In combination, the structural and cultural components of the organisation help answer the question, "*Will people act creatively?*"

Direct and Indirect Leadership Influence

As a leader, every day you are shaping your organisation's creative conditions through both overt decisions and subtle signals. You directly influence the environment by the way you allocate resources, set goals, evaluate performance, and role-model the behaviours that are deemed suitable.

At the same time, you indirectly influence creativity through your informal communication. Your tone in hallway conversations, openness in staff forums, and willingness to welcome dissenting views all contribute to an unspoken sense of what is permissible or encouraged. These informal cues can be as powerful—if not more so—than formal policies in shaping creative risk-taking and experimentation.

The ripple effect of these behaviours extends throughout teams: supportive leadership enhances team trust and psychological safety. At the same time, negative or disengaged conduct stifles confidence and innovation.

Decades of research demonstrated that daily leader behaviours— how feedback is given, how setbacks are handled, how success is celebrated—significantly influence whether individuals and teams feel safe and empowered to act creatively, or whether they will deem the risks far too great. Ultimately, leaders set in motion a dynamic system: every action and interaction, whether intended or not, triggers responses that either reinforce or undermine creative engagement across the entire organisation.

A summary of the mechanisms through which leaders shape creative conditions is shown in table on the following page.

Table 10 – The mechanisms leaders use to shape creative conditions

ABILITY	
Training and Development	Providing targeted skill development programs and creative thinking workshops builds both domain expertise and creative problem-solving capabilities
Growth mindset	By openly discussing failures as learning opportunities and celebrating "intelligent failures," leaders foster belief that creativity can be developed
Knowledge sharing	Creating opportunities for cross-functional learning and expertise exchange
Recruitment and selection	Hiring for both domain expertise and creative potential while valuing diverse perspectives
Coaching programs	Pairing experienced creative practitioners with developing staff to transfer skills and confidence
MOTIVATION	
Performance evaluation	Recognizing and rewarding creative contributions encourages sustained innovation and signals what is valued
Encouragement and support	Supportive communications and behaviours from leadership increases intrinsic motivation and collective creative confidence
Vision communication	Connecting individual work to larger purpose, sharing inspiring organizational stories, and articulating clear meaningful objectives creates drive and direction
Valuing ideas	Soliciting diverse perspectives and acting on ideas signals creativity's value
Autonomy provision	Allowing freedom in how work is done, and decisions are made enhances intrinsic motivation and ownership
Mastery support	Providing opportunities for skill development in meaningful areas
Recognition systems	Implementing formal and informal recognition for creative efforts, not just successful outcomes
Goal setting	Setting challenging, clear, and aligned goals that inspire creative solutions
OPPORTUNITY	
Resource and time allocation	Prioritising time, funding, and tools for creative thinking, experimentation and reflection
Delegation	Delegating meaningful decision authority and providing autonomy
Psychological safety	Admitting to mistakes and uncertainties, as well as positive approaches to sharing ideas and failures creates psychological safety for others
Facilitating connections	Creating informal meeting spaces and encouraging cross-functional dialogue enables knowledge sharing and creative collaborations
Process flexibility	Designing adaptable procedures and reducing rigid approvals to allow for local innovation and experimentation
Role modelling	Leaders demonstrate openness to new ideas, and learning from failure
Experimentation platforms	Creating formal mechanisms (innovation labs, pilot programs, hackathons) for testing new ideas
Positive risk culture	Establishing clear risk appetite statements, differentiated risk frameworks for innovation vs. compliance, and formal learning-from-failure protocols

The Leader's Helicopter View: Creating Coherence Across Boundaries

On the one hand, you play a crucial role in influencing individuals and teams to enhance their creativity. On the other hand, your leadership position provides a unique helicopter perspective—the ability to step back and see your organisation from a high-level vantage point, understanding how all moving parts interconnect and influence each other. This elevated perspective enables you to identify patterns, spot opportunities for creative connection, and align disparate initiatives toward common creative goals.

Those leaders who can effectively span boundaries—bridging gaps between departments, hierarchies, and external stakeholders—are seen as significantly more influential and drive superior innovation outcomes (Ernst et al., 2025; Liu et al., 2022).

> This is because your cross-boundary visibility allows you to forge connections between ideas, teams, and resources that others cannot see, creating coherence across the organisation and the communities you serve. This role is powerful, providing the basis for meaningful change far beyond your team or organisational fences.

By aligning creative efforts across different levels and functions, you become the architect of organisational coherence—ensuring that creativity flows effectively throughout the system rather than being trapped in isolated pockets. This critical capability will be explored in detail in the coming chapters, where we examine specific strategies for building and leveraging the advantage of your holistic view.

Your Leadership as the Catalyst: Shaping a Creative Future

As a leader, your role is nothing less than transformative—you are the architect, engineer, and electrician of creativity within your organisation.

This is because organisational conditions are the strongest predictors of creative performance (Amabile, 1996). However, leaders often underestimate their role in creating these conditions. As Teresa Amabile's research reveals, even highly creative individuals struggle in unsupportive environments. At the same time, ordinary people achieve extraordinary outcomes when the right conditions exist. This situation is described perfectly by Landry & Caust (2017).

"There is a reservoir of hidden potential and talent locked up in public bureaucracies. People can do much more if given the chance. This can unleash their discretionary effort. The desire to do more than you need to. But hard wired, rigid approaches within and across administrative systems, organizations, and individuals constrain what is possible." (Landry & Caust, 2017, p. 6).

The ability to foster creativity does not happen by chance; it is carefully crafted through continuous, deliberate choices, behaviours, and a clear vision. The AMO framework provides a powerful blueprint, but it is your leadership—your purpose-driven commitment to creating conditions—that truly turns potential into performance.

Above and beyond individual skills, motivation, or opportunities, you hold the unique power to build a culture where creative confidence flourishes—where risks are embraced intelligently, ideas are valued, and boundaries are seamlessly crossed. Your helicopter view enables you to see the subtle patterns, connect diverse parts, and align effort toward a shared purpose, inspiring others to innovate boldly. The future of public sector leadership depends on this unwavering dedication to building creative confidence across every agency.

In the chapters ahead, you will discover clear strategies that will enable you to enact your role as a creative catalyst and establish the creative conditions that transform risk aversion into proactive opportunity advancement.

21 You Build Creative Ability

"More than rigor, management discipline, integrity or even vision—successfully navigating an increasingly complex world will require creativity" **(IBM, 2010).**

Two of the most fundamental responsibilities of any leader are to ensure that their people:

1. Have the skills to fulfil their roles safely, efficiently, and effectively.

2. Are provided with opportunities to build upon these skills and achieve their fullest potential.

Over the past decades, the nature of work has significantly shifted from routine to non-routine tasks, fundamentally altering the skills required for organisational success.

HR Executive (2022) reports that, *"the growth rate in non-routine jobs is almost 25 times higher than the growth rate in routine jobs,"* while the Reserve Bank of Australia (2017) confirms that *"most of the employment over the past 30 years or so has come from non-routine cognitive jobs"* found across healthcare, education, and professional business services. This shift is not merely statistical—it represents a fundamental change in what organisations need from their people.

The World Economic Forum's Future of Jobs Report (2025) crystallises this reality, drawing on a comprehensive survey of over 1,000 employers across 55 economies, representing 22 industry clusters and a workforce of 14 million people. The report reveals that creative thinking now ranks fourth among essential skills, with 57% of employers considering it crucial—outranking other seemingly critical capabilities, including customer service, AI and big data, technological literacy, cybersecurity, teaching and mentoring, quality control, and environmental stewardship.

In my mind, this ranking makes sense because, within a complex and ever-changing context, creativity enables the continual adaptation and success of all the other skills.

What is also striking is how many of the other top-ranking skills for the future rely on creativity. Creative thinking is not just a standalone skill—it is foundational to many of the other competencies. For example, analytical thinking, the top-rated skill at 69%, relies on creativity to ask the right questions, reframe challenges, make sense of complex information, connect disparate ideas, and generate novel solutions to unfamiliar problems.

Similarly, resilience, flexibility, and agility —the second most valued skill set at 67%—are all about responding to change, overcoming setbacks, and finding new ways forward when the old paths no longer work, all of which are the hallmarks of creativity.

Leadership and social influence (61%) are also inseparable from creativity. Effective leaders inspire others by using their imagination to see beyond the status quo, telling the story of the organisation's future, encouraging diverse perspectives, and creating the conditions where all can flourish.

Creativity Is A Core Capability For The Public Sector

Every year, more data comes to light, and conversations occur that recognise creativity as the missing piece of the change puzzle. It is becoming more obvious that creativity is fundamental to organisational capability across all industries, particularly in the public sector. For example, the Australian and New Zealand School of Government (ANZSOG) recognises that *"creativity is a crucial part of policy capacity in governments"* (ANZSOG, 2023c) and is an essential contributor to important social change.

The OECD goes further to assert that the future of good governance actually depends on creative public servants (OECD, 2017c). While it is recognised that agencies currently rely on hiring external innovation specialists, the comprehensive challenges faced by our communities demand that creativity become a widely available in-house competency.

"In addition to the continued use of innovation specialists and external experts, government increasingly need to improve the skills and capabilities of existing staff" (OECD, 2017a, p.6).

Public sector officials must shift their thinking about creativity from viewing it as an outsourced function, brought in on a project basis, to understanding that it must emerge from within the public service itself. In-house capability is essential because creativity is not a competency required only in discrete innovation projects, but an ongoing ability to ask the right questions, to identify the gaps, find common threads and connect the dots. (OECD, 2017c).

Creativity is so crucial for the effectiveness of the public sector that it can no longer be delegated to consultancy firms and addressed at arm's length. It must become part of the public service culture, and this is where it becomes a clear leadership responsibility.

The Components Of Creative Ability

So, how do we build the creative confidence of our people? What skills and experiences do we need to provide so that when we are met with the question, *"Can our people be creative?"*, the answer is a resounding, "Yes!" What investments do we need to make in training and development programs to ensure they have what it takes to generate novel and valuable solutions?

The answer is not simply to make everyone complete an online mandatory training course on creative thinking. Creative ability is multifaceted, built on four interconnected foundations:

1. Domain expertise
2. Creative growth mindset
3. Creative self-efficacy
4. Intellectual risk-taking
5. Creativity skills.

These dimensions apply equally to leaders as they do to all staff, for it is the leader's own creative development that serves as both a role model and catalyst for organisational creative confidence.

Rather than hoping creativity will emerge naturally with the wave of a magic wand and some wishful thinking, effective leaders systematically build the conditions that enable people to grow and act on their creative potential. They recognise that creative ability is not fixed—it can be developed, strengthened, and unleashed through deliberate investment and practice. In other words, leaders enact their own growth mindsets to build creative confidence across the organisation.

Domain-Specific Skills: The Foundation of Creativity

The romantic notion that creativity springs from pure inspiration, with no requirements around skills or experience, is not only wrong—it is counterproductive. Research consistently demonstrates that creativity requires substantial domain expertise, and it very rarely crosses into other, unrelated domains (Baer, 2016). Pablo Picasso perfectly describes this reality.

"Learn the rules like a pro, so you can break them like an artist."

Across numerous studies, it has been confirmed that domain knowledge and experience significantly predict creative performance (An et al., 2016; Ward, 2008). With expertise comes the ability to understand the constraints, the stakeholders, the unintended consequences of past approaches, and the subtle interdependencies that novices miss. This deep knowledge becomes the raw material from which creative insights emerge.

Even more compelling is the finding that *"students with a higher level of domain knowledge benefit more from creativity training"* (Sun et al., 2020). This outcome clearly shows that expertise amplifies rather than constrains creative potential.

For leaders, this means that building creative capacity starts with building genuine expertise. Teams need time to develop deep technical knowledge, understand complex systems, and build sophisticated mental models of their work environment so that creativity skills can deliver their maximum effect.

Creative Growth Mindset: Creativity Can Be Developed

The most powerful factor in creative development is the simple belief that creativity can be developed. Growth mindset research shows that beliefs about ability significantly impact creative performance, with many studies finding correlations between growth mindset and both innovative thinking and behaviour (McCracken, 2024; Lieu et al., 2022).

Project ROAR (2023) also reports that employees at organisations promoting growth mindsets are:

- 34% likelier to feel a strong sense of ownership and commitment to the company
- 65% likelier to say that the company supports risk-taking
- 49% likelier to say that the company fosters innovation.

When people believe their creative abilities are fixed, they avoid challenges that might reveal limitations. When they believe creativity can be developed, they seek out opportunities to develop their creative capabilities and embrace challenges as opportunities to grow. For leaders, fostering a creative growth mindset means modelling and communicating the belief that everyone can develop creative capabilities through effort, learning, and practice.

Creative Self-Efficacy: Confidence in Creative Potential

Even when people possess domain expertise, creativity-relevant skills, and a growth mindset, they may still hesitate to act creatively if they lack confidence in their creative potential. Creative self-efficacy is the belief that one can produce creative outcomes. Unlike knowledge, which can be gained from a textbook or online course, self-efficacy is a sense of confidence and can only be developed through practice.

Just like domain-specific knowledge, there is an essential threshold of experience required to become confident in creative tasks. That is why creative self-efficacy is directly and positively related to employee creativity (Tierney & Farmer, 2022)—because effort has been invested in getting better at it.

Creative self-efficacy has also been shown to promote intrinsic motivation, especially for creative activities (Oh & Pyo, 2023). This relationship between self-efficacy and motivation results in positive cycles where confidence leads to engagement, which leads to success, which builds further confidence.

Bandura's self-efficacy theory (1997) provides a roadmap for building creative confidence through four sources:

Mastery experiences involve providing people with successful creative challenges that build confidence through achievement.

Vicarious learning occurs when people observe credible role models successfully engaging in creative work.

Verbal persuasion involves encouraging creative efforts and risk-taking through supportive feedback and recognition.

Emotional states matter because positive environments reduce the anxiety and fear that can inhibit creative expression.

To build creative confidence, then, leaders must design experiences that allow people to succeed creatively, share stories of creative successes within the organisation, provide encouraging feedback that focuses on creative process and growth, and create environments where creative risk-taking is supported rather than punished.

Creativity is a practice, and the role of leaders is to provide the necessary knowledge and space for people to sharpen their creative skills.

Intellectual Risk-Taking: Willing to Venture Into Uncertainty

Creative ideas by their very nature involve stepping into unknown territory. Intellectual risk-taking is the willingness to do this—to propose novel ideas, challenge established assumptions, and experiment with untested approaches—despite the possibility of failure, criticism, or looking foolish. It is distinct from recklessness; rather, it is the deliberate choice to venture beyond what is known and proven in service of discovering something better.

Without this willingness, people default to "safe" solutions that fit within existing frameworks—even when those frameworks are inadequate. In organisational contexts, this manifests as people remaining silent in meetings rather than proposing alternative approaches or adhering to established processes even when circumstances have changed. Over time, this risk-aversion becomes institutionalised and becomes just part of "the way we do things around here."

Leaders play a key role in modelling intellectual risk-taking behaviours—by acknowledging uncertainty, proposing experimental approaches, and treating intelligent failures as learning opportunities. When they do, they create psychological safety and provide the permission for others to do the same. Conversely, when leaders punish failure or treat it as a character flaw rather than a necessary part of discovery, they extinguish the willingness to take intellectual risks across their organisations and continue to embed a risk-averse culture.

Building intellectual risk-taking capability requires deliberate investment in creating environments where experimentation is expected and where intelligent failures are treated as data rather than disasters. This involves designing work that includes small-scale experiments with low stakes, celebrating attempts that fail but yield insights, and providing explicit permission to venture beyond established boundaries. It also requires leaders to be vulnerable and to admit when they don't know the answers. Openly reflecting on what they learn from setbacks, and showing others that success is not always inevitable helps create a climate where people feel confident dealing positively with risk.

Creativity Skills: The Cognitive Toolkit

Domain expertise provides the raw material for creativity. However, creativity-relevant skills provide the cognitive tools to transform that knowledge into something new and valuable. These skills encompass the mental processes that enable people to generate ideas, evaluate possibilities, and navigate the creative process effectively.

Research by Rawlings & Cutting (2025) reveals that creativity requires a dual capacity: the ability to think divergently, which allows for the generation of unique ideas, and the ability to think convergently, which enables a person to critique these ideas and understand their relative value.

The ACER Creative Thinking Skill Development Framework provides a clear, structured approach to teaching and assessing creative thinking by breaking it down into three interconnected strands and seven specific aspects (Heard et al., 2025).

The ACER framework illustrates the comprehensive suite of skills required for creative thinking:

Strand 1: Generating Ideas (Divergent Thinking)
- Generates several ideas (Fluency) – quantity of ideas.
- Generates a range of ideas (Flexibility) – diversity and distinctness of ideas.

Strand 2: Experimenting with Ideas (Synthetic Skills)
- Shifts perspectives and boundaries – reframes problems, is open-minded and can tolerate uncertainty.
- Adapts and manipulates ideas – recognises creativity comes from a combination of existing ideas, not necessarily something completely new.

Strand 3: Identifying Quality of Ideas (Convergent Thinking)
- Ensures effectiveness – considers usefulness, practicality and purpose-driven nature.
- Considers novelty – how it challenges conventional thinking and is appropriate for the context.
- Elaborates ideas – works out how the idea would function.

While designed for primary and secondary educational contexts, this framework exemplifies how creative thinking can be decomposed into teachable, observable behaviours, making it a valuable model for any organisation seeking to invest in a rigorous, evidence-based suite of creativity skills.

Leaders can develop these skills through targeted training programs that develop both idea generation and evaluation capabilities, and which show people how to think about the problems they face from new perspectives.

Modelling The Creativity You Seek to Build

There is one massive mistake that leaders make when attempting to boost creativity across their organisation: focusing on building creative confidence in others while neglecting their own creative development. This approach fails because, as we have heard, vicarious learning is a powerful strategy to boost self-efficacy.

People learn most effectively from observing credible models who demonstrate the behaviours they seek to develop. Given their authority and visibility, leaders are likely to be the most influential role models, whom officers across the organisation watch to see how creativity is treated.

> When leaders actively pursue their own creative development, they are also initiating powerful ripple effects throughout their organisations. They demonstrate that creativity is valuable and worthy of investment, show vulnerability and a growth mindset in action, provide authentic examples of learning from failures, and build credibility when encouraging and supporting others to take creative risks.

The modelling effect cannot be underestimated. Team members quickly recognise when leaders are "talking the talk" without "walking the walk". Their words do not become well-regarded, and they lose the trust of the people they are hoping to influence.

Conversely, leaders who are genuinely committed to their own creative growth generate authentic inspiration that spreads throughout their organisations. When leaders are engaged in their own creative journey, they can speak with the authority of experience and the vulnerability of ongoing learning.

The need for leaders to invest in their own creativity does not mean they must bounce around like a ballerina, set up an easel in their executive offices or call in their staff for a clay workshop. It means they must approach their leadership work with creative intentionality, continuously seeking new approaches, learning from experiments, sharing their experiences and modelling the creative confidence they seek to build in others.

The Reinforcing Cycle of Creative Ability

Creativity is a skill that can be developed. Understanding the interconnected dimensions of domain expertise, creative skill, growth mindset, and self-efficacy provides the framework for achieving this. Knowing this, there is no excuse for leaders to systematically build the conditions that enable everyone to develop and apply their creative potential.

All it takes is the commitment to grow creativity and back this commitment through deliberate investment, practice, and the right environmental conditions.

However, building creative ability is only half the equation. People may possess all the creative capabilities and confidence in the world. However, if they are not motivated to use them, that capacity remains dormant. While motivation, like ability, is a very personal phenomenon, leaders have a huge role to play in getting people excited about expending effort.

So now, we turn to the crucial question, *"Do people want to be creative?"* and explore how leaders create the motivational conditions that inspire people to embrace their creative potential and boldly apply it to the challenges they face.

22   You Shape Motivation

As non-routine work continues to rise, most of your efforts in the future will focus on encouraging creative effectiveness. So now is the time to understand what drives people to invest their energy and intellect in innovation and ingenuity.

Just as you are creative, so is every single team member you lead. They are all potential powerhouses of great ideas. They come to work every day with a unique blend of skills and experiences that can be used to develop new and valuable products, services and ways of working. They each have an enormous contribution to make to the communities you serve.

> However, they are far more than just a human resource, an input into your desired innovations. They are thinking, feeling entities with a complex internal world. Each one chooses where, how and how much to invest their effort. They know the difference between being employed for someone else's ends and being fully engaged in delivering something exciting.

Moreover, this is where many leaders get unstuck when it comes to motivating their people to develop something new. They rely on lazy superficial stimulants and fall back into comfortable formal controls. But these mechanisms don't work for the increasingly non-routine, creative tasks that make up our days.

The Personal Risks Behind Non-Routine Work

We have heard that the work of leadership is non-routine (also known as heuristic). The fact is that most of your people's work is likely to be the same. If your teams are developing anything new, or are in the business of reshaping, transforming or reforming what already exists, then there will not be any clear procedures in place. They are being asked to use their imagination and intuition to forge new pathways where there is no clear outcome, and in the process, be judged for their ideas and their implementation of them. Even just in describing the nature of their creative work, you can feel the risk and fear rising.

Because when you ask people to step outside the bounds of routine work, you are asking them to take profound personal risks. By asking them to develop and share ideas, you are also asking them to reveal themselves to others, with the real possibility of being ridiculed or rejected. By not providing a procedure or set pathway, you are allowing them to make mistakes, with potentially dire consequences for their reputation and social standing.

The contrasting nature of the different kinds of tasks makes it clear that routine work is driven by outside forces – policies, procedures, command and control. Creative work is driven from the inside out – people must be willing to bear the risks, be internally motivated to share themselves, and feel safe enough to do so. And here is the kicker: enabling internal motivation is about creating the right conditions. Therefore, any leader seeking greater creativity in their people must first find it in themselves and recognise their role in building environments where personal expression is encouraged.

There Is No Choice – You Will Need To Motivate Creativity

The need to get good at motivating creativity is real as the fundamental nature of work is changing, and leadership must change with it. As algorithms increasingly handle the routine, the value of human contribution shifts decisively to the heuristic—managing people, applying deep expertise, and navigating complex social interactions (Manyika et al., 2017). Indeed, the World Economic Forum (2025) reports that 'creative thinking' is growing in importance faster than any other skill. This presents a new leadership reality: you are no longer managing compliance in a transactional workforce; you are managing energy in a creative one.

To succeed, you must move beyond traditional incentives and master the drivers of intrinsic motivation, for it is only through deep internal drive that people invest their full intellect and ingenuity in the non-routine problems of the future.

The Catalysts to Creativity

Thanks to decades of deep research, we now understand what compels people to put their energy into creative tasks, which are inherently uncertain, complex and uncomfortable. The three things that will get people to choose creative courage over comfortable conformity are:

Autonomy: the desire to be self-directed and have control over how, when, and with whom we accomplish our work, creating a sense of ownership, agency and coherence that drives engagement over mere compliance.

Mastery: represents our innate drive to continually improve and develop our skills in areas that matter to us, seeking to get better at something important through practice, feedback, and the pursuit of excellence.

Purpose: is the deep human need to contribute to something meaningful beyond ourselves, connecting our work to a larger mission that transcends personal gain and creates a sense of significance.

Autonomy – The Desire To Do It My Way

You cannot ask someone to undertake a creative project, bringing all their expertise, experience, and excitement to the fore to develop something new and valuable, and then tell them they have to do it your way. Even if you are the decision maker of the final solution, they are sharing themselves throughout the process, so they need to feel a sense of ownership over it. They need to have both control over and personal pride in their work, which is found in the independence to make decisions about their work methods and the freedom to collaborate meaningfully with others.

This control is important because it creates coherence between the person and their work environment. When people can align their work methods with personal values and preferences, there is a flow of energy that improves personal effectiveness. Research clearly shows that individuals with greater freedom and independence in their work consistently produce more innovative outcomes (Amabile, 1998). When people are given the autonomy to explore and experiment, their creative capacity actually expands.

In practice, organisations achieve creative autonomy by clearly distinguishing between outcomes and processes. While controls and accountability are placed around achievement of key goals, and performance outcomes are made abundantly clear, people are free to self-select projects, and teams can determine when, where and how work gets done.

Mastery – The Push to Improve

Mastery is the powerful inner drive to build competence and continually refine one's skills. When people have an interest or passion in a particular field, the opportunity to move from novice to expert provides an incredible incentive. This intrinsic motivator pushes people to pursue knowledge, experience the joy of learning, and provides immense satisfaction from progress made. It compels people to undertake dedicated and deliberate practice, embrace challenges, and push beyond personal limits.

As Pink explains, mastery:

"Requires the capacity to see your abilities not as finite, but as infinitely improvable... it demands effort, grit, and deliberate practice. And... it's impossible to fully realise, which makes it simultaneously frustrating and alluring" (Pink, 2018, p. 208).

In this way, mastery is the application of a growth mindset to something that provides personal meaning.

Leaders can cultivate a culture of mastery through:

1. assignment of projects and tasks based on personal strengths and passions, and celebrating progress

2. providing rapid and specific feedback

3. offering ongoing skill development opportunities in things that the person cares about.

Note, however, the importance of aligning work and skill development with areas of personal interest, which is crucial for coherence. A leader cannot simply tell someone they will become a master of compliance or customer service. There needs to be a sense of purpose and passion for the area, and this is where work assignments become imperative.

Suppose people feel they are being pushed into disciplines where they have no desire to advance, and decisions about their development are based on organisational demands rather than personal preferences. In that case, they will simply feel like pawns. This imposed mastery will be counterproductive and negatively impact intrinsic motivation.

Purpose – The Motivator of Meaning

Purpose is the powerful driver that helps people find real meaning in their work, forging a vital connection between daily tasks and something much bigger than themselves. As Daniel Pink describes, purpose is the innate desire to be in *"the service of a cause larger than ourselves"* (Pink, 2018, p. 146). It is all about creating a legacy and contributing to something they believe really matters.

When employees have a sense of alignment between their work and what they believe is important, they experience higher motivation and productivity, increased engagement and commitment, greater resilience and innovative thinking – all integral inputs to creative work. It makes sense – we are willing to invest ourselves and our precious resources of time, skill and energy into those things that we care about. The reverse also holds – when we see our work not having any impact that aligns with our values, we will not spare any of our resources to improve on it.

If you are fostering a sense of autonomy and mastery, you are likely also achieving a sense of purpose; people will be choosing projects and processes that are meaningful to them. However, leaders also have a key role in addressing purpose directly, through two key mechanisms:

- Authentically crafting and communicating a compelling vision for their organisation.
- Ensuring every team member understands how their contributions connect to this bigger picture mission and achievement of organisational goals.

Why External Rewards and Punishments Don't Work

You would not be the first leader to consider offering bonuses or threatening negative consequences if creative outcomes are not achieved. Dangling carrots and waving sticks are what we know, and they do work for routine tasks.

Nevertheless, for creativity, it is counterproductive. Rewards make creativity contingent on external motivators, shifting the focus from the inherent joy and fulfilment of the creative process to a transactional, "If I do this, then I will get that" mentality.

When extrinsic rewards are layered on top of work people already find enjoyable, they cheapen the experience and make people feel that it is simply something they are being paid to do. Extrinsic rewards dilute the sense of meaning and purpose attached to the work, which, in turn, dampens motivation and reduces overall performance. What was once work that was imbued with passion and play has been turned into mere labour.

> People's sense of autonomy, mastery and purpose are far too important to be "paid off". When you attempt to do so, you insult people's innate sense of inspiration.

While such tactics may spark a short-term spike in output, in the long term, they inflict serious damage. They instil a dependency similar to addiction: over time, people come to expect the rewards and become desensitised, needing increasingly greater incentives to regain the same ignition of inspiration.

When it comes to punishments, well, these are the antithesis of creativity as they foster a sense of fear. Criticising, penalising, or disciplining people will only shut down their sense of engagement, agency, and trust, and block the brain's divergent thinking systems. The work stops being interesting, challenging and captivating and instead becomes linked with negative consequences.

Motivating Creativity Takes Courageous Leadership

There is no two ways about it, motivating creativity takes courageous leadership. Leaders must move away from command-and-control mechanisms and a focus on rules and routines, and instead see themselves as creators of the conditions that enable creativity in others. This means letting go of the security blankets of traditional structures and systems to build psychological safety, trust, and actively support people in their purpose and potential.

It is a bold shift that can feel deeply uncomfortable, but is not discomfort at the very heart of creativity? Leaders who cannot find their own creative selves in the way they lead will quickly lose credibility. Because asking your people to be creative without showing it yourself is simply asking for a charge of hypocrisy. Calling on your people to be courageous without also making brave changes in the way you view and work in the world is a sure-fire way to lose support.

Your people are sitting there with so much untapped potential. They possess abilities that enable their autonomy, passions that fuel their purpose, and a drive to master the skills they care about. What is either helping them or hindering them from achieving all of this and delivering the creative solutions you require is the environment you have created.

23   You Orchestrate Opportunities

The task and environment components in your organisation combine to either encourage people to share ideas for improvement or send a clear warning that creativity is not welcome.

In the previous chapters, we have looked at the conditions under which people can be creative (ability) and want to enact their creative potential (motivation). The final element of opportunity answers the question *"Will people be creative?"* Because even when an organisation has talented and passionate employees, organisational conditions can either help or hinder the enactment of their creative potential. Without opportunity, even the most skilled and motivated employees will find themselves constrained or sidelined and their creativity crushed.

While ability and motivation are very much individual constructs, opportunity looks more broadly to consider the organisational elements which are beyond the control of an individual but which either *"enables or constrains that person's task performance"* (Blumberg & Pringle, 1982, p. 565). It comprises the mesh of organisational, environmental, and job conditions that leaders construct, consciously or otherwise.

The OECD also reports that government agencies with strong opportunity structures—such as participatory cultures, enabling leadership, and transparent resource allocation—convert individual creativity into real innovation, whereas those without remain stagnant even with motivated, skilled staff (OECD, 2017).

Houtgraaf's research in public administration likewise shows that novel ideas are seldom generated (and even less often implemented) unless environmental signals and support mechanisms indicate creative action is genuinely possible, valued, and safe (Houtgraaf et al., 2022).

So, while opportunity may be the last of the AMO elements, it is certainly not the least important.

Before delving into the opportunity elements in greater detail, it must be noted that there is significant overlap and interaction between the AMO components (Bos-Nehles, 2023), and some opportunity factors have been covered previously in discussions around ability and motivation. The focus of this chapter, then, will be on those organisational elements not covered in prior chapters, and which have a direct and substantial impact on creative practice.

Opportunity = Task + Environment

Opportunity is not a static organisational feature but is a dynamic interplay of several systems and processes, with the combined effect being acutely felt by individuals in the flow of daily work. The opportunity elements span a spectrum from decision-making authority, access to resources and information, to basic features of organisational life such as psychological safety and team structure. Broadly, however, they fall into two main categories:

1. The *tasks* people undertake
2. The *environments* they inhabit

Task conditions include such factors as variety, challenge, scope for autonomy, and meaningful goals. Environmental conditions encompass the social, cultural, and physical contexts that either support or inhibit creative activity.

In practical terms, an employee is more likely to act creatively when presented with an appropriately challenging task that is novel (neither overwhelming nor trivial), within an environment where new ideas can be voiced and developed, and where there is support for "beautiful risks" and "intelligent failures".

Conversely, it is easy to understand how environments characterised by rigid procedures, unclear communication, lack of set goals, and fearful, unsupportive leaders sap creative energy before it can find expression.

Enablers Of Creative Confidence

Task Components

The task aspects of opportunity refer to the degree to which individual job design enables employees to experiment, take initiative, and apply creative solutions within the scope of their assigned work. There are two key aspects of tasks that can be beneficial for supporting the development of creative confidence: job design and resource availability.

Job Design. As we have heard in previous discussions about motivation, when jobs are designed to provide autonomy and discretion, individuals are given genuine freedom to explore new approaches, make independent decisions, and experiment in their work process. Such autonomy, embedded in the task itself, means that individuals can pursue methods and solutions that match both organisational goals and personal preferences.

Similarly, task variety and significance play a crucial role. Daily activities that are non-repetitive and perceived as meaningful provide stimulation for the application of creative thinking and the encouragement to take ownership of their contributions. In this way, task design becomes a direct lever for opportunity, structuring work to encourage engagement, initiative, and inventive responses.

Resource Availability. Another core element at the task level is the provision of sufficient resources—including time, tools, and support—to pursue creative work (Amabile et al., 1996). When employees have the tangible resources specifically allocated to their tasks, they are empowered to iterate, problem-solve, and innovate without being hampered by practical constraints. Adequate resourcing built into the job itself is a foundational feature of opportunity-enhancing task design.

Environment Components

Beyond the specific job design, four core elements of the environment contribute to climates and cultures conducive to creativity. These cover empowerment, access to information, psychological safety and leadership advocacy.

Participative Decision-Making. Practices that involve employees in participative decision-making and empowerment shift the work environment from one of passive compliance to active collaboration (OECD, 2017). These include organisational mechanisms—such as cross-functional teams, suggestion programs, and shared governance—that allow employees to influence processes and outcomes beyond their immediate responsibilities.

Empowerment at the systems level gives people confidence that their creative inputs will be valued and acted upon. With this comes a sense of agency and responsibility for their work environments, encouraging them to make meaningful change.

Access to Information. They say that information is power, and so when the environment is rich in information flow and open communication, people will feel empowered to enact change. When organisational structures facilitate ready access to knowledge and foster lateral communication and internal/external networking, they multiply both the sources of inspiration and the pathways by which ideas can be shared, vetted, and improved. Such environments serve as breeding grounds for cross-pollination of ideas, creating a dynamic in which creativity becomes a collective process rather than a solitary effort.

Psychological Safety. Perhaps most critically, environmental opportunity is maintained through climates of psychological safety and organisational encouragement. When leaders and peers foster safety—where respectful dissent is welcomed, failure is viewed as part of learning, and new ideas are visibly encouraged—individuals are far more likely to take the interpersonal and reputational risks inherent in creative action (OECD, 2017; Amabile et al., 1996).

Organisational encouragement, signalled through both policies and informal norms, tells people that their creativity is valued and that experimentation aimed at achieving beneficial outcomes is not only permitted but celebrated.

Leadership Advocacy for Creativity. Finally, the ongoing support and endorsement of creativity by leaders acts as a pervasive and powerful environmental signal. When leaders promote, reward, and model creative behaviour, they set the tone for the entire organisation, creating a culture where creativity is not only permitted but expected.

Together, the above task and environment components form a synergistic architecture that enables or inhibits creative confidence. By designing tasks that foster autonomy, variety, and are properly resourced, and by shaping environments that empower, inform, protect, and encourage, leaders construct the opportunities necessary for people to create confidently and effectively. Collectively, they place a clear sign on the door that says,

"Please share your ideas for how we can improve and be more innovative."

Table 11 – The opportunity enablers

Enablers of Creative Confidence	
Task Conditions	**Environmental Conditions**
Job design - Structuring roles to provide autonomy, variety, and meaningful work that stimulates creative thinking and experimentation.	Participative decision making - Involving employees in organisational decisions and processes to foster ownership and creative input.
Resource availability - Providing adequate time, tools, materials, and support necessary for creative exploration and implementation.	Access to information - Ensuring open knowledge sharing and communication channels that fuel creative connections and insights.
	Psychological safety - Creating climates where risk-taking, experimentation, and failure are viewed as learning opportunities rather than threats.
	Leadership advocacy - Leaders who actively promote, model, and reward creative behaviour throughout the organisation.

Constraints to Creative Confidence

Task Components

The way roles are structured and resourced can severely constrain a person's ability to act creatively. The two key task-related components that create blockages are resource constraints and stifling structures.

Resource Constraints. When employees are not afforded the time, materials, or support required to complete their tasks, their work can begin to feel undervalued and overwhelming. Chronic under-resourcing or relentless short deadlines drain energy and focus, leaving little room for exploration or experimentation, and sending subtle signals that innovation is a low priority.

Stifling Job Structures. Excessive repetition, low variety, or rigid prescription of work methods foster disengagement and checklist thinking, rather than challenge and creative engagement. Without adequate autonomy or task variety, employees see little reason or reward in trying something new and instead begin to believe they are there simply to be a robot.

These task-level constraints narrow opportunity by making creative action hard, unrewarding, or simply impossible within day-to-day work. Employees stuck in such tasks reasonably avoid creative risks, instead defaulting to routine behaviours.

Environment Components

Other inhibitors stem from the broader organisational environment—its level of formalisation, fear and lack of support.

Bureaucratic Rigidities. When formalisation is high and control is tightly centralised—signalled by rigid hierarchical structures or an overabundance of rules—space for creative action shrinks. With every subsequent organisational layer, the real and imagined barriers to proposing ideas or improvements increase. People learn that information does not flow freely across status levels and silos, so they do not even consider making the effort to climb the mountain.

Psychological Unsafety, Fear of Failure, and Blame. Cultures that punish risk, stigmatise error, or breed mistrust see creative confidence shrivel, as individuals become risk-averse and self-censor their ideas to avoid negative consequences. Fear-based management discourages feedback, experimentation, and the sharing of insights, leading to stagnation and turnover.

Lack of Leadership Encouragement. When leaders fail to actively endorse or reward innovative thinking, employees receive the message—explicitly or implicitly—that creativity is risky and possibly futile. This lack of advocacy reinforces avoidance, solidifies stereotypes of conformity, and further erodes confidence in creative engagement.

All these inhibitors increase both psychological and practical resistance to creative effort. They raise the perceived risk of creative action, boosting both the reality and the fear of negative consequences. In combination, they work to place a very clear sign on the door:

"Beware! Creativity is not welcome here."

Opportunity Impacts Risk Perception

Whether a person will enact their creative potential ultimately comes down to their evaluation of the risks and rewards. Organisational opportunity structures—such as autonomy, participative decision-making, resource availability, and psychological safety—all contribute to a person's assessment of just how risky taking action will be.

Table 12 – The opportunity barriers

Inhibitors of Creative Confidence	
Task Conditions	**Environmental Conditions**
Resource constraints - Insufficient time, materials, or support that makes creative work feel unfeasible and undervalued.	Bureaucratic rigidities - Excessive formalisation, rigid rules, and centralised control that restrict creative action and innovation.
Stifling job structures - Repetitive, low-variety tasks with rigid procedures that discourage experimentation and creative thinking.	Psychological unsafety - Cultures that punish mistakes, stigmatize risk-taking, and foster fear of negative consequences for creative efforts.
	Lack of leadership encouragement - Absence of visible support for creativity, failing to advocate for or reward innovative thinking and behaviour.

Where there are positive opportunities and clear support for creativity, a person will likely judge sharing new ideas and implementing them as less risky. However, where there are rigid rules, a lack of clarity and communication, and leadership based on fear, it is understandable that a person would assess this situation as one of great personal risk. In this case, there would be significant concern in moving forward with new ideas.

Psychological safety, in particular, lowers the subjective threat of failure or criticism, granting employees the confidence that they can propose and implement novel ideas without negative consequences. Access to resources and information further assures individuals that creative efforts are supported, reducing the uncertainty and fear associated with venturing beyond established routines.

Conversely, rigid hierarchies, resource scarcity, and environments intolerant of error amplify the perceived dangers of creative engagement, making risk avoidance a very rational choice. Thus, the construction of opportunity is not simply about enabling action, but also about shifting the psychological calculus around risk—transforming creativity from a gamble into a valued, supported and viable organisational option.

> It is relatively easy to state that you want your people to be less risk-averse. Still, the question is whether, as a leader, you are creating opportunities for them to feel that their creative actions are sufficiently supported. How are the systems and structures you have established helping them reduce their risk assessment?

Opportunity Across Boundaries: Where Conditions Are Coherent

Constructing opportunity is necessary for individual and collective creativity. However, so is alignment across team, organisational and community boundaries. Even the most opportunity-rich environments can falter when individual and team efforts lack integration and shared purpose.

Therefore, the next chapter will extend the leader's role from engineering the conditions for opportunity within an organisation to orchestrating coherence first and foremost within themselves, and then also between teams, stakeholders and the communities they serve. With a focus on coherence, creativity has the opportunity to flow across boundaries, building pathways for ideas to multiply, connect, and deepen, as well as for the development and diffusion of innovation across domains.

24   You Craft Coherence

Crafting coherence is an intuitive art involving continuous harmonisation of purpose and skill within the organisation and across institutional boundaries.

Creative coherence is the alignment of individual creative purpose and skill with organisational systems and the broader social context, allowing creativity to flow naturally and fostering creative confidence across all levels.

With coherence, organisations can achieve superior innovation outcomes and sustained creative performance (Massie et al., 2022; Creative Systems Theory, 2022). When individual creative aspirations are aligned with organisational creative capacity and community needs, there is a multiplication and amplification effect across the organisation and your communities. Everyone is enabled to contribute their best creative work while supporting collective innovative achievement. This coherence becomes the foundation that makes all other creative leadership practices possible and effective.

However, without coherence, even the most talented and motivated employees remain siloed, and their potential to influence and inspire beyond their office walls is wasted. Likewise, without coherence, the knowledge, ideas and innovations existing outside the organisation do not have the chance to infiltrate and shape the organisation, ensuring its continued relevance and achievement of meaningful results.

Building on our understanding that leadership itself is creative work, this chapter focuses specifically on your role as the creator of organisational coherence, where you craft the conditions by which individual creativity multiplies into collective innovation.

The Act of Coherence Making

Coherence does not emerge spontaneously—it requires a continuous process of making and remaking meaning across organisational levels and with the stakeholders who receive and shape the services. This coherence-making process is fundamentally creative work, requiring leaders to synthesise diverse perspectives, competing priorities, and conflicting demands into unified organisational direction and purpose.

It requires leaders to be simultaneously:

- System architects: designing structures that enable creative alignment across boundaries.

- Intuitive artists: synthesising and amplifying meaning from organisational and community contexts.

- Alignment monitors: sensing and investigating gaps in alignment and directing action to amend the shortfalls.

As a system architect, you are looking at the organisation and its stakeholders from a helicopter perspective. You build the organisational structures, processes, and mechanisms that enable alignment across them, including workflows, communication channels, decision-making processes, and resource allocation systems.

As a meaning synthesiser, you gather diverse perspectives, values, and purposes and weave them into a unified narrative that enables coordinated creative action. This requires the unique ability to find common ground among competing viewpoints while preserving the diversity that fuels innovation.

As an alignment monitor, you continuously maintain and adapt organisational coherence over time, aware of organisational evolution and environmental changes that may impact its alignment with external influences. This ongoing creative challenge requires sensitivity to coherence gaps and the ability to redesign alignment mechanisms as needed.

In this way, crafting coherence calls on many creative skills, such as imagination, synthesis, pattern recognition, and innovative problem-solving. Yet coherence crafting operates at a significantly higher level of complexity than the development of a single system.

It requires leaders to create alignment across multiple organisational systems simultaneously while also supporting diversity, which is critical to continued creativity. It also requires building a sense of stability while also facilitating the flexibility necessary for continued innovation and adaptation.

Key Leadership Coherence Mechanisms

There are four key mechanisms leaders use to craft coherence, being:

1. Visionary integration
2. Boundary spanning and bridging
3. Temporal coherence management
4. Cultural balancing.

Visionary Integration. Research by Cai and colleagues (2023) demonstrates that leaders create coherence by forming and communicating an inspirational and unifying vision, aligning diverse stakeholders around shared possibilities. Such visions create a sense of meaning for individuals while also connecting them to the broader organisational purpose. This vision is often captured and communicated through strategic planning processes, which are discussed specifically in the following section.

Boundary Spanning and Bridging. Effective coherence is all about stepping outside the organisational boundaries and discovering unique and valuable capabilities that exist within other groups, industries and communities. It is about building bridges between previously disconnected individuals and groups to enhance overall creative capacity; designing integration mechanisms that enable mutual inspiration and support to achieve shared goals.

Temporal Coherence Management. Leaders must creatively balance consistency with adaptation over time, maintaining organisational coherence while enabling continuous evolution and innovation. This temporal dimension of coherence crafting requires managing the tension between stability (which provides psychological safety and predictable frameworks) and change (which enables growth and improvement). To achieve this, the core elements that maintain stability must be identified, along with the adaptive elements that enable change. Strategies are developed to ensure consistency in the former while supporting the flexible nature of the latter.

Cultural Balancing. There is a careful balance needed between diverse perspectives and cultures within an organisation and consistency of purpose and identity. Cultural coherence involves building organisational environments that support both individual authenticity and collective alignment—enabling people and groups to contribute their unique creative capabilities while working toward common goals.

Strategic Planning As A Creative Coherence Process

Most organisational strategic plans fail because they have devolved into mechanical compliance exercises rather than being harnessed for the powerful coherence artefacts they are. Traditional strategic planning processes typically produce documents that satisfy administrative requirements but fail to generate the genuine alignment necessary for coherent organisational action. They become a wish-list of motherhood statements that reinforce silos, fail to deliver a shared, inspirational purpose, and do not connect different units and cultural groups around a common cause. This represents an enormous lost opportunity.

> Strategic plans have exceptional potential as coherence artifacts. The planning processes and the documents that result, can bridge the creative potential within individuals, teams, and communities. However, when strategic planning becomes formulaic and uncreative, or communication falls short, organisations miss their chance, leaving creative potential fragmented and unrealised.

Many organisations continue to use a top-down approach to strategy development, missing the chance to fully understand organisational complexity and construct a vision that connects its diverse groups. By dictating the strategic plan, the chance to understand the interconnections and integrations across perspectives is lost.

Equally critical is the need for compelling and consistent communication of the strategic vision both within and outside the organisation. Strategic coherence degrades rapidly without ongoing reinforcement through clear, inspiring messaging that maintains alignment over time (Lusiani & Langley, 2019).

Internal communication must translate strategic vision into a meaningful context for different organisational units, while external communication ensures stakeholders, partners, and communities understand and can align with the organisation's direction. Without this consistent narrative reinforcement, even the most thoughtfully crafted strategic plans lose their coherence-creating power, as organisational memory fades and competing interpretations emerge.

The strategic plan must therefore include explicit communication strategies that maintain shared understanding and sustained commitment to the creative vision across all organisational boundaries.

When strategic planning becomes a coherence crafting process, organisations develop plans that truly guide creative action rather than simply satisfying administrative requirements and sitting upon the shelf until they require review. These plans become living documents that enable distributed creative decision-making, facilitate organisational learning, and maintain alignment between individual creative contributions and collective innovative capacity.

The Ongoing Coherence Challenge

Organisational coherence requires continuous creative attention—it degrades without intentional maintenance and adaptive redesign. Sustaining it depends upon the leaders' ongoing creative engagement with organisational meaning-making. This alignment is a daily practice that includes:

Coherence Sensing: Developing sensitivity to coherence gaps and misalignments through regular organisational assessment. This involves paying attention to signs of fragmentation—

conflicting priorities, miscommunication, duplicated efforts, or creative initiatives that do not align with organisational direction.

Creative Problem-Solving: Using creative approaches to resolve coherence challenges as they emerge. When misalignment occurs, avoiding mechanistic solutions in favour of creative synthesis that addresses root causes while preserving organisational diversity and creative potential.

Meaning-Making Communication: Continuously reinforcing and evolving organisational coherence through creative communication that connects individual contributions to collective purpose. This involves storytelling, vision reinforcement, and celebration of creative achievements that demonstrate coherent organisational action.

Adaptive Coherence Design: Redesigning coherence mechanisms as organisations evolve. This requires ongoing assessment of whether existing structures, processes, and cultural elements continue to support coherence with stakeholders and communities, or whether they need modification to maintain alignment under changing circumstances.

Maintaining organisational coherence is almost a full-time job in itself and certainly not just a task for one specific leader to shoulder alone. It requires developing coherence capacity across a broad range of managers and leadership teams, enabling distributed responsibility for this imperative process.

To achieve effective and continuous coherence, the organisation needs to enable others to understand its importance, the mechanisms by which it is maintained, and to identify and address coherence challenges as they arise. One readily available tool for this is leadership team meetings.

Leadership Team Meetings: A Key Coherence Tool

Agencies and organisations routinely convene their senior leadership teams, yet too often these gatherings default to operational updates, budget reviews, and compliance reporting—missing a critical opportunity to build the creative coherence upon which innovation depends.

> The question leaders must ask is whether we are using these precious forums to align on the foundations of creativity itself. Executive team meetings should serve as deliberate spaces for exploring shared approaches to risk, articulating collective beliefs about what creativity is and how it manifests across the organisation, and connecting key innovation projects back to strategic purpose. These conversations create the coherence necessary for creativity to flourish.

Leaders must also use this time to surface and address inconsistencies between stated values and actual behaviours—examining where commitments diverge from actions, where resource allocation contradicts priorities, or where leadership responses inadvertently undermine the creative confidence they claim to support.

Executive teams function most effectively when they dedicate time to strategic alignment and shared sense-making, not just tactical coordination (Wageman et al., 2008). By intentionally transforming leadership team meetings into coherence-building forums, senior leaders model the very alignment they seek to create throughout the organisation.

These meetings become powerful mechanisms for ensuring that all leaders speak a consistent creative language, make decisions that reinforce rather than fragment creative capacity, and collectively maintain the integrity of the creative foundation upon which organisational innovation depends.

The Ultimate Leadership Challenge

Coherence crafting reveals the ultimate paradox of creative leadership: to enable authentic creativity in others, you must first create the conditions where individual creative expression serves rather than fragments collective purpose. This requires you to move beyond managing within existing organisational frameworks to actively creating new forms of alignment that enhance both individual fulfilment and collective achievement.

However, crafting coherence, while essential, is not the final dimension of creative leadership. Once you have created the organisational conditions where creativity can flourish, you face your most visible and influential leadership responsibility: living the creative behaviours you seek to inspire in others.

In our next and final chapter of this section, *You Act As A Role Model,* we will explore how your personal creative practice becomes the most powerful tool for inspiring creativity throughout your organisation. While coherence creates the conditions for creativity across your communities, your modelling of creative behaviour provides the inspiration and permission that transforms potential into action.

25 You Act As A Role Model

"People do what people see, not what they hear." ~
John Maxwell

If you have been in the workforce long enough, you have likely experienced the launch of some exciting new change initiative. The leader may have announced the need for a new approach in a town hall meeting or through an enthusiastic all-employee email. Perhaps a formal project was set up, or maybe a permanent team was established, all with the promise that this would future-proof the agency and foster a culture of innovation.

However, you may have also noticed that in the weeks and months following, this project progresses in one of two very different ways. This is a tale of two teams.

Leader Discomfort Delivers Cynicism

In one team, the leader who espoused the need for the new may initially be very engaged, providing much praise and offering assistance to advance the great work. However, behind the scenes, they continue operating very much from the old playbooks. They continued to avoid or escalate uncertain decisions, causing significant delay and impeding progress.

This leader does not advocate upwards for taking "beautiful risks"; they defer changes to established processes in favour of baby steps, apologise profusely when resources cannot be found to fund the ideas, and show visible discomfort when team members propose unconventional approaches.

After receiving very negative responses to setbacks, the team decides not to discuss them anymore, internalising the despondency. As months pass without much progress, whispers spread about the unit being shut down, but there is no clear communication from the leader. In fact, the executive sponsor is becoming largely absent, and when present, they are both abrupt and evasive.

The team, who were previously asked to attend regular executive meetings, became increasingly sidelined and, instead of receiving attention, was increasingly left alone. The outcome? Within a year, maybe two, the initiative quietly fades away, leaving cynical employees and an unstated commitment not to speak of it again.

The executives are informed that, despite the best efforts, it was impossible to progress due to technology, environmental factors, stakeholder resistance, or budget shortfalls (take your pick). The end. The team melts back into the mainstream, their hopes for making a meaningful difference quashed.

Leader Courage Delivers Change

However, elsewhere, a second story unfolds, one in which the leader is doing the challenging work of facing uncertainty and being authentic. Here, when the same announcement is made, the leader steps forward not with polished certainty and a plethora of promises, but with grounded openness and the commitment to provide growth opportunities. They admit what they do not know, inviting others into the process. This leader encourages small experiments and emphasise learning over perfection.

When missteps and mistakes are made early on, they are celebrated as signs of progress and used as critical learning experiences. The leaders are continually communicating about the vital outcomes the work will deliver for their communities and encouraging their people to bring their best selves each day.

The team begins to build trust among themselves and with the leader, feeling supported to push themselves and take risks to deliver important results. In this team, there is a sense of equality and safety, where information is shared, and collective responsibility is evident.

In this team, updates from experiments — both successful and not — are met with curiosity rather than critique. The leader promotes a positive balance between optimism and caution, novelty and value, and spends time developing a shared language and understanding of the objectives and boundaries. They manage the risk–reward relationship thoughtfully and openly, discussing the dichotomy with others before coming to a team decision.

Over time, the team not only delivers new products and services but also a renewed culture — one rooted in trust, creative confidence, and excitement for the future.

Two teams. Two leaders. One difference.

A complex combination of individual, organisational and social factors causes the outcomes achieved in both examples. Nevertheless, there is no doubt that the leader in the latter example achieved significant success through recognising one simple fact: you cannot simply instruct others to be more creative or innovative. You must lead the way. You must be willing to become uncomfortable and courageous first.

Your people are watching, learning, and modelling their behaviour on what you do, not what you say. Your staff are looking at you to determine how risks are handled, challenges navigated, and creativity supported. They are checking to see if you are being honest about what you claim is valued, or whether your actions merely show hypocrisy. Your people are full of potential, but they will only expend effort for those whom they see as authentic and trustworthy.

> Leaders are called leaders for a reason – through the example they set and the conditions they build, they guide and influence the behaviour of others. That is why if you want to boost creativity in your organisation, it needs to begin with you.

The Science of Social Learning

Decades of social research have confirmed that individuals learn primarily through observing, imitating, and modelling the behaviours of significant others in their environment. In organisational contexts, leaders are the most influential figures, as they decide how resources are allocated, performance is judged, and which work processes are deemed acceptable.

Just as children look to parents and peers to understand the behaviours that ensure they are cared for, people look to their leaders to understand what approaches will gain them social and professional approval. They look at the way leaders solve problems, share information and are willing to be vulnerable themselves before taking steps to improve organisational situations.

Most importantly, they use the leaders past behaviours to inform their risk/reward assessments, assessing if they fail, whether they will be supported or shamed.

How You Influence Creativity

As a leader, you have two broad mechanisms through which you influence others, being:

Showing people what to do + Supporting others to do it.

More specifically, you have four levers that work in combination to develop creative confidence:

1. Role modelling behaviours
2. Encouraging followers
3. Providing mastery experiences
4. Enhancing emotional states.

Let's look at each of these role model mechanisms more closely.

Figure 14- Leadership levers for creative confidence

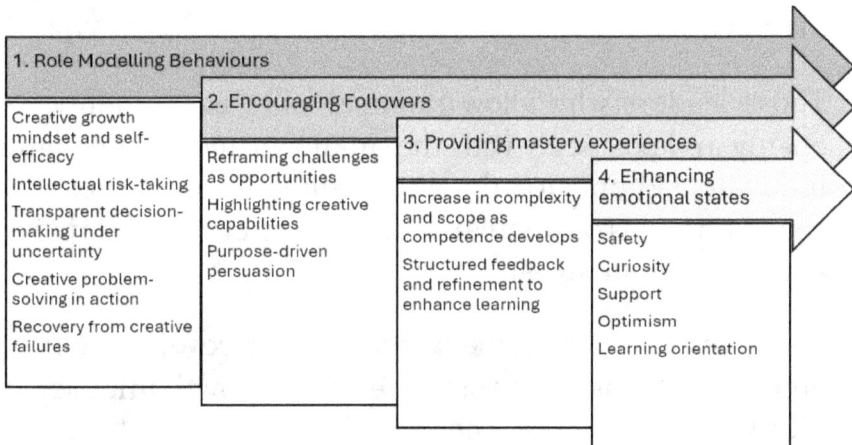

1. Role Modelling Behaviours			
Creative growth mindset and self-efficacy	**2. Encouraging Followers**		
Intellectual risk-taking	Reframing challenges as opportunities	**3. Providing mastery experiences**	
Transparent decision-making under uncertainty	Highlighting creative capabilities	Increase in complexity and scope as competence develops	**4. Enhancing emotional states**
Creative problem-solving in action	Purpose-driven persuasion	Structured feedback and refinement to enhance learning	Safety
Recovery from creative failures			Curiosity
			Support
			Optimism
			Learning orientation

1: Role Modelling Behaviours

"What you do speaks so loudly, I can't even hear what you say!"
~ Sam Rutigliano

We have spoken about the importance of a creative growth mindset and self-efficacy as core components of creative confidence. Now, what is important to consider is that these capabilities are built by observing others successfully performing tasks, particularly when those others are in positions of authority and influence (Bandura, 1977).

This is crucial for all leaders to understand; employees can develop creative confidence through witnessing you successfully navigating uncertainty, risk-taking and utilising creative problem-solving (Zhou et al., 2024). People learn what a growth mindset looks like, and how to foster one for themselves when they first have a chance to see it in action.

However, it must be noted that there is a real difference between authentic creativity and performative behaviour, with employees readily able to distinguish between those who genuinely are practising creative skills and those putting on a show (Černe & Škerlavaj, 2012).

Those leaders who allow themselves to be authentic, to work openly and positively with the unknown and the uncomfortable, motivate others to do the same. Those whose creative commitment is only superficial merely serve to dampen support and increase mistrust.

Three specific leader behaviours send powerful examples to others regarding what someone with a growth mindset and self-efficacy actually does. These are:

Transparent decision-making under uncertainty. When leaders openly share their thought processes when facing ambiguous challenges, they demonstrate how to navigate uncertainty creatively and show followers that uncertainty is a normal part of creative work (Hughes et al., 2018).

Creative problem-solving in action. Leaders who engage in creative problem-solving, utilise creativity during work processes, and solve problems with unconventional methods provide direct models for followers to emulate.

Recovery from creative failures. When leaders model how to learn from setbacks, adapt approaches based on new information, and maintain persistence in the face of challenges, they demonstrate the resilience and continuous improvement that followers need to develop their own creative confidence (Amabile, 1996).

The ripple effect of creative role modelling cannot be understated. It extends throughout organisational culture, with leaders' creative behaviour acting as a clear example of what a creative growth mindset, creative self-efficacy and intellectual risk-taking looks like, and showing people what is possible with practice.

2: Encouraging Followers

Verbal persuasion represents the second lever that leaders use to influence follower creativity. The power of encouragement does not lie, though, in generic motivational speeches made from a podium, but in specific, personalised coaching that builds on individual strengths and addresses creative challenges. Three persuasion strategies that effectively enhance follower creativity include:

Reframing challenges as opportunities. When leaders consistently frame problems as creative opportunities and emphasise the potential for breakthrough solutions, they influence followers' cognitive appraisals around risk and rewards and increase willingness to engage in creative problem-solving (Zhou & George, 2001).

Highlighting creative capabilities. Leaders who specifically acknowledge and encourage followers' creative capabilities help build the confidence necessary for sustained creative effort.

Purpose-driven persuasion. When leaders connect creative challenges to meaningful outcomes and organisational mission, they tap into intrinsic motivation that sustains creative effort even when facing obstacles.

However, as important as coaxing and coaching are, persuasion alone is insufficient. It must be accompanied by behavioural modelling, mastery experiences, and supportive emotional climates to create lasting creative confidence.

3: Providing Mastery Experiences

As discussed in previous chapters, leaders play a crucial role in providing opportunities for employees to build both the technical competencies and creative skills necessary for innovative performance. Creativity is a practice, and must be developed through an ongoing cycle of action and reflection. In this way, leaders influence creative confidence by giving people the chance to practice and perfect creative thinking skills, problem-solving approaches, and innovative methodologies.

When leaders provide challenging, creative assignments with appropriate support and feedback, two important processes occur (Huang, 2016):

1. The employees gain a clear understanding of the leaders' creative expectations.
2. The employees establish their own creative role identity.

Both the leaders and their employees come to know each other better, and expectations and creative identities are integrated through shared experiences.

The research reveals that effective mastery experiences follow a progressive model where creative challenges increase in complexity and scope as individuals develop competence (Gong et al., 2009). Leaders must carefully calibrate creative challenges to ensure they are neither too easy (providing no growth) nor too difficult (leading to failure and reduced confidence). They also require structured feedback and refinement cycles that help individuals learn from both successes and failures.

4: Enhancing Emotional States

The fourth lever by which leaders can influence creativity involves promoting and sustaining positive emotional states that support creative thinking and risk-taking. As we will see in the following section, the emotional climate profoundly influences creative performance with positive emotions broadening individuals' thought-action repertoires, leading to increased creativity, flexibility, and innovative problem-solving (Fredrickson, 2001).

Leaders play a crucial role in establishing the team climate. Their emotional states are contagious and significantly influence others and the overall atmosphere (Barsade, 2002). Through their own behaviour, they signal to others what the acceptable emotional responses are when challenges arise.

The most foundational and influential behaviour that leaders can model is how they create a space of psychological safety. Edmondson defines psychological safety as *"a shared belief held by members of a team that the team is safe for interpersonal risk taking"* (Edmonson, 1999, p. 350) and research consistently shows this safety is beneficial for creative expression and innovative behaviour.

Leaders create psychological safety through their responses to creative attempts, failures, and unconventional ideas. Positive modelling behaviours include responding to risks with curiosity rather than criticism, support rather than punishment, and a learning orientation rather than blame.

This emotional influence extends beyond momentary mood states, with individuals more likely to form an emotional attachment to their work and a deep commitment to the organisation and its objectives. When leaders consistently model positive emotional engagement with creativity, followers develop similar emotional orientations that sustain creative effort over time.

The Prerequisite: Why Leaders Must Nurture Their Own Creativity First

"The bottleneck is at the top of the bottle. Where there is a lack of innovation, it is leadership that must change." ~ Gary Hamel

Despite understanding these four levers for influencing creativity, leaders cannot effectively utilise any of them without first developing their own creative capabilities and identities. The most important reason leaders must nurture their own creativity first is authenticity, as it is authentic leadership behaviours that create the trust and psychological safety necessary for creative risk-taking (Rego et al., 2012).

Conversely, leaders who lack genuine creative development cannot provide the authentic role models that followers need for vicarious learning. Those who have not faced the discomfort that comes in moving into the unknown cannot demonstrate how to overcome uncertainty. Those who have not born personal and professional risk in the pursuit of innovation cannot create the emotional resonance required for people to feel genuine support.

People are looking for a sense of coherence and integrity from their leaders, that they are "walking the talk", "putting their money where their mouth is" and are willing to "put in the hard yards" that they are asking of them. Where there is no alignment between the creativity that is espoused as important and the leaders' own individual behaviours, this inconsistency between word and deed will reduce trust and increase the risk evaluations of future actions.

> Most importantly, Zhou (2020) found that leaders' personal sense of creative power actually spills over to their followers, activating the follower's own creative potential. This direct effect operates through what the researchers termed "creative self-efficacy transmission"—the process by which leaders' creative confidence influences followers' beliefs about their own creative capabilities.

Creative confidence cannot be transmitted by leaders who lack it themselves. There is no escaping the reality - leaders must first develop confidence in their own creative abilities before they can effectively influence others' creative development. Moreover, it is essential for delivering cultural change, as shifts in "the way things are done around here" are achieved not through policy announcements, but through consistent behavioural modelling (Hughes et al., 2018).

The evidence is clear: leaders cannot give what they do not have. Creative leadership requires creative leaders—individuals who have invested in developing their own creative capabilities and can authentically model, encourage, guide, and inspire creativity in others through their genuine creative competence.

Your Influence Can Be Inspirational

For leaders serious about fostering innovation, the path forward requires honest self-assessment and committed investment in personal creative development. The spillover effects of genuine creative leadership—such as increased follower creative self-efficacy, enhanced psychological safety, a strengthened innovation culture and sustainable community outcomes—justify this investment many times over.

The question for leaders is not whether they have time to develop their own creativity, but whether they can afford not to. In a world demanding constant innovation and adaptation, creative leadership has become essential. Leaders who recognise this reality and invest in authentic creative development will build the conditions for organisational creativity that directive approaches alone can never achieve.

In the next section of this book, we will present a practical model to help you develop these essential creative capabilities: The Creative Energy Equation. This synthesis of all the research we have explored throughout this book provides a simple tool to help you remember what really matters when it comes to creativity and foster the conditions for yourself and others to deliver meaningful change.

The Creative Energy Equation will translate all the evidence we have examined into an actionable framework for developing your authentic creative leadership and the organisational culture that will allow people to contribute to their fullest potential.

4

THE CREATIVE ENERGY EQUATION

From the previous sections we now have a wealth of research to draw upon to spark imagination and innovation in our agencies. However, while the creativity research is rich and diverse, it can be overwhelming. Most frameworks are either too complex for daily use or too niche to drive real change. What we need is a concise, clear model for making creativity an everyday reality. This is where the Creative Energy Equation comes in:

Creativity = Emotion x Meaning x Connection (self and others).

$$C = EMC^2$$

The Creative Energy Equation is inspired by one of the most imaginative and courageous people of our time, Albert Einstein. It also recognises the energetic nature of creativity and captures this in a simple, memorable and meaningful way.

The Creative Energy Equation bridges the gap between research and reality, distilling proven findings into an actionable equation anyone can use at any time to remind themselves of what is truly important when it comes to harnessing and nurturing creative potential.

26 The Formula: C=EMC²

The Creative Energy Equation offers a blueprint for creating the conditions (physical and mental) where creativity flows naturally and inspiration is transformed into meaningful change.

I hope, by now, that one thing is clear – creativity is a vital force in both our personal and professional lives. There is not one job, organisation, home or community where creativity is not used to bring about meaningful change. Due to its essential nature, creativity has been extensively studied; however, the focus of the research has shifted over time.

In the 19th Century, Francis Galton used families and statistical methods to investigate the heritability of eminence and exceptional ability. His pioneering work, documented in *Hereditary Genius* (1869), marked the beginning of systematic scientific inquiry into human genius—viewing creative capacity as an inherited trait possessed by the gifted few.

Then, in 1950, J.P. Guilford addressed the American Psychological Association, advocating and gaining acceptance for creativity as a distinct field of research in psychology. This pivotal moment shifted the research focus from rare inherited genius to the recognition of creative potential as a capability accessible to all people.

Today, our understanding has evolved once more. Rather than asking whether creativity is inherited or learnable, contemporary research explores the conditions that activate and amplify the creative potential we all possess—the environments, emotions, and connections that foster our innate creativity.

We now have an incredible wealth of information to draw on to spark and sustain imagination and innovation. However, we do not have a concise, clear model for how to make it work in practice.

This is where the Creative Energy Equation comes in.

While creativity research is rich and diverse, most frameworks struggle to translate theory into everyday practice.

The Four C Model (mini-c, little-c, Pro-c, Big-C) offers educators a useful taxonomy for categorising types of creativity. Yet, it does not provide actionable steps for generating creative breakthroughs in the moment.

The AMO model (Ability, Motivation, Opportunity), while useful for understanding workplace performance, treats Opportunity as a catch-all category encompassing everything from resources and time to organisational culture and social support—a diverse mix of factors too broad to provide clear direction. And while concepts such as psychological safety are important, by themselves they are insufficient and incomplete.

Other frameworks focus on specific techniques, broad systems or narrow contexts, leaving us with fragmented insights rather than a unified approach. No single model captures the full picture in a way anyone can apply at any time. And they all seem to lack a deep consideration of the actual source of creativity—people.

The Creative Energy Equation bridges the gap between research and reality—distilling proven findings into a single, actionable equation anyone can use anytime to incite and increase creative energy. It captures concisely the human core of creativity and is inspired by one of the most inspirational and imaginative people of our time, Albert Einstein.

Einstein - A Creative Visionary

Albert Einstein was not just a master physicist—he was a visionary who reshaped our understanding of the universe. Remarkably, Einstein's breakthroughs emerged not simply from strict scientific methods but from a beautiful blend of calculation, creativity, professionalism, and playfulness.

Before his theories were proven, Einstein famously relied on thought experiments—vivid acts of the imagination, such as picturing himself riding a beam of light or falling freely in an elevator, to probe the mysteries of space and time. His creative process embodied what he later called combinatory play: forging connections between seemingly unrelated concepts and forming authentic ideas through new associations.

Einstein declared:

"Imagination is more important than knowledge. Knowledge is limited. Imagination encircles the entire world." (Einstein, 1929, p.117)

Importantly, Einstein's statement did not diminish the value of knowledge—knowledge provides the foundation, but imagination allows us to transcend existing boundaries.

Other scientists often accused Einstein of lacking seriousness, suggesting his methods lacked rigour and credibility within the scientific academy. For years, he was viewed as a nonconformist among physicists, a characteristic not encouraged by his peers.

Yet, it was precisely his boundary-pushing approach—his ability to use imagination to open his mind and expand his thoughts—that enabled him to see beyond existing paradigms and discover radical truths about energy and the universe. His willingness to combine child-like curiosity with deep professional skill proved to be the key to his most crucial discoveries.

From Cosmic Energy to Human Creativity

Einstein's iconic equation, $E=mc^2$, revolutionised science by revealing a fundamental law of the universe: mass and energy are interchangeable, and under the right circumstances, even a tiny amount of mass can unleash extraordinary energy when multiplied by the speed of light squared. The power of the equation lies in showing how a simple, small entity, when combined with an exponential multiplier, can release something vast and valuable.

This scientific principle offers a powerful metaphor for creativity in human life. In Einstein's formula, energy (E) is not created out of nothing; it emerges when existing potential (M, mass) is activated by optimum conditions (light, c^2). In the same way, the creative energy within individuals, teams, or organisations can be immense—but only if the right internal and external conditions come together.

The Creative Energy Equation draws inspiration from this insight. It pays homage to Einstein by preserving the structure of his famous equation, but shifts the focus from mass to human potential. Where Einstein showed how physical energy can be liberated from matter under the right conditions, $C=EMC^2$ reveals how creative energy can be activated in people when emotion (E), meaning (M), and connection (C) work together.

The formula reminds us that just as cosmic energy depends on powerful multipliers, human creativity needs more than just knowledge or talent—it flourishes exponentially when the right emotional, purposeful, and connective conditions are present.

The Creative Energy Equation - Overview

Creativity = Emotion x Meaning x Connection^2 (self and others).

$$C = EMC^2$$

E = Emotion: The Spark of Creative Energy

Most of the models we have discussed so far—the AMO model of Ability, Motivation, Opportunity and well-known motivation frameworks such as Pink's autonomy-mastery-purpose—are really means to an emotional end. They prescribe organisational structures, systems, and practices not for their own sake, but because they help people feel good—and therefore perform better. These models work precisely because they evoke the emotional states we need for creativity: helping people feel empowered, excited, bold and brave.

Ability is important because it brings a sense of confidence in the skill and resources one has to apply to a task. Motivation awakens excitement and energy for action, and Opportunity is all about fostering the feelings of safety and support that fuels courage. Understanding this reveals why focusing on emotion as the first element of $C = EMC^2$ is essential:

> Every organisational intervention ultimately aims to construct empowering emotional states.

You may remember the Cognitive Behavioural Therapy (CBT) model from Section 1. It shows clearly that emotions are the essential precursor to action. Our beliefs and thoughts are bundled up and channelled into emotions whose sole purpose is to get us to move physically or psychologically. Without emotion, we would not do anything; emotion energises us, focuses our attention, and compels us to act.

However, not all emotions contribute equally to creative energy. Some emotions, like shame, guilt, and fear, can prevent us from moving forward, keeping us stuck in cycles of self-doubt or hesitation. Others, such as anger or pride, may propel us into action, but often in reactive, unhelpful, or hyperactive ways.

To fuel constructive creativity, we must foster positive emotions like courage, willingness, acceptance, gratitude, and joy. Research by psychologist Barbara Fredrickson demonstrates why these emotions are particularly powerful: her broaden-and-build theory shows that positive emotions literally expand our thinking, broaden our awareness of possibilities, and construct sustainable psychological resources (Fredrickson, 2001).

When we experience joy, interest, or contentment, our thought-action repertoires widen, allowing us to see connections we might otherwise miss and generate novel ideas more readily.

Importantly, this does not mean we must feel positive emotions all the time. There is tremendous energy released when someone moves from a distressing or debilitating emotion toward an empowering one. And so, a key part of nurturing creative energy is ensuring there is support for processing and progressing away from the emotions that hold us back and toward those that help us be our best. Engaging in creative acts can help with this transformation as the relationship between emotion and creativity is bidirectional—engaging in creative acts improves improve our emotional states, creating a reinforcing, upward spiral.

In the Emotion element of the Creative Energy Equation, our goal is to nurture both confidence (the belief in our skills and creative abilities) and courage (the willingness to move forward, take risks, and trust we will be supported). When we feel capable in our abilities and secure in our environment, we can free up the energy needed to imagine new possibilities and take bold steps to bring them to life.

M = Meaning: The Compass for Creative Focus

Creativity gains direction and deep personal commitment when anchored in purpose.

You may feel fantastic and full of life when you walk through the office doors. However, suppose you do not feel the work you are doing is important, makes any significant community contribution, or is aligned with your personal vision and values. In that case, the vital component of meaning is missing. As a result, the effort and energy you will expend will only be average.

Meaning—the belief that what you are doing is important— ignites intrinsic motivation, which drives continued commitment and resilience in the face of challenges. As we explored earlier with Pink's principles of autonomy, mastery, and purpose, intrinsic motivation arises when work connects to our internal drivers rather than external rewards.

Teresa Amabile's decades of research on creativity reinforces this: people produce their most creative work when motivated by interest, challenge, and personal significance rather than money, deadlines, or other extrinsic pressures. Her componential theory identifies intrinsic motivation as an essential ingredient for creativity, demonstrating that without it, even skilled individuals with supportive environments will produce mediocre results.

When the work aligns with our core motivations, it will be seen as meaningful, and we will willingly and generously commit our resources to make it a success, and constantly seek ways to improve it. Moreover, when we believe we are contributing to a cause or a community that shares our vision and values, we become courageous, moving beyond ourselves and persisting through challenges for the sake of others.

It is meaning that translates positive emotional states into focused and determined action. With it, you have an army of creative warriors standing bravely to take on uncertainty and complacency. Without it, you have a crew of passive and piecemeal participants unwilling to share their full potential.

So, in the Meaning element of the Creative Energy Equation, our goal is to ensure a clear sense of purpose—both with our individual work and with the broader mission of the team or organisation. When personal purpose aligns with both task and collective mission, creativity flourishes as we work on challenges that solve real problems, create products that matter, and contribute genuine value to the world.

C^2 = Connection: The Multiplier Effect

Like light in Einstein's equation, connection (C) is creativity's exponential force.

There are two important aspects to connection:

1. Connection to self
2. Connection to others.

Connection to Self

As we heard in the first section of this book, we are all unique. This fact means we are sitting on an incredible creative resource—our authenticity. When we tap into this individuality, we have a ready platform for new ideas and innovations.

To do this, we require intrapersonal intelligence, a fancy term for self-awareness and insight. It is having a sound sense of one's values, skills, motivations, and emotions. It is also about supporting ourselves to shine and showing ourselves kindness and compassion, especially in the face of challenges and failures, which are inevitable on the creative path.

Connection to Others

Each person's authenticity is an awesome creative power. Imagine then what happens when we combine it with other awesome creative powers? The results can be atomic.

Through cooperation and collaboration, connection to others amplifies creativity by adding different perspectives, encouraging consideration of diverse experiences, combining various skill sets, and sparking new and valuable associations. This is why cognitively diverse teams—those with different knowledge processing styles and perspectives—consistently outperform homogeneous groups in solving complex problems. Studies show that diverse teams make better decisions 87% of the time and produce significantly more creative solutions than uniform teams (Larsen, 2017).

However, diversity alone is not enough. Teams need both creative diversity—different creative thinking styles and authentic perspectives—and strong collaboration skills to realise these performance benefits. When people feel safe bringing their whole selves to work and genuinely collaborate across differences, the multiplication effect becomes extraordinary. In an AI world where the threat of homogenisation is real, it is precisely this connection with others that will keep creativity alive.

In the Connection element of the Creative Energy Equation, we focus on two essential goals. The first is consciousness—

developing awareness of our own strengths, interests, and emotional states so we can contribute authentically. The second is collaboration—amplifying creative potential through genuine partnership with others. When we combine self-knowledge with the willingness to connect across differences, we unlock the exponential power that makes C^2 the multiplier in our equation.

Figure 15- The Creative Energy Equation

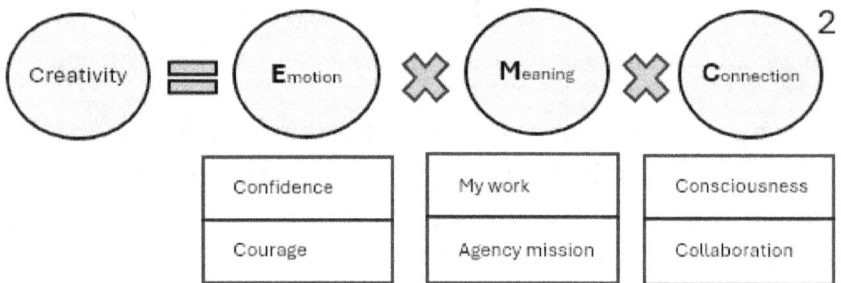

| Confidence | My work | Consciousness |
| Courage | Agency mission | Collaboration |

Why This Equation Works

The Creative Energy Equation, $C=EMC^2$, distils over seventy years of creativity research into a simple framework that can be used by individuals, teams, and organisations alike. While the formula appears elegantly simple, it is sophisticated in its research foundation. Each element draws on established bodies of scientific evidence:

The Emotion component integrates findings from positive psychology, particularly Barbara Fredrickson's broaden-and-build theory, along with insights from affective neuroscience and the relationship between emotional states and creative thinking.

The Meaning component synthesises decades of motivation research, especially Teresa Amabile's intrinsic motivation principle and self-determination theory, demonstrating why purpose and personal significance are essential for sustained creative effort.

The Connection component brings together research on authenticity, intrapersonal intelligence, cognitive diversity, and team creativity, showing how self-awareness combined with collaborative partnerships produces powerful creative outcomes.

Additionally, even though there is a deep scientific foundation to this model, a person can intuitively understand the intention behind each element. They can readily skim the equation and determine, at a high level, how well they align with each component. Even with just a birds-eye view of the equation, the answers will readily identify where they can improve and what actions they can take to enhance their creative energy. For example, I know readily if I feel confident in my work and supported to share ideas. I know immediately if I think my work is meaningful and whether I feel inspired by the agency's mission. I can also identify the extent to which I understand and encourage my own creative expression and engage with others.

The elements of the Creative Energy Equation—emotion, meaning, and connection—are ever-present and accessible to everyone, regardless of background or credentials. The Creative Energy Equation does not rely upon expensive education or the latest technological gadgets. It works because it is based on clear, concise, scientifically proven components. It does not require any fancy new tricks but concentrates on the foundations necessary to bring out the very best of human creativity.

Crucially, these elements are also scalable, working with equal power whether you are navigating a personal creative challenge alone in your studio, leading a team through innovation, or designing organisational culture for thousands of people. The same fundamental principles apply when writing a poem, launching a startup, or transforming a multinational corporation. This universality is what makes $C=EMC^2$ not just a theory but a practical tool for creative action at any level.

This equation is valuable because it focuses on what is truly important—ensuring the conditions are conducive to embracing and expanding the creative energy that already exists. It offers a blueprint for designing environments (physical and mental) where creativity flows naturally and inspiration is transformed into meaningful change.

Equation Limitations

It is important to note that the Creative Energy Equation has been deliberately focused on the conditions that enable creativity rather than specific creative techniques. You will not find instructions here for brainstorming methods, free-thinking frameworks, or design thinking principles. Instead, $C=EMC^2$ concentrates on the foundational environment—emotional, motivational, and relational—that must be in place for any creative technique to work effectively.

Think of it as caring for the the soil rather than teaching specific planting methods. This approach is based on the belief that if the conditions are right (emotion, meaning, and connection aligned), people naturally generate creative solutions and can integrate whichever techniques best suit their context.

The Creative Energy Equation is therefore complementary to, rather than competitive with, process-based and technique-focused models. It ensures you have the right internal and external environment to support any specific creative tool or method you choose to use.

A Concise Framework for Creativity

One of the most valuable contributions of the Creative Energy Equation is that it clarifies that creativity is not the exclusive domain of those with expensive educations or specialist expertise. It emerges from the intersection of elevated emotions, self-awareness, purpose, and authentic connection—capacities available to every human being.

Rather than privileging one element over the others, the equation shows that creativity flourishes from a synthesis: when emotion energises us, meaning directs us, and connection multiplies our possibilities, we access the full spectrum of our creative potential.

In the chapters that follow, we will explore each element in depth, beginning with the foundation of all creative action—emotion. Let's discover how cultivating the right emotional conditions can unlock creative potential.

27 Emotion: The Spark For Creativity

At their core, all interventions aimed at increasing creativity, boosting innovation, and reducing risk aversion target the same thing: a person's emotional state—specifically, their confidence and their courage.

For generations, emotions have been cast as the enemy, especially in the world of work. We have been taught that feelings are unprofessional, disruptive, and best ignored in favour of objectivity and productivity. The prevailing wisdom says: suppress or deny emotions for the supposed benefit of all.

Nevertheless, our emotions drive every decision and every action, whether we acknowledge them or not. Even when we mask our feelings behind a polite face, those hidden emotions shape what we choose to do and what we choose not to do. Moreover, as discussed in Section 1, emotions play a significant role in people's assessment of the value of our ideas. Therefore, mastering creativity requires understanding not only our own emotions but also the emotional lens through which others view our work.

So, instead of disregarding emotions or engaging with them only when they feel comfortable, we must recognise and respect their incredible influence over our ability to be innovative. Rather than denying or avoiding them, we must explore and embrace emotions as one of our most vital sources of intelligence and creative energy.

What Are Emotions? They Too Are Energy—In Motion

We have spoken about creativity as energy; emotions are energies, too. Their very name suggests their nature—"e-motion," energy in motion. They are currents cast forward from our minds to make us move, either psychologically or physically (or both) and always either away from pain or towards pleasure (or both).

"Emotions are our source of energy" (Landry & Caust, 2017 p. 18)

It is easy to dismiss emotions as sporadic or erratic reactions. When we accuse someone of being "too emotional," we imply their responses lack reason or basis. Countering this claim, the work of psychologist Lisa Feldman Barrett demonstrates that emotions are real, meaningful physical experiences and are carefully calculated from a combination of body signals, memories, and environmental cues (Barrett, 2017).

Specifically, every emotion we feel arises from the synthesis of three key inputs being our current physical state, memories of past experiences and the specific context in which we find ourselves.

Figure 16- How emotions are constructed

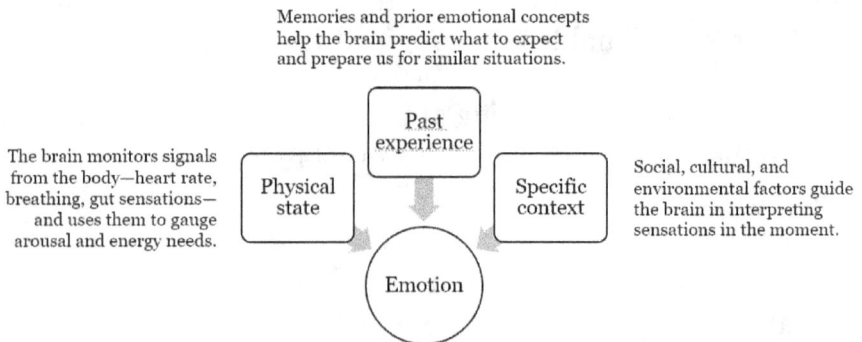

Memories and prior emotional concepts help the brain predict what to expect and prepare us for similar situations.

Past experience

The brain monitors signals from the body—heart rate, breathing, gut sensations— and uses them to gauge arousal and energy needs.

Physical state

Specific context

Social, cultural, and environmental factors guide the brain in interpreting sensations in the moment.

Emotion

In this way, emotions are not hardwired, automatic responses— they are dynamically constructed in the moment, shaped by our body, our history, and our surroundings.

This constructed nature of emotions is clearly illustrated in the following examples of Emma and Sarah, who have two very different experiences when tasked with delivering a presentation about their ideas.

Emma

As Emma prepares to present a new project to her colleagues, she notices her heart racing and her palms sweating. The physical signs of stress are unmistakable. Her mind flashes back to a previous presentation when she stumbled over her words and felt the sting of embarrassment after her boss cruelly counselled her afterwards.

The current context—a high-stakes meeting with senior management—only amplifies her nerves, which are not helped by her rumbling stomach and the air-conditioning being too cold. Emma's boss was too busy to spend time with her before the presentation, and the only feedback she received on the copy she sent him was an email with three words: "It looks fine".

Drawing on these elements, Emma's brain constructs a powerful sense of anxiety, self-doubt and distraction. As a result, Emma is concentrating on just keeping it together and thinking only about what she will say next. She misses important cues and audience comments that could help her better understand the issues and build connections.

Emma finds questions the questions her colleagues ask confronting and races through the answers quickly. She holds no curiosity about the concerns raised or the value they may add to the project. Her mission is to make it out alive. Emma walks away feeling relieved that it is over, but incompetent and determined to avoid sharing her ideas ever again. Speaking up, she feels, is just a sure way to get shot down.

Sarah

Sarah has a starkly different emotional experience. She also feels her heart pounding and her palms damp. However, she recalls how a supportive manager helped her recover gracefully from a previous slip-up and has invested in her presentation and public speaking skills. She is also well-fed and has spent some time in the meeting room earlier, navigating the space and setting it up to her liking. In contrast to Emma, Sarah had a meeting with her boss the day before, during which she walked through the presentation. He provided some constructive suggestions, support and assurance that her ideas were awesome.

The context is also different: the team recently celebrated a win, and management has emphasised learning and growth over perfection. Now, Sarah's brain interprets her body's signals as excitement. She is eager to show her work to others and is motivated by her peers' interest in her ideas. Instead of shrinking back, she steps forward, energised and ready to contribute, viewing this as a chance to see how these ideas can evolve rather than an event to fear.

These examples show how emotions are formed from various factors. Most importantly, though, they make clear that the environment we find ourselves in has a massive impact on how we process our emotions and how we proceed.

> The contextual nature of emotions has profound implications for creativity: we cannot control emotions directly, but we can shape the conditions that influence their construction.

By designing environments that support healthy physical states (adequate rest and nutrition, manageable workload), reinforce positive emotional concepts (celebrating experimentation), and provide supportive environments (psychological safety and encouragement), we enable brains to construct emotions that energise creative action.

However, knowing how emotions are constructed is only the first step. We must also understand how different emotional states either facilitate or flatten creative action.

How Emotions Help or Hinder Creativity

Barbara Fredrickson's broaden-and-build theory proposes that positive emotions do far more than make us feel good—they expand our awareness and encourage us to think and act in more open, flexible, and creative ways (Fredrickson, 2001). Positive emotions such as joy, gratitude, interest, hope, amusement, awe, and love all share the ability to enlarge our thought–action repertoires. For example, joy sparks the urge to play and experiment, interest drives exploration and learning, and love fosters connection, collaboration, and support for one another's highest potential.

Over time, these broadened mindsets help us build enduring personal resources—intellectual, social, psychological, and physical—that we can draw upon when facing challenges. In turn, positive emotions increase resilience, deepen relationships, and enhance wellbeing, enabling us to deal constructively with the challenges that arise in creative projects. Importantly, positive emotions can also undo the lingering effects of negative emotions, helping us transform painful past experiences, recover more quickly from stress and return to a state of openness and growth.

In contrast, negative emotions—such as fear, anger, and anxiety—tend to narrow our focus and trigger survival-oriented actions like fight, flight, or withdrawal. In life-threatening situations, this narrowing is adaptive and purposeful, enabling rapid, decisive responses to protect ourselves. However, in everyday contexts, a predominance of negative emotions can limit our ability to see new possibilities or build supportive connections. For instance, shame, guilt, and fear can trap us in cycles of self-doubt or hesitation, while anger or pride may drive action, but often in reactive, aggressive or unhelpful ways.

Yet recent research reveals a more nuanced picture, and the value does not necessarily come from being happy all the time. The relationship between emotion and creativity is not simply "positive emotions good, negative emotions bad." Instead, it is about understanding how different emotional states serve different creative functions, the energy that comes from transforming negative states, and learning to work with the full spectrum.

To navigate this emotional landscape intentionally, we need a comprehensive map that shows us the spectrum of emotional states and their impact on our creative capacity. This is where Dr David Hawkins' Map of Consciousness becomes invaluable.

Mapping the Emotional Spectrum—From Force to Power

While Fredrickson's broaden-and-build theory shows us *how* positive and negative emotions function, psychiatrist Dr David R. Hawkins developed a Map of Consciousness that provides a comprehensive view of the full emotional spectrum and its impact on our capacity to act creatively (Hawkins, 2012). His model presents two broad types of emotions, Force and Power.

Crucially, Hawkins identifies courage as the threshold at which Power first emerges and life shifts from threatening to exciting. Hawkins' model is shown in the diagram on the following page.

It is worth noting that, like Gardner's model of nine intelligences, Hawkins' model has faced criticism for relying on applied kinesiology and for lacking traditional empirical validation. Despite this, this model has immense practical value, offering an accessible framework for recognising emotional patterns and charting pathways for growth—precisely what we need to navigate creative energy.

Figure 17- Levels of Consciousness - Dr David Hawkins

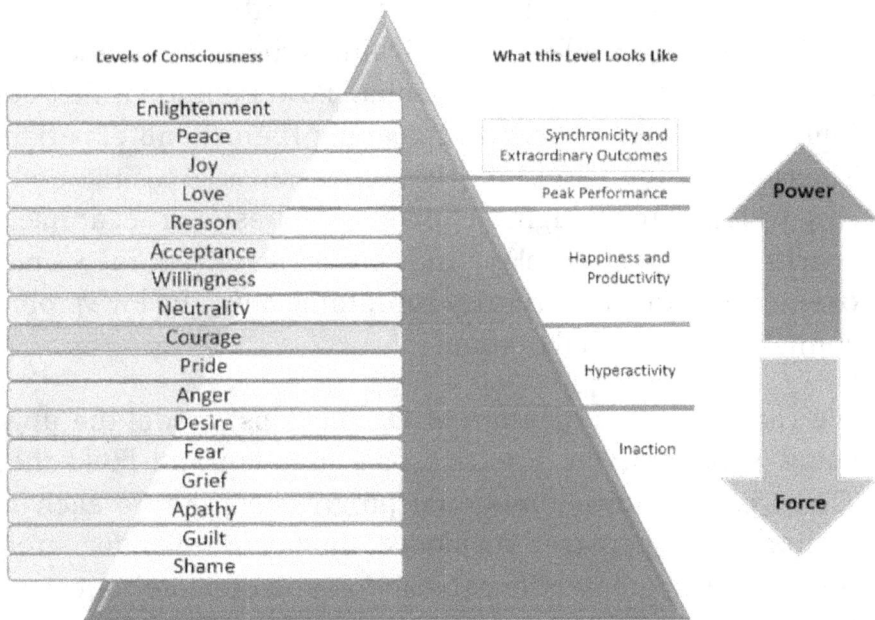

Levels of Consciousness	What this Level Looks Like	
Enlightenment		
Peace	Synchronicity and Extraordinary Outcomes	Power
Joy		
Love	Peak Performance	
Reason		
Acceptance	Happiness and Productivity	
Willingness		
Neutrality		
Courage		
Pride	Hyperactivity	
Anger		
Desire		
Fear	Inaction	
Grief		
Apathy		Force
Guilt		
Shame		

Force Emotions: Lower-level emotions such as shame, guilt, fear, anger, and pride are categorised as force emotions. These states often feel heavy and constraining, exerting pressure that can lead to inaction, and come with a sense of being stuck. Alternatively, they can come with aggressive, excessive effort, and a sense of being out of control. Hawkins described these as life-destroying energies, not because they are bad, but because they drain vitality and keep us cycling through old patterns. These are the emotions Barbara Fredrickson explains in her broaden-and-build theory as negative—such as fear, anger, and anxiety—which narrow our focus and prompt specific, survival-oriented actions like fight, flight, or withdrawal. They close us off to new experiences and possibilities as our energy turns inward for self-preservation.

Power Emotions: In contrast, emotions of power—courage, acceptance, love, joy, and peace—are life-affirming. They draw on intrinsic strength, allowing individuals to act authentically and move toward their highest potential. Power emotions lift people, filling them with energy and opening them to all experiences. These are the emotions Fredrickson classifies as positive and that can widen our thought-action repertoires. For example, joy sparks the urge to play and be creative, courage enables overcoming uncertainty to try something new, and love promotes connection and collaboration.

We can see in the diagram of Dr Hawkins' model the upward spiral spoken of in Fredrickson's broaden-and-build theory. There is a positive emotional progression, where each rung higher offers increased resilience, the opportunity for stronger relationships, greater life satisfaction and creative contribution. In this way, even advancing one rung forward releases creative potential.

Understanding this distinction between force and power is essential for $C=EMC^2$. Our aim is not to eliminate force emotions but to create conditions that help individuals and teams move toward the courage threshold—where creative action is possible.

Because some force emotions—for example, those that lead to hyperactivity, such as desire, anger, and pride—can create a sense of urgency that demands expression and fuels creative action. For example, anger played a vital role in Maya Angelou's work. She believed that anger, when acknowledged and channelled constructively, could become a powerful tool for positive and purposeful change. Angelou famously said,

"You should be angry...use that anger. You write it. You paint it. You dance it. You march it. You vote it. You do everything about it. You talk it. Never stop talking it." (Angelou, 2006)

However, it must be noted that in these situations, the creative work itself becomes the *vehicle* for transformation, moving creators from force toward power, from limitation toward liberation. The emotions were not denied or suppressed; they were acknowledged, channelled towards meaningful pursuits and ultimately transcended through creative action.

Confidence + Courage

Most workplaces inadvertently keep people in force emotions— shame, guilt, fear, anger, or pride—through excessive pressure, micromanagement, blame cultures, lack of support, unclear purposes, resource scarcity, and political competition. In these states, creativity becomes sporadic, defensive, non-sustainable or impossible, leading to disengagement, high turnover, and missed opportunities for innovation.

> Instead, what individuals and organisations must work towards is achieving a combination of confidence and courage.

Confidence: the belief in our domain-specific skills, ability to develop new skills (growth mindset) and creative capacity (creative self-efficacy). Confidence says, *"I have the skills I need to make meaningful change, and if I need new ones, I know I can develop them."*

Courage: the willingness to experience and work through uncomfortable emotions while taking creative risks. Courage says, *"I will move forward even when the outcome is uncertain, and I trust that I will be supported."*

When organisations foster confidence (through skill development, recognition, autonomy and appropriate stretch assignments) and courage (through psychological safety, supportive leadership, and permission to experiment), they create the conditions for sustained movement from force to power, and to higher levels of productivity, performance and most importantly, wellbeing.

Psychological Safety Is Not Sufficient – People Need Confidence Too

Psychological safety—feeling secure enough to take interpersonal risks without fear of punishment—is essential for fostering courage, but it only clears the way for creative action; it does not equip individuals with the confidence to act. It is the combination of psychological safety and creative confidence which provides the optimum conditions for innovation (Ahmad et al., 2025). Interestingly though, it has been found that high levels of creative confidence can actually overcome lower levels of psychological safety to deliver innovative improvements (Liu et al., 2024).

This situation is best explained through an example. Imagine a design team in which members feel free to propose wild concepts—psychological safety is high and they feel fully supported to share their ideas. Yet if team members doubt their expertise or creative skills, if they lack confidence in their ability to develop new approaches, they may still hold back, fearing that their ideas are inane. They can feel safe within the team, but also still believe their ideas are stupid.

Conversely, if a person does not feel safe within the team environment, but wholeheartedly believes in the change they seek to make, and in their ability to deliver it successfully, then they may undertake maverick actions, going outside protocols and implementing what is known as "bootleg innovation".

It is confidence—rooted in domain knowledge, well-practised creative techniques, and a track record of small successes—that empowers individuals to move beyond brainstorming ideas to implementing tangible innovations. Without it, safe spaces risk becoming filled with silence or tentative suggestions rather than being energised environments filled with the sharing of ideas and the building of breakthrough innovation. Confidence delivers the beliefs necessary to leverage expertise and safe environments for innovative ends.

> If we were to use the analogy of a car, psychological safety takes the foot off the brake of fear, enabling risk-taking, while creative confidence is the engine that propels people forward. The creativity car is not going anywhere without sufficient attention to both.

Cultivating Emotional Foundations for Creativity

As we have seen, emotions are the enabler of creative action. From understanding how the brain constructs emotions to navigating the full spectrum from force to power, the Emotion element of $C=EMC^2$ reveals that:

- Emotions energise and direct our behaviour, shaping both individual creativity and how others perceive the value of our work.
- Both positive and negative emotions can serve creative functions—broadening, focusing, signalling problems, and spurring change.

- The Map of Consciousness shows that courage is the crucial threshold where sustainable creative energy emerges.
- Psychological safety fosters courage, but without creative confidence (self-efficacy and growth mindset), safe spaces cannot translate into creative action.
- True creative performance requires intentionally building both confidence and courage through supportive conditions, skill development, and emotional intelligence.

As discussed in the previous section, leaders play a crucial role in influencing emotional states. To establish a climate where emotions are enhanced and creativity thrives, organisations must:

- Recognise and respect the fundamental role of emotions in creative work—and understand the emotional lens through which others assess our ideas.
- Monitor the emotional climate of teams continuously, identifying when people operate in force emotions and introduce supports to more positive states.
- Treat emotional intelligence as a core organisational capability, providing education and resources to help people become aware of and manage their own emotions.
- Balance psychological safety assessments with measures of growth mindset and creative self-efficacy to foster both courage and confidence.

In summary, it is the quality of our emotions that determines the energy we have to invest in creative effort. In the next chapter, we turn to the second element of the Creative Energy Equation—Meaning—to discover how purpose and significance can transform this energy into focused, sustained creative impact.

28 Meaning: The Compass For Focus

Leaders can ask their people to bear creative risk and invest effort in innovation, but these will only be sustained if supported by a strong sense of purpose.

We have already discussed the Emotion (E) element, showing how positive emotional states broaden our perspectives, but also how some negative emotional states can spark incredible inspiration. However, a person can feel wonderful, energised, optimistic, and all fired up for the day—but this does not guarantee creative capacity. They may come to the table stirred by anger, pride, or a burning desire to make a difference. Still, these emotional states do not automatically translate into meaningful creative outcomes.

While emotions are essential for excitement and energy, creativity needs an organising principle. It needs direction and focus; otherwise, it is like sailing in wild winds without a rudder. There may be abundant energy available, but little intentionality about how it is invested. Creative direction and endurance come from meaning—the belief that what we are doing is important.

This meaning operates on two interconnected levels:

1. Personal meaning: the sense that your individual work aligns with your values, strengths, and aspirations—that what you do each day matters to *you*.
2. Shared meaning: the conviction that your team or organisation's mission is significant and worth contributing to—that your work matters to *others* and serves a purpose beyond yourself.

Without a sense of purpose or significance at either level, even the most enthusiastic effort can become scattered or superficial. It is meaning that transforms fleeting enthusiasm into lasting commitment, anchors creative energy in something worth pursuing, and turns creative potential into real, impactful results. In this chapter, we explore how to cultivate both dimensions of meaning to give creativity the compass it needs.

What Is Meaning?

Meaning is the sense that our actions, goals, or work are important and align with our deepest values, beliefs, and aspirations. It is the feeling that what we do matters—not just to ourselves but often to something larger than us.

"Meaningful work is work that is significant, purposeful, and worthwhile. It is work that people feel matters in some important way, either to themselves, their organisation, or the broader world." (Amabile & Kramer, 2011)

When we find meaning in our work or creative pursuits, we experience a sense of purpose, significance, intention, deep resonance, and fulfilment that compels us forward.

The Science of Purpose and Intrinsic Motivation

Viktor Frankl endured many excruciating years in a concentration camp during WWII. Years later, he released his seminal work *Man's Search for Meaning*, in which he shared his overwhelming observation from this experience: humans are fundamentally driven by a "will to meaning."

Even in the most challenging circumstances, it is our sense of purpose that sustains us. After the war, Frankl continued to work as a psychologist and applied this insight to help many of his patients navigate their daily struggles and lead thriving lives.

As Frankl famously wrote,

"Those who have a 'why' to live can bear almost any 'how." (Frankl, 1946)

This statement is as true for our creative pursuits as it is for our personal lives. A clear sense of purpose enables us to navigate the challenges inherent in creative work and commit to realising our creative potential. Since Frankl's work, countless studies into human motivation and creativity have confirmed the importance of meaning and purpose.

For example, in his book *Drive (Pink, 2018)*, Daniel Pink identifies purpose as the ultimate motivator—the force that compels us to create, innovate, and persist over the long term. When we feel that our work matters, we are far more likely to invest our energy, overcome obstacles, and pursue excellence.

Amabile and Kramer's research at Harvard Business School shows that small wins in meaningful work provide powerful fuel (Amabile & Kramer, 2011). Most importantly, they confirmed that intrinsic motivation—working for the love of the work rather than for external rewards—is the key ingredient in breakthrough creative ideas. When purpose is present, creativity flourishes.

Martin Seligman's PERMA model (Seligman, 2011)—a cornerstone of positive psychology—identifies meaning as one of the five essential elements of flourishing. When our daily efforts are tied to something significant, we are more likely to feel fulfilled and energised, even in the face of challenges.

> In short, meaning is the medium that keeps us focused, resilient, persistent and willing to continue investing the creative energy needed to achieve lasting impact.

It makes sense—if we do not believe in the importance of what we are doing, we are far less likely to want to make any additional effort to improve it. And if leaders are asking their people to put in discretionary effort, it is virtually impossible without a sense of purpose.

Meaning Is a Creative Imperative

Meaning works directly on the Beliefs aspect of the Cognitive Behaviour Therapy (CBT) model. The belief that our work is important—or not, that it aligns with our skills and passions—or does not, or that it is meaningful—or meaningless, powerfully shapes our emotional state. These beliefs set the stage for emotions such as courage and joy, or apathy and fear, which, in turn, drive our motivation and ultimately determine our creative results.

Example 1: The Social Entrepreneur

Consider the story of a social entrepreneur, let's call him Peter, who believes passionately that his work helps marginalised communities thrive. Motivated by this sense of significance, he is driven to find sustainable solutions despite setbacks and limited resources. Peter considers the long-term impacts and the necessary inputs to achieve them. He feels passionate and prepared to put in the work necessary to deliver his vision.

Peter's unwavering commitment leads him to build plans, take action and embed accountability. He seeks collaborations that contribute resources and skills he does not have. He also invests his energy in advocating for those in power to develop supportive policies. Peter continually seeks new ideas to implement and add value to his community. He feels committed to bringing about positive change.

The challenges Peter encounters he sees as natural responses to change, and views each as an opportunity to enact systemic shifts. He is in this game for the long haul and understands the importance of self-care, taking time out to restore his energy and come back renewed. It is Peter's strong belief in the significance of what he is doing that sustains him.

Example 2: The Disengaged Corporate Employee

Compare this to Steve's experience as a corporate consultant. Steve began his career excited to contribute to his clients' success. He threw himself into his work and undertook extensive additional study, all so he could deliver the best advice to his clients as he was compelled to help them grow and thrive. Steve truly wanted to play a part in establishing successful and sustainable businesses because he knew this would have positive flow-on effects for their shareholders and communities.

Over the years, though, Steve sees very little change. He works long hours preparing reports and presentations that are accepted and applauded at board meetings but not implemented. He invests an incredible amount of energy in proposing viable new pathways that are praised but not pursued. Without his clients taking action on his recommendations, Steve feels his time is being wasted. It does not help when he hears the agency partner say their role is to "tick the boxes" for their clients.

This rattles Steve, who now sees his work as merely a compliance exercise for clients who wish to demonstrate that they have sought professional advice. He loses the sense that he is contributing, and while he is being paid well, it is not enough to sustain his creative energy. Steve becomes bitter, reduces his effort on each project, and recycles previous recommendations. He slips into apathy, the latter a natural process of numbing himself against doing the work he believes no one cares about.

For Steve, motivation has become almost non-existent because there is very little meaning. He now puts in minimal effort, avoids taking risks, and resists collaboration with colleagues. Over time, this lack of engagement leads to stagnant projects, low team morale, and will likely lead to Steve leaving. There is no creativity in this environment; it is merely about churning out work in exchange for cash.

These examples highlight how much meaning influences our willingness to invest our precious assets—time, energy, and effort—in any endeavour and our ability to sustain this commitment over time. If we lose sight of the importance of our work, then the drive to find new ideas and add value also diminishes. We choose to preserve our energy for higher priorities. This outcome is not sabotage or selfish; it is a perfectly understandable state for someone with limited energy and who may need it later for more pressing priorities.

Personal Meaning: Why Your Work Matters to You

Personal meaning is the belief that your work is significant to your own values, strengths, and aspirations—that what you do matters deeply to *you*, not just to others or external measures of success. When work resonates with who we are and what we care about, it becomes intrinsically rewarding rather than merely a means to an end.

As we explored earlier with Pink's autonomy-mastery-purpose framework, the need for purpose is not a luxury but a core human driver: we are wired to seek work that feels significant.

The coherence that comes from doing work that is personally meaningful enables a smooth flow of creative energy, resulting in many valuable outcomes, such as higher levels of creative performance, persistence through setbacks, and improved personal wellbeing (Steger, Dik, & Duffy, 2012).

These results are possible because personal meaning transforms tasks from obligations into opportunities for self-expression and growth, and allows us to contribute to things we actually care about.

> The journey to discovering and living our purpose is deeply personal, requiring us to reflect on our values, beliefs, and aspirations and to courageously pursue work that resonates with our unique sense of meaning.

This awareness of what matters to us and the work we consider important is a core part of the self-connection element of the Creative Energy Equation, which will be covered in the next chapter.

However, meaning does not exist in a vacuum. While our individual compass guides our personal journey, the greatest creative breakthroughs often emerge when our sense of purpose connects with that of others. A shared sense of purpose can unite, inspire, and multiply creative energy for collective impact.

Shared Meaning Fosters Safety and Performance

Shared meaning is the conviction that your team's or organisation's work matters beyond any single person, that together you are pursuing something significant. A strong sense of collective mission is among the most powerful predictors of high-performing, resilient teams and organisations.

> When a group rallies around a common "why," collaboration flourishes, trust deepens, and creativity emerges, with studies confirming that a strong sense of shared purpose yields more breakthrough ideas and innovation (Lindstrom, 2024).

Meaning does this by mediating another concept that has received increasing attention recently—psychological safety. Amy Edmondson's pioneering research on psychological safety highlights that teams with a strong sense of shared meaning are far more likely to foster an environment where everyone feels comfortable contributing. Collective clarity also fosters a sense of belonging and community as employees see how their work contributes to a larger, meaningful goal.

In these teams, members know that their voices matter because they are working toward something significant together. This shared purpose encourages candour and experimentation, helping teams recover from setbacks and learn from mistakes. Additionally, when team members are motivated by a shared mission, leaders can "back off" and afford them greater ownership and autonomy, creating an upward spiral that contributes to greater job satisfaction, a sense of safety, and work-life harmony.

Ultimately, the power of shared purpose lies in its ability to connect people to one another and something bigger. When individuals identify with a group's mission, their motivation and concern for collective outcomes are enhanced, increasing the likelihood of meaningful collaboration.

The ability of collective purpose to transform a group of individuals into a unified, creative force is the motivation behind Simon Sinek's call to "start with why". His Golden Circle model (Sinek, 2009) reveals that truly inspiring leaders and organisations communicate from the inside out, starting with purpose (why), then explaining their distinctive approach (how), and finally describing their offerings (what). This sequence matters because decisions driven by purpose tap into our emotions, fostering trust and loyalty and prompting us to take action—while the "what" of our work appeals only to the rational mind and holds very little inherent inspiration.

Figure 18- The Golden Circle – Simon Sinek

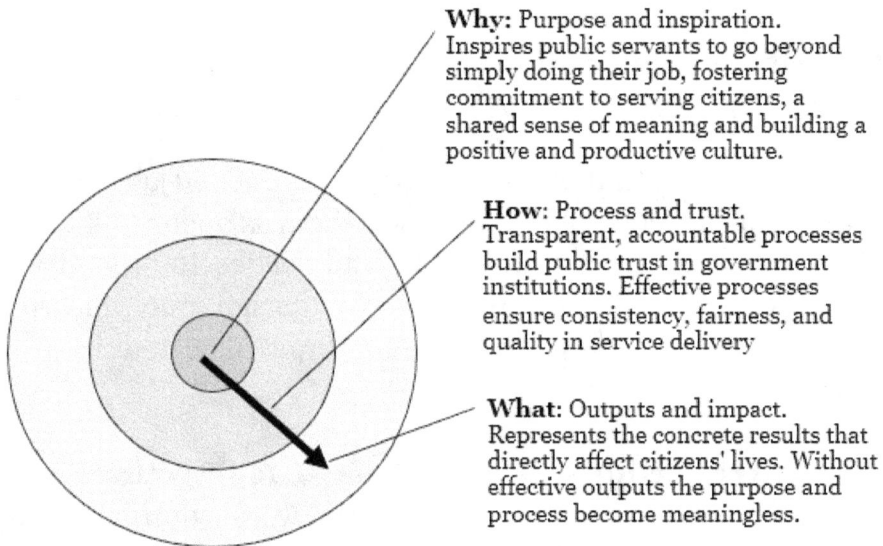

Why: Purpose and inspiration. Inspires public servants to go beyond simply doing their job, fostering commitment to serving citizens, a shared sense of meaning and building a positive and productive culture.

How: Process and trust. Transparent, accountable processes build public trust in government institutions. Effective processes ensure consistency, fairness, and quality in service delivery

What: Outputs and impact. Represents the concrete results that directly affect citizens' lives. Without effective outputs the purpose and process become meaningless.

By starting with why, organisations create emotional resonance and coherence that compel commitment, attract aligned customers and employees, and differentiate themselves in ways others cannot easily replicate. It sets the organising principle by which all policies, processes, services and products are assessed and choreographs all future actions to ensure coherence.

Designing for Meaning

Personal and collective meaning are most powerful when they align and reinforce each other. Individuals who see how their unique strengths and values contribute to a shared mission experience the deepest sense of purpose. Organisations that successfully bridge personal and collective meaning create environments where creativity thrives—where people invest their full energy because their work matters to them *and* serves something greater.

Some of the most effective practices that bring together both personal purpose and collective mission include:

Role design: Rather than treating roles as fixed job descriptions or just a collection of outputs, view them as opportunities to link individual strengths, interests, and values to organisational mission goals. This tailored role design may incorporate strengths-based assignments and time allocated to passion projects.

Team reflections: Dedicate time in retrospectives or team meetings to discuss how the team's work contributes to the organisational mission, and reflect on the purposefulness of recent and future projects.

Meaningful metrics: Alongside traditional engagement metrics, assess perceived meaningfulness of work and personal alignment with organisational values. Tools like the Work and Meaning Inventory (WAMI) or custom pulse surveys can track both personal and collective meaning over time.

Constant and purposeful communication: Leaders must consistently and continually tell the story of the organisational mission and why the agency matters. They must recognise their role to "rally the troops" around meaningful goals and share this compelling vision with stakeholders.

When personal and collective meaning align, when systems embed purpose, and when emotional foundations support both confidence and courage, organisations unlock the sustained creative energy needed to navigate uncertainty, overcome obstacles, and achieve extraordinary outcomes.

From Direction to Multiplication: The Power of Connection

We have now explored two foundational elements of the Creative Energy Equation. Emotion provides the spark—the energising force that compels us to move, to imagine, and to act. Without emotional energy, creativity remains dormant. Meaning provides the compass—the sense of purpose and significance that organises scattered enthusiasm into focused, sustained effort. Without meaning, even the most energised individuals drift aimlessly or burn out when challenges mount.

However, there is one more element that amplifies creative potential: Connection. Like the speed of light squared (c^2) in Einstein's equation, Connection is creativity's exponential force. It operates on two dimensions: consciousness (deep awareness of your own strengths, interests, and emotional states) and collaboration (multiplying creative potential through genuine partnership with others).

In the following chapters, we will explore how to cultivate both dimensions of Connection—the consciousness that brings your authentic self forward and the collaboration that turns diverse perspectives into creative breakthroughs.

29 Connection With Self: Authenticity As A Creative Asset

Every person is already unique and valuable just as they are. By fostering a strong self-connection, we support our authenticity and achieve sustainable creativity.

In earlier chapters, we confirmed that creativity is not the privilege of a few but a universal capacity that resides in every person. You are, simply by being yourself, both unique and valuable, and so are already creative. You have an original combination of experiences, perspectives, expressions and passions that no one else on Earth can replicate. Your individuality is your greatest creative asset.

However, in a world that prizes productivity and performance, it is easy to lose touch with our authenticity. We have heard that there are harmful stereotypes and biases around creative leaders, so it is no wonder we hide our true selves behind masks of rationality and logic. Sacrifices of the self are made for the benefit of success. However, the constant push to achieve can lead us into conformity, which is the mortal enemy of creativity and a real danger to our wellbeing.

As Dr Gabor Maté argues, the cost of disconnecting from our authentic selves extends far beyond creative stagnation. It causes an inner conflict that manifests as illness, both physical and mental.

Maté identifies a fundamental tension between attachment and authenticity. In professional contexts, this tension manifests daily: when we suppress genuine concerns to maintain relationships with peers, conform to team norms that conflict with our values, or silence creative ideas to avoid standing out, we sacrifice authenticity for comfort.

We develop patterns—people-pleasing, hyper-responsibility, perfectionism, emotional stoicism—that workplaces often reward, never recognising them as signs of disconnection from our true selves or considering the harm that lies beneath.

The consequences of internal conflict or suppression extend beyond frustration or burnout. In his research, Maté observed that people with chronic illnesses shared a common pattern: they had learned to censor the authentic self to meet others' expectations.

When we repeatedly betray ourselves, the conflict creates a toxicity that, sooner or later, manifests as physiological disease. In pursuit of being "normal", we create an internal war that undermines both creativity and vitality. True wellbeing depends on connecting with our authentic selves.

Each person is inherently unique and valuable, but understanding and honouring that truth requires deliberate effort.

"To be yourself in a world that is constantly trying to make you something else is the greatest accomplishment." ~ Ralph Waldo Emerson

The creative potential that arises when we tap into our authenticity is why, in the Creative Energy Equation, there is a whole element dedicated to this endeavour. It is the foundation of sustainable creativity, enabling us to transform force emotions, understand our personal motivations, and achieve coherence between our inner and outer worlds.

When we reconnect with ourselves—our values, emotions, and aspirations—we activate our greatest creative power: authenticity. We are also creating internal coherence between who we are and what we do, reducing conflict and facilitating the flow of our inherent creative energy.

Authenticity: What It Really Means

The Cambridge Dictionary defines authenticity as

> *"The quality of being real or true."*

The Oxford Review describes it as

> *"The genuine expression of one's identity, beliefs, and values without fear of judgment or discrimination."*

From my experience, I would amend this latter definition slightly. I would say it is:

> *"The genuine expression of one's identity, beliefs, and values <u>despite</u> the fear of judgment or discrimination."*

Because let's be honest—when you speak up in a meeting with an idea that challenges the status quo, when you advocate for a value that others overlook, or when you lead in a way that reflects your personal principles rather than corporate convention, there will always be at least a little trepidation.

As tribal creatures, we are wired to fear standing out. However, authenticity is feeling the fear and doing it anyway. It is being true to your personality, spirit, and character—living in alignment with your values and beliefs, regardless of whatever external or internal pressures try to interrupt. It is taking "beautiful risks", focusing on the rewards, and not allowing oneself to become consumed by the negative consequences that may arise.

In professional life, the pressures to conform are relentless. There are implicit rules about how leaders should behave, what ideas are safe to propose, how much emotion is acceptable to show, and what risks are worth taking.

Organisations often reward those who fit established moulds—reliable, agreeable, predictable—while creative disruptors, questioners, and authentic voices may face resistance, even when their contributions ultimately drive innovation.

Because there is so much overt pressure to suppress our authenticity, achieving it rests on dedicated, disciplined practices of self-awareness and congruence. What this means is that to be authentic, a person has to:

- Understand what is important to them personally—their core values, strengths, passions, and aspirations.
- Be aware of how they respond to others and to any pressure to conform—recognising when they compromise authenticity for acceptance.
- Choose the words and actions that genuinely reflect their inner values and motivations—even when those choices carry risk.

Acting on one's authenticity is not an ad-lib process but a careful authoring of one's behaviours to ensure continued alignment with personal purpose and values. Bearing this in mind, then, true creative expression—whether in how you lead a team, design a product, solve a problem, or challenge a process—is a dynamic process that requires ongoing self-reflection and adjustment as one grows and evolves.

The ability to recognise misalignment and recalibrate to reconnect with one's authenticity is built upon two foundations:

1. Self-Awareness
2. Insight.

Self-Awareness: Knowing What You Do

Self-awareness is the essential first step on the path to authenticity. Defined as a flexible attentiveness to our environments and internal cues (Dahl et al., 2020), self-awareness allows us to tune into what feels right within us and to notice how we respond when faced with pressures to conform or suppress our ideas.

Knowing our emotions, values, and motivations, we can better discern which actions align with our true selves and which are driven by external expectations. It allows us to recognise when a project energises you versus when it drains you, notice patterns in how you react to feedback or conflict, or understanding which aspects of your role feel meaningful versus merely obligatory. This clarity is vital for creativity, enabling us to act intentionally, draw inspiration from our inner world, and courageously challenge ourselves to grow.

When we see ourselves clearly, we are more confident and more creative. We make sounder decisions, build stronger relationships, and communicate more effectively. Self-aware leaders foster more satisfied and successful teams. At the same time, individuals who cultivate self-awareness experience greater job satisfaction, better emotional regulation, and enhanced resilience.

Despite its importance, self-awareness is rarer than most people realise. Research by organisational psychologist Dr Tasha Eurich found that while 95% of people believe they are self-aware, only 10-15% truly are (Eurich, 2018). This gap is particularly pronounced among senior leaders and executives—ironically, those whose decisions have the greatest impact. The more power someone obtains, the less honest feedback they tend to receive, creating an insulation from reality that erodes self-awareness over time.

Without self-awareness, we risk drifting into patterns that stifle originality or lead us to betray what is meaningful to us. We might pursue career paths that look impressive externally but drain us internally. We might adopt leadership styles that feel safe but do not reflect our authentic values or allow others to express their authentic, creative selves. We might suppress ideas, concerns, or feedback that could drive innovation, simply because we have not developed the self-knowledge to recognise their importance.

Insight: Understanding Why You Do It

While self-awareness helps us recognise what we do and how we feel, insight takes us deeper—it is the understanding of how emotions, thoughts and beliefs shape our subjective experience, and especially our sense of self (Dahl et al., 2020).

Insight is the intelligence that connects the dots between our motivations, beliefs, and behaviours, revealing the underlying patterns that shape our professional and personal lives. This deeper understanding is essential for authenticity because when we know *why* certain habits or reactions arise, we can change those that no longer serve us and reinforce those that align with our true values and aspirations.

Insight is not limited to self-reflection but extends outward, enabling us to perceive what drives others. Both are crucial for creative work and for implementing meaningful change.

When we develop insight into others—their motivations, fears, and hopes—we become more effective collaborators, leaders, and innovators. This social insight enables us to anticipate reactions, tailor our communication, and build stronger, more empathetic relationships—all essential for successful creative endeavours.

Equally important is cultivating insight into how others perceive us. Understanding the gap between our intentions and the impact we have can be transformative, providing valuable feedback for personal and professional growth (Eurich, 2018).

A manager might believe they are being direct and efficient when colleagues experience them as dismissive and rushed. An innovator might think their passion comes across as inspiring, but team members actually find it overwhelming. When we are open to this perspective, we become more adaptable, receptive to change, and better able to build trust with those around us.

Why Does This Matter For Leadership?

The link between authentic, self-aware leadership and individual performance, team productivity, and innovation is now well-established. In fact, research by Cornell University found that self-awareness was the strongest predictor of overall executive success, with self-aware leaders building more engaged, satisfied and successful teams (Butler et al., 2014).

> Teams led by self-aware leaders are more collaborative, handle conflict more effectively, and demonstrate greater agility, continually examining objectives, strategies, and processes to ensure alignment with their goals (Lyubovnikova et al., 2017).

These results are possible through the psychological safety and trust that authentic leaders create. When leaders are secure in themselves, they provide the permission for other employees to feel safe, take interpersonal risks, express unconventional ideas, and engage in innovative work behaviours (Schuckert et al., 2018).

Conversely, leaders lacking self-awareness create teams characterised by negative energy, less harmony, reduced camaraderie, and destructive behaviours that require costly organisational interventions.

For organisations navigating complexity, uncertainty, and rapid change, for those who seek to increase creative confidence and innovation, fostering authentic, self-aware leadership is not a soft skill luxury—it is a strategic imperative.

Authenticity at Scale

Just as authenticity is essential for leaders, organisations must also cultivate this capacity to build creativity and collaboration. Organisational authenticity—the coherence between an organisation's stated mission, values, and its actual practices—builds trust, drives performance, and attracts aligned stakeholders (Eldor, 2025).

Employees who perceive their organisation as authentic show significantly higher work performance, as they trust the organisation enough to put in their full effort (Eldor, 2025). The result of consistently aligned purpose, strategy, and culture is impressive, with sustained performance improvement recorded 96% of the time (Boston Consulting Group, 2024).

Yet authenticity cannot be faked or simply declared—it requires the organisational equivalent of:

- Self-awareness - regularly auditing whether actions align with stated values.

- Insight - understanding stakeholder perceptions through surveys, transparency reports, and third-party audits.

When organisations are clear about their values, enact them transparently and consistently, they build trust and reputational capital that attracts and retains top talent, inspires motivation and creativity, and fosters resilient cultures capable of navigating complexity and change – all of which are needed in our modern-day public sector.

The Skills of Self-Connection

Self-awareness and authenticity do not emerge spontaneously but are cultivated through dedicated practice of four specific skills.

1. Introspection
2. Emotional intelligence
3. Courage
4. Self-compassion.

Introspection: Tapping the Inner Landscape

Introspection is the process of accessing our rich internal mental landscape, including idle thoughts, fleeting impressions, and emergent feelings. Rather than dismissing internal dialogue as a distraction, skilled introspection employs it to understand experiences and develop diverse perspectives—all without requiring input from others. This internal resource unlocks endless original combinations of thoughts, feelings, desires, and dreams. Introspection transforms self-reflection into a vast reservoir of creative material grounded in genuine experience.

Emotional Intelligence: Understanding the Why Behind Feelings

While introspection provides awareness of *what* we think and feel, emotional intelligence illuminates *why* we respond as we do, the meaning behind emotions, and the implications of our behaviours. We have seen how creativity is inherently an emotional exercise: it demands we recognise fear, understand what fuels it, and choose behaviours that move us beyond it rather than retreat into safety.

This intricate internal process—identifying an emotion, tracing its source, and consciously selecting a response—is the extensive emotional intelligence that creative work calls us to enact daily. Self-awareness enables us to act intentionally and create the psychological safety for ourselves and others that fuels creative confidence.

Overriding Vulnerability: The Courage to Share

Generating creative ideas is not merely an intellectual exercise— it is inherently self-revealing. Research by Goncalo and Katz (2020) demonstrates that sharing ideas is also an act of self-disclosure, because our ideas reveal much about ourselves, including personal preferences, experiences, and values. As they eloquently describe, *"your soul spills out"* when you share creative work, making the act feel vulnerable and exposing. This self-disclosing quality of creativity creates a temptation to perform for validation rather than express authentically. However, genuine creative contribution requires revealing something fundamental about oneself, demanding considerable courage. As Brené Brown asserts,

"You can choose courage or you can choose comfort, but you cannot have both".

Self-Compassion: The Foundation for Resilience

Creating something new inevitably comes with failure—not only in the final product but in our ability to act authentically. There will be times when we choose comfort over courage, cower into conformity, or fail to dare differently. For this reason, self-compassion—treating ourselves with kindness—becomes an essential skill.

It is also a skill that facilitates creative originality, particularly among individuals prone to self-judgment (Zabelina & Robinson, 2010). In their study, participants induced into a self-compassionate mindset produced significantly more original answers on the Torrance Test of Creative Thinking than those in control conditions, with the effect strongest for highly self-critical individuals.

> Self-compassion reduces self-censorship, transforms creativity from a pursuit of external validation to one of internal motivation and mastery, and provides a firm foundation supporting resilience through the creative journey's inevitable ups and downs.

Honouring the Self-Connection Behind Creativity

Beneath every creative act, whether it be a strategic plan, a bold new policy proposal, or an unconventional service solution, lies an immense amount of self-connection. To move through the uncomfortable unknowns and the vulnerability inherent in sharing ideas, there is required to be an immense amount of introspection, emotional intelligence, courage, and self-compassion. What peers and stakeholders see when they view the new product, process, or policy is merely the tip of the iceberg; beneath the surface is the extensive work of self-connection that made authentic expression possible.

Therefore, when someone speaks up about an issue they care deeply about, challenges the status quo, or puts forward an idea that reflects their unique perspective, they have bravely faced themselves, worked through their fear, and given themselves permission to stand out. In a world where conformity is all too common, this needs to be celebrated.

So, the next time a colleague takes a creative risk or offers an authentic perspective, recognise not only the contribution itself but the profound internal journey that brought it forward. Behind every act of creative courage is someone who chose authenticity over comfort—and that deserves genuine acknowledgement.

From Self to Others

The journey of self-connection is not merely an inward or stand-alone pursuit; it is the essential foundation for building another foundational element of creativity—strong, meaningful connections with others. When we understand who we are, what drives us, and how we show up in the world, we become more open, empathetic, and authentic in our relationships. This inner clarity allows us to engage with others from a place of confidence and genuine curiosity, setting the stage for trust and exciting collaboration.

In the next chapter, we explore how the work of connecting with ourselves contributes to connecting with others, and where individual creative potential can be multiplied exponentially. When authentic selves come together in genuine collaboration, the creative energy generated far exceeds what any person could achieve alone.

30 Connection With Others: Collaboration As Amplification

"A bureaucracy that engages with people, within an organisation and outwardly across a system, with stakeholders in the community, and citizens is creating the dynamic it needs to face the future." **(Landry & Caust, 2017, p. 72)**

In his groundbreaking work at the University of Wisconsin-Madison's Centre for Healthy Minds, Dr Richard Davidson identifies Connection as one of the four fundamental pillars of wellbeing (Dahl et al., 2020). The other three pillars — Awareness, Insight, and Purpose — have been covered in the earlier Self-Connection and Meaning chapters.

Connection is defined as the qualities and skills that support healthy relationships and a prosocial orientation toward others—including kindness, compassion, empathy, and appreciation. As confirmed by Dr Davidson and his team, connection is not merely an optional soft skill; due to its measurable effects on brain function and behaviour, it is also a skill we consciously need to invest time and effort in.

Connection is imperative for creativity because our brains are fundamentally wired for social engagement. As identified by Abraham Maslow in his motivational hierarchy, belonging and the emotional support it encompasses are a core need, second only to physical and psychological safety. Therefore, when we practise empathy, gratitude, and compassion, and establish positive affiliations with others, we gain a feeling of achievement and reward from fulfilling this foundational requirement.

Connection with others also has positive effects on every other element of the Creative Energy Equation. Engaging with others in productive ways fosters uplifting feelings that can act as a creative spark. Connection with others also enables the development of shared meaning, which can focus and sustain innovation through the most challenging times. Additionally, when we engage empathetically with others, we learn more about ourselves, deepening the self-awareness and insight necessary to nurture our own creative potential.

Through these mechanisms, connection has direct effects on a leader's own wellbeing and creative capacity, and, crucially, by focusing on this element, leaders can also influence the conditions for the development and expression of others' creative potential.

Connection: Crucial For Leadership Development

For leaders in public service, Connection serves as the catalyst for their own creative development. An authentic connection with others acts as a mirror, deepening leaders' self-awareness of their own values, assumptions, strengths, and blind spots. When colleagues ask clarifying questions, challenge thinking, or offer different perspectives, leaders investigate and articulate beliefs they had not fully examined and discover insights they could not access on their own. Through others, they come to know themselves more fully, strengthening the self-connection element and thus, creative potential.

In exciting neurological research, it has also been shown that empathetic leadership activates brain regions associated with cognitive flexibility and creative thinking (Boyatzis et al., 2012).

Leaders who cultivate compassion experience greater psychological safety, which reduces fear of judgment and increases the willingness to take creative risks (Han et al., 2019). Moreover, the positive emotions generated through authentic connection — such as trust, curiosity, and joy — broaden perspectives and enable divergent thinking, which is essential to innovation (Fredrickson, 2001).

Connection also provides the emotional regulation necessary for sustained creative effort. When leaders feel genuinely supported and understood by others, their stress responses are moderated, allowing access to the executive brain functions—strategic thinking, reflection, and creativity—that are suppressed under chronic stress (Boyatzis & McKee, 2005; Rock, 2008). This neurobiological reality explains why isolated leaders often experience creative stagnation. At the same time, those embedded in meaningful and supportive relationships maintain innovative capacity even under pressure.

Connection: Leaders Enable Creative Expression in Others

Beyond personal benefits, Connection enables leaders to fulfil their role as creators of the conditions that foster others' creativity. Employees with highly empathic leaders report markedly higher levels of creativity and engagement and are more likely to display innovative behaviours (Van Bommel, 2025; Ma et al., 2024). These results are due to the positive connection behaviours of leaders influencing many other mediating factors, including:

Creation of psychological safety: Leaders who demonstrate genuine empathy and compassion create psychological safety— the foundational condition for creative expression (Edmondson, 1999). When team members experience leaders as emotionally attuned and supportive, they feel safe to voice unconventional ideas, admit mistakes, and take interpersonal risks essential for innovation (Han et al., 2019). Studies show that psychological safety accounts for nearly half the variance in team creativity outcomes, making it perhaps the single most critical leadership intervention for innovation (Sharma & Mehta, 2023).

Transference and amplification of positive emotional states: Neuroscience research reveals that positive emotions are contagious through neuronal mirroring systems (Hatfield et al., 1994).

Leaders who embody Connection—expressing genuine curiosity, appreciation, and care—activate similar emotional states in their teams. This emotional contagion creates upward spirals of positive affect that broaden thinking, increase openness to experience, and enable the cognitive flexibility necessary for creative problem-solving (Fredrickson, 2001).

Recognition and activation of individual strengths: Connected leaders develop a deep understanding of each team member's unique capabilities, motivations, and creative potential (Buckingham & Clifton, 2001). By recognising and affirming individual strengths while providing personalised support for growth, they enable people to contribute in ways that align with their passions and talents—a critical condition for intrinsic motivation and creative expression.

Fostering inclusive collaboration: Leaders grounded in Connection create inclusive environments where diverse perspectives are not merely tolerated but actively integrated. Their capacity for empathy enables them to navigate differences with curiosity rather than defensiveness, fostering the cognitive diversity essential for breakthrough innovation while maintaining the relational cohesion necessary for implementation.

The Imperative for Public Service Leadership

Public service leadership is fundamentally relational, with influence occurring through trust, authenticity, and shared purpose rather than hierarchical authority alone. In government contexts, therefore, where leaders must address complex, multi-stakeholder challenges while maintaining public trust, Connection becomes both a leadership competency and a democratic imperative.

However, the demands of public service—political pressure, resource constraints, public scrutiny—can easily erode the very connections that fuel creativity and effectiveness. Leaders who prioritise Connection develop protective factors against burnout while building the relational infrastructure necessary for innovation (Boyatzis & McKee, 2005). They model the empathy and collaboration they seek to foster across sectors, creating coherent cultures of safety and support that enable the creative problem-solving essential for addressing wicked policy challenges.

Additionally, by cultivating connection capability, leaders establish the crucial foundation for collaboration, which is necessary to co-create community solutions and implement them effectively and sustainably.

Building On Connections: Collaborative Governance

The delivery of public value is no longer the exclusive domain of government but is increasingly becoming a shared responsibility across all societal sectors. Citizens, businesses, non-profits, and public agencies are now working in concert to address complex challenges (Thabit et al., 2025).

> More public service initiatives are now implemented through multi-actor channels rather than traditional hierarchical structures. This expansive nature of modern-day service delivery means that governments must get great at collaborative value creation.

Collaboration, however, rests on a foundation that many public sector agencies have historically undervalued: authentic connection—both with self and with others. When diverse participants bring their unique perspectives, expertise, experience, and authentic selves to shared projects, there is potential for exponential, very exciting outcomes.

As author Maria Popova eloquently expresses,

"Creativity, after all, is a combinatorial force... To truly create and contribute to the world, we have to be able to connect countless dots, to cross-pollinate ideas from a wealth of disciplines."

In an era where artificial intelligence threatens to homogenise approaches and standardise solutions, it is our connections with others—enacted through collaboration and co-creation that keep creativity alive, public services responsive, and governments relevant.

Collaboration Is Now How Value Is Created

This shift towards multi-actor value creation has given rise to the term "collaborative governance" becoming part of mainstream public sector administration. Collaborative governance is about bringing public and private stakeholders together in consensus-oriented decision-making to develop or implement public policy (Ansell & Gash, 2008).

It represents a fundamental departure from centralised and hierarchical modes of policy-making, replacing them with processes in which government, community, and the private sector communicate and work together to achieve outcomes that no single sector could deliver on its own.

Another term commonly used is one coined by the Blair government in the 1990s, being "joined-up government", which describes the same concept, being the coordination and collaboration of public, private, and voluntary sector bodies across organisational boundaries towards common goals.

The popularity of these terms reflects recognition that complex, contemporary challenges facing governments (such as climate adaptation, health equity, economic resilience, and social cohesion) cannot be addressed through control and command by centralised government agencies. The wicked problems of our day demand open, collaborative approaches that cross organisational boundaries and meaningfully engage external stakeholders.

Collaborative governance is no longer an option, but an essential mechanism to achieve:

- enhanced policy coherence
- improved efficiency in service delivery
- better utilisation of expertise across sectors
- more effective resource allocation
- increased public trust and legitimacy (United Nations Office for Sustainable Development, 2011).

Getting the Government's Backyard In Order

While collaboration with organisations outside government is imperative, it must not overshadow the work needed to improve collaboration within the sector and across agencies. The term "whole-of-government" is commonly used to denote coherence across public-sector agencies and serves as a foundation for constructive, productive collaborations with other entities. Because if we cannot overcome departmentalism and siloed thinking within stagnant public sector structures, how are we to capitalise on the opportunities that collaboration with other entities presents?

The need for the government to get its own backyard in order and become "whole" is well documented. A report published by the Australian Public Service Commission (APSC) found that the public service typically operates in silos and rigid hierarchies and traditional ways of working present barriers to effective service delivery (APSC, 2024). The consequences are significant: only 11% of Australian public sector employees report being able to access the data they need for their roles, and one-third regularly undertake tasks without complete information due to departmental fragmentation (IDM, 2023).

Structural reorganisations offer no panacea. UNSW researchers studying machinery-of-government changes concluded: *"silos exist just as much within MOG'd departments as between departments"* (Carey & Buick, 2019). The Victorian Public Sector Commission describes the underlying mentality that prevents them from being able to harness the power of internal collaboration:

"People working within the silo typically see no need to share knowledge and resources with people from outside the silo and refuse to do so" (VPSC, 2015).

Perhaps most damning, the Robodebt Royal Commission revealed how information silos enabled catastrophic policy failure, concluding that *"the Scheme was permitted to commence and expand, in large part, due to relevant information being unduly compartmentalised"* (APSC, 2024). The solution, the Commission found, lies not in further restructuring but in *"genuinely collaborative real world and digital workspaces"* that assemble relevant information through parallel rather than sequential processes.

These findings point to a fundamental truth: the collaborative capabilities required for distributed value creation must be deliberately built, not assumed.

> However, if public sector leaders cannot foster collaboration within their own agencies—breaking through hierarchies, tapping into the incredible expertise available in other teams, enabling information flow, and coordinating across divisions—they will struggle to orchestrate the far more complex task of multi-actor governance.

The trust governments and their agencies seek to foster with outside parties will be hampered by the view that they are hypocrites—espousing the need for collaborative governance without doing their own inner work.

When Collaboration Enhances Creativity

For public sector organisations, the question is not whether collaboration is valuable—it is often essential. Addressing wicked policy problems, delivering services across fragmented systems, and achieving outcomes that transcend organisational boundaries all require coordinated action that no individual or single agency can accomplish alone. The creative ideas generated by brilliant individuals, no matter how insightful, fragment and fail without collaborative mechanisms to translate them into coherent implementation.

> Nevertheless, unlike the myth that two heads are always better than one, the advantages of collaboration are neither automatic nor guaranteed. Collaboration does enhance creativity, but only when specific conditions are deliberately cultivated.

Without intentional design and skilled facilitation, groups often underperform individuals working separately due to issues around coordination, blocking and interference. So, under what conditions does collaboration unlock creative potential rather than suppress it?

The following conditions must be present in order for collaborative work to match or enhance individual creative performance:

Psychological safety: Team members need to feel genuinely safe expressing unconventional ideas without fear of criticism, judgment, or negative consequences. This is why studies show psychological safety has a direct and positive influence on creative outcomes, making it a critical condition for effective collaborations (Sharma & Mehta, 2023).

Shared purpose with autonomy: Teams need alignment around common goals and success measures while preserving space for individual creative exploration and diverse approaches. This balance—coherence without conformity—enables creative energy to flow productively rather than being lost to conflict or fragmentation.

Deep information elaboration: Teams must actively exchange, discuss, integrate, and build upon task-relevant information and diverse perspectives. Simply having diverse people in the room is insufficient—the real value emerges through the quality of interaction and information synthesis (Kerrissey et al., 2020).

Cognitive diversity with integration: Beyond demographic diversity, cognitively diverse groups—those with varied intelligence strengths, expertise, thinking styles, and problem-solving frameworks—can outperform homogeneous teams, but only when differences are actively integrated through dialogue rather than allowed to fragment into silos. This diversity of information enables teams to access different knowledge networks, apply distinct frameworks, and identify blind spots that similar thinkers miss (Rock & Grant, 2016).

Structured processes and facilitation: Effective collaborative creativity benefits from deliberate practices such as alternating between individual and group ideation (hybrid approaches), using techniques that minimise production blocking, establishing clear protocols for building on ideas, and providing skilled facilitation to manage group dynamics (Paulus & Yang, 2000).

How Well-Designed Collaboration Enhances Creativity

When these conditions are met, collaboration activates several mechanisms that can enhance creative outcomes:

Cross-pollination of ideas: Diverse collaborators bring different perspectives, experiences, knowledge, and working styles. This diversity provides raw material for novel combinations—the essence of creative thought. One person's partial insight sparks another's breakthrough; a different perspective fills the missing piece of the puzzle.

Communicative spark and reformulation: Interaction itself stimulates thinking. When others ask questions, offer alternative viewpoints, or request clarification, we reformulate our ideas, often discovering insights we had not fully articulated even to ourselves. This dialogic process makes implicit knowledge explicit and surfaces hidden assumptions.

Co-construction of knowledge: Collaborative creativity thrives on dialogue—whether verbal, visual, or digital. Through shared language and iterative exchange, participants collectively build understanding and generate solutions that transcend what any individual brought to the conversation.

Amplified motivation and persistence: Being part of a collaborative effort can motivate people to develop and refine ideas more thoroughly. Team members create both accountability (responsibility to contribute meaningfully) and support (encouragement when facing difficulties), enabling persistence in the face of creative challenges that might cause individuals to give up.

Distributed cognitive load: Complex problems often exceed the cognitive capacity of any single person. Well-designed collaboration distributes different aspects of creative work— information gathering, analysis, synthesis, evaluation, refinement—across team members with complementary strengths.

However, these mechanisms only function when teams actively work to overcome natural process losses: production blocking (cognitive interference from waiting to speak), evaluation apprehension (fear of judgment), social loafing (reduced individual effort in group settings), and coordination costs (mental resources diverted to managing group dynamics rather than creative thinking). Effective collaborative creativity requires deliberate practices to unlock potential benefits while minimising these inherent challenges.

The critical realisation here is that collaboration is both essential to government effectiveness and must be deliberately built. Government leaders cannot simply mandate teamwork or cross-agency collaboration and expect enhanced creativity.

Instead, they must invest in creating the conditions that enable the partnership to fulfil its potential and recognise that these conditions come from their own level of connection capability. The challenge for government is to be intentional, disciplined, and evidence-informed in building collaborative capabilities that unlock rather than suppress the creativity essential for delivering excellent community outcomes.

Collaboration Creates Coherence

In public sector contexts, collaboration serves an additional critical function: it creates the coherence necessary for creativity to translate into coordinated action. When diverse actors work in isolation, even excellent creative ideas fragment, duplicate, and fail to meet community needs cohesively.

However, effective collaboration builds coherence, balancing central strategic priorities with local operational autonomy. Through alignment around shared purpose, resources, and data, and robust governance principles, creative energy can flow across distributed actors, enabling them to function as a coherent creative system rather than competing silos.

Importantly, coherence does not mean uniformity or suppression of creative differences. Effective collaborations value diverse perspectives and specialised approaches while creating shared language, aligned success measures, and coordinated activities. This balance—honouring creative difference while building unity of purpose—transforms isolated creative initiatives into coherent movements capable of addressing challenges and of transcending any single organisation's boundaries.

The Unacknowledged Collaborations

Even when public sector leaders believe they work independently, they never truly create in isolation. Every decision you make, every framework you employ, every approach you adopt represents a collaboration with colleagues, theorists, predecessors, and even critics whose ideas have shaped your thinking. As Isaac Newton acknowledged in 1676,

"If I have seen further, it is by standing on the shoulders of giants."

His revolutionary insights emerged not from solitary brilliance but from building upon Galileo's, Kepler's, and Descartes' prior discoveries.

Your leadership operates the same way.

When you implement place-based approaches, you collaborate with decades of community development theorists.

When you adopt co-design processes, you build on participatory action research traditions.

When you apply evidence-based policy frameworks, you leverage statistical methods developed over centuries.

> The governance principles guiding your decisions, the change management models informing your reforms, the stakeholder engagement techniques structuring your consultations—all represent inherited wisdom from others' experiences, research, and creative labour.

These examples illustrate the reality of what is termed "distributed creativity": the understanding that creative work is a product of dispersed actions, spanning across people, objects, and time (Glăveanu, 2014). People create based on others' ideas, using tools others made, addressing problems others identified, within cultural contexts collectively shaped.

Therefore, creativity is a much larger concept than the individual who appears to make it happen. It is born from an accumulation of knowledge and communities that have already implemented new ideas. While you may consider yourself the inventor of an idea, in truth, you are merely a collaborator with all the creators that have come before.

This reality is revolutionary. It means you are never alone in developing new approaches; thousands have already walked the same road. It also means that fostering creativity in your organisation does not require finding rare geniuses but creating conditions where people can access diverse knowledge networks, engage across differences, and build openly on others' contributions.

When leaders acknowledge they always stand on the shoulders of giants—and create space for others to stand on theirs—they unlock the cumulative, exponential power of collaboration across time and space.

From Self-Connection to Collaborative Synergy

Throughout this exploration of the Creative Energy Equation $(C=EMC^2)$, we have seen how each element builds upon and amplifies the others. Emotions provide the spark for creative work. Meaning channels that energy toward purposeful goals. Connection with self establishes the authenticity and self-awareness necessary for genuine contribution. And finally, connection with others multiplies creative capacity exponentially, transforming individual insights into collective breakthroughs capable of addressing the wicked problems facing contemporary governance.

Nevertheless, understanding these principles is insufficient. Transformation requires honest assessment of where you and your organisation currently stand, not only to identify challenges but to celebrate and amplify the creativity that already exists.

The questions in the following section provide a framework for reflection across all elements of the Creative Energy Equation and offer important insights into the current flow of creative energy in your agency or organisation. Take time to engage with them thoughtfully and to identify opportunities for growth. For the challenges ahead will require every ounce of creativity we can muster, across all dimensions of society. We will not be able to address the pressing problems of our time without it.

31   The Whole Is Greater: Synergy Across The Equation

As systems thinker Russell Ackoff wisely observed,

"A system is never the sum of its parts; it's the product of their interaction." (Ackoff, 1971)

This fundamental truth lies at the heart of the Creative Energy Equation.

While we have explored emotion, meaning, and connection as distinct elements throughout this section, their real power emerges only when they interact—when each element amplifies and shapes the others in dynamic, ever-evolving ways. The synergy gained across elements is shown in the table on the following page.

As is clear from the analysis, together, the elements of the Creative Energy Equation form a self-reinforcing cycle: positive emotions inspire meaningful work; meaningful work deepens connection; and connection, in turn, generates new emotional and creative momentum.

However, this cycle thrives not in isolation but within cultures and systems deliberately designed to support it. In public sector contexts where we have seen how creativity is critical for meaningful change, the challenge becomes translating understanding into action.

The next phase of this journey, then, requires honest assessment: Where do you and your organisation currently stand across these elements? Where is creative energy flowing freely, and where is it being constrained? What conditions already exist that are empowering creative potential? And importantly, what must change so that this potential may be realised for the benefit for the communities you serve?

To assist with this review and reflection, the following chapter provides a set of questions which will enable you to identify not only the obstacles to creative energy but also to celebrate and build upon the creative capabilities that already exist within your agency.

Table 13– The synergy between creative energy elements

	EMOTION (The Spark)	MEANING (The Compass)	CONNECTION (The Multiplier)
EMOTION (The Spark)	Positive emotions spark and sustain creativity. In turn, creativity benefits emotions resulting in an upward and self-reinforcing cycle.	Heightened emotions signal areas of passion and fuel curiosity, motivating us to explore and act on what we care about.	Positive emotional states create the sense of safety, optimism and openness necessary to build constructive and authentic connections.
MEANING (The Compass)	Purpose directs emotional energy and provides emotional endurance and resilience by anchoring effort in significance.	When personal purpose aligns with collective mission there is internal coherence, commitment and increased creative potential.	Shared meaning creates a sense of belonging, trust and responsibility that enables psychological safety and authentic connection.
CONNECTION (The Multiplier)	When individuals feel genuinely seen and valued, positive emotions intensify. Emotions are contagious; quality connection with leaders shapes the team's shared emotional state.	Through supportive connections, a deeper understanding is gained of what individuals and teams deem meaningful. Collaboration enables collective action towards common goals.	Connections provide mirrors for us, allowing for greater self-awareness and authenticity. In turn, greater self-knowledge makes more positive and productive collaborations possible.

32 Reflection Questions For The Creative Energy Equation

The following reflection questions are designed to help you explore how creative energy flows—or is constrained—within yourself, your work, and your organisation. These prompts are not a survey or assessment tool to be completed, but rather a resource for ongoing self-discovery and professional development.

You might want to skim through all questions at once, focus on one element that feels most relevant to your current situation, or return to different questions as your context evolves. Use these prompts in the way that works best for you to foster honest reflection and meaningful insight.

Consider journaling your responses, discussing them with colleagues, or using them as thought-starters for team conversations about creativity.

1. Creativity: General Creative Capacity

This element explores your overall relationship with creativity—how you understand it, experience it, and make space for it in your life and work.

1. How do you personally define creativity in the context of public sector work? Has this definition changed over your career?
2. What beliefs do you hold about who gets to be creative in your organisation? Are these beliefs serving or constraining creative potential?
3. When was the last time you felt genuinely creative at work? What conditions made that moment possible?
4. When you encounter a complex problem, do you instinctively reach for established solutions or explore novel approaches? What drives this tendency?
5. How much time do you currently dedicate to creative thinking—both scheduled and spontaneous? Is this sufficient for the challenges you face?
6. What creative activities (if any) do you engage in regularly? How might you cultivate the time and space for more?
7. How does your team or organisation define and measure success? Do these definitions inspire or constrain innovation?
8. When you look at your agency's most pressing challenges, what would become possible if everyone accessed their full creative potential?
9. What organisational structures, systems, or cultural norms currently support creativity in your workplace? What conditions hinder it?
10. If you could redesign one aspect of your work environment to enhance creativity, what would you change and why?

2. Emotion: The Spark

This element examines the emotional climate that either ignites or extinguishes creative energy—both within yourself and across your teams.

1. What emotions do you most frequently experience at work? Where would these emotions sit on Dr Hawkins' Map of Consciousness (force vs. power emotions)?
2. When was the last time you felt psychologically safe enough to share an unconventional idea? What conditions created that safety?
3. How aware are you of your own emotional states throughout your workday? What practices help you develop this awareness?
4. Do you experience fear, anxiety, or doubt about sharing an idea? If so, do you lean into the discomfort or decide to play it safe?
5. How would you describe the emotional climate of your team or organisation? Is it characterised more by courage and joy, or by fear, anxiety or even apathy?
6. What specific practices does your organisation have in place to support emotional wellbeing? Do you believe they are sufficient?
7. How confidently do you believe in your own creative abilities (creative self-efficacy)? What evidence supports or undermines this confidence?
8. When someone on your team takes a creative risk that does not work out, how do leaders typically respond? What message does this send?
9. How comfortable are you expressing emotions at work? What implicit or explicit rules govern emotional expression in your workplace?
10. Suppose you could shift your team or organisation to enact more courage. What specific practices would you implement to make this possible?

3. Meaning: The Compass for Creative Focus

This element explores whether your creative energy is anchored in purpose and significance—personally and collectively.

1. Can you clearly articulate why your work matters—both to you personally and to the broader community you serve?
2. How aligned is your daily work with your personal values and aspirations? Where do you experience coherence or conflict?
3. How well do you know the mission of your organisation? Do you feel genuinely inspired and connected to it? Why or why not?
4. How well does your organisation communicate its purpose and why the work matters? Is this message consistent and compelling?
5. When was the last time you felt your work was truly meaningful? What made it feel significant in that moment?
6. How much autonomy do you have to shape your role around your strengths, interests, and sense of purpose?
7. Do you see a clear connection between your individual contributions and the broader mission of your agency? How is this connection reinforced (or not)?
8. Does your team collectively understand and articulate its purpose? Is there genuine shared meaning about why the work matters?
9. When recruiting or onboarding new team members, how much emphasis is placed on connecting them to the organisation's purpose versus teaching them processes?
10. If you could redesign your role to maximise personal meaning while serving organisational goals, what would you change?

4. Connection with Self: Authenticity

This element explores how well you know yourself—your values, strengths, emotions, and authentic identity—and whether you can bring your whole self to your work.

1. How well do you understand your core values? When was the last time you consciously examined whether your work aligns with them?
2. How often do you take time out for introspection or reflection? What barriers prevent more regular practice?
3. When do you feel most authentically yourself at work? When do you feel you must wear a mask or suppress aspects of your identity?
4. How aware are you of your emotional patterns and triggers? Can you recognise when you are operating from fear versus courage?
5. How well do you know your creative strengths—the unique perspectives, experiences, and capacities you bring that no one else can replicate?
6. How often do you compromise your authentic self to fit in, avoid conflict, or meet others' expectations? What is the cost of this compromise?
7. How do you typically respond to yourself when you make mistakes or fall short? With self-criticism or self-compassion?
8. Does your organisation create space for employees to explore and develop self-awareness? What resources or practices support this?
9. How congruent is your work with your inner values and beliefs? Where do you notice misalignment?
10. What do you think would happen if you brought your full, authentic self to work tomorrow?

5. Connection with Others: Collaboration

This element examines the quality of your relationships and collaborative practices—the multiplier that transforms individual potential into collective breakthrough.

1. How genuinely connected do you feel to your colleagues? Do relationships feel transactional or truly supportive?
2. When you interact with team members, how much curiosity do you bring to understanding their perspectives, motivations, and creative potential?
3. How skilled are you at empathy—genuinely understanding and sharing the feelings of others? How might developing this skill enhance your work?
4. How psychologically safe is your team environment? Can everyone voice unconventional ideas without fear of judgment?
5. How diverse is your team—in terms of thinking styles, backgrounds, experiences, and perspectives? Is this diversity actively leveraged for creativity?
6. When your team collaborates, do you experience genuine co-creation and synthesis, or do contributions remain separate and siloed?
7. How does your organisation recognise and celebrate collaboration versus individual achievement?
8. When conflicts or disagreements arise, how do you and your team navigate them? Are differences seen as creative opportunities or threats?
9. How well do you know the unique strengths and creative capacities of each person on your team? How do you actively support their development?
10. How well does your team discuss, integrate and build upon ideas, rather than simply sharing them?

Closing Reflection

As you reflect on these questions across all elements of the Creative Energy Equation, consider:

- Which element currently feels strongest in your personal practice, professional role, and organisational culture?

- Which element represents your greatest opportunity for growth and development?

- What one small change could you make tomorrow to strengthen creative energy—for yourself, your team, or your organisation?

Remember: creativity is the energy that powers all public sector change, and you create the conditions for it to flow. How well you nourish the emotions of confidence and courage, foster individual and collective meaning, and build connections with self and others will determine the value you can deliver for the communities you serve.

CONCLUSION

Some confine creativity to stages and studios. I see it everywhere—woven through the everyday work of the elected officials and public servants who are shaping our societies.

I began the journey of this book because I witnessed something that troubled me deeply. I was part of a small, purposeful team—the kind where everyone brought their full selves to work, where ideas flowed freely and where problems were solved creatively. We were driven, we were energised. We were making a real difference.

Then the organisation grew. And with that growth came layers—administrative structures, coordination mechanisms, distance from decisions and endless escalation processes. The creative dynamism that had defined us dwindled away. Stimulating became stable. Agile became apathetic. And somewhere in the process, I watched talented, capable people transform from being creators into being simply compliant, their creative energy dampened not by their own limitations, but by systems and cultures that had lost sight of why creativity mattered.

I realised then that this wasn't a problem unique to that one organisation. It was symptomatic of growth itself, but it was also a recognised feature of how large public sector systems operate—hierarchical, risk-averse, bound by compliance requirements and political pressures. And I began to wonder: What if the solution to our greatest public sector challenges wasn't more policy or process, more plans or presentations, but more creativity?

This book is my answer to that question.

What We've Discovered: The Public Service IS Creative

When I began writing this book, the question being asked was: *"Is the public sector creative?"* Thanks to recent research, we can definitively answer this question. Yes, it is. Our public service is constantly producing new and valuable ideas, products, services and processes. However, we must dive deeper to understand *how* and *where* that creativity is happening.

The public sector excels at pragmatic creativity—small, incremental improvements to existing products, services and practices. This focus is understandable given the demands on governments to ensure stability and continuity of service. And these small changes matter; over time, they accumulate into significant efficiency gains and service improvements.

But alongside pragmatic creativity sits pioneering creativity (Houtgraaf et al., 2024)—the bolder, braver work of breakthrough innovation. This is where the public sector is far less confident, with only a small proportion of effort invested in proactive and profound change. And yet, as the OECD makes clear:

"Breakthrough innovation—creating new and more effective solutions that better respond to a changing context and the citizenry's needs—is required to respond to the current set of demands and constraints faced by the public sector." (OECD, 2017c p.15)

> You can only apply Band-Aids for so long. In a rapidly changing world, it's only a matter of time before incremental fixes become irrelevant, and so does the government that delivers them.

This is why there is such urgency around innovation, transformation, reshaping and reform. These terms acknowledge that current systems must be markedly changed to remain beneficial. We need both types of creativity, but we're underinvesting in the pioneering work that will future-proof our nation.

Creativity Is Core To Public Sector Work

Yet this dichotomy—pragmatic versus pioneering—doesn't capture the full picture of public sector creativity. Creativity emerges in the informal moments of problem-solving, in how we communicate and collaborate, in the wisdom experienced practitioners bring to their work, and in the countless small acts of human ingenuity that make government function day by day. It appears in how we navigate ethical dilemmas, respond to citizen concerns, build relationships across diverse groups, and adapt established practices to serve real human needs.

> Creativity flows through strategic conversations, community engagement, policy design, and the countless moments where public servants exercise professional judgment in service of others. There is a vast, often unmeasured landscape of creative thinking and action that animates public sector work every single day.

This book has shown that creativity is absolutely integral to the work we do. It impacts our ability to develop and diffuse innovation, improve productivity, solve wicked problems, build resilience and form the relationships necessary for shared value delivery. Creativity is at the core of all that government seeks to achieve.

And here's the paradox: while creativity is synonymous with change, it's also vital to maintain the stability and security that government seeks. In a rapidly changing world, stability is no longer achieved through rigidity, but through adaptive capacity. Citizens' continued sense of safety and security depends on governments being creative enough to respond to evolving threats and challenges that traditional approaches cannot address.

It is clear—governments must get better at creativity if they are going to deliver what they promise, protect their people and ensure prosperity into the future.

The Dangers of Denial

Despite the pervasive need for creativity in public sector work, it is often dismissed as airy-fairy or relegated to the arts— something pleasant but optional, even indulgent. This fundamentally misunderstands what creativity truly is.

Creativity is the serious work of developing new and valuable solutions to the wicked problems plaguing our communities. It is not nice-to-have; it is essential and urgent.

As long as we continue to cling to limiting beliefs about creativity—that it belongs only to artists, that it's frivolous, or that only special people possess it—we will deny ourselves and our citizens the best possible outcomes. We will leave solutions on the table for problems that demand our most rigorous and creative thinking.

The consequences of this denial are profound. Communities suffer when their governments are constrained by outdated thinking. Innovation stalls. Prosperity diminishes. And the idealism that drew many of us to public service erodes into frustration and burnout.

Without recognising that creativity is core to public service effectiveness, we will not focus on providing the capability or infrastructure that enables public servants to do this well. We will miss the opportunity to build the base of skills and systems that allow creativity to flourish.

You Are A Creator

Leadership presence and modelling are a significant influence of cultural change. When you shift, others shift with you. Your daily choices—how you respond to ideas, what you reward, who you promote, what risks you take and which ones you protect—these set the tone for everything that follows.

In this way, you are a creator. You are building the conditions in which people either flourish or diminish.

Every day, you are crafting an environment that either helps or hinders people in being their best and either spark or stifle their creative potential. Creativity goes well beyond tangible process, product and service improvements. It is central to building strong, positive relationships that characterise great leadership. It is the foundational capability that facilitates workplaces where clear purpose and courage exist.

> The fact that you are a creator is non-negotiable. The choice you have is whether you are establishing cultures that suppress people's potential, deskill them, and deny your communities the future they deserve—or whether you are consciously building the conditions where creativity can thrive.

You are a creator. Now is the time to be intentional about the kinds of creations you wish to make and the legacy you wish to leave through your leadership.

You may face obstacles. Budget cuts may tempt you to treat investment in creative capability as a luxury you cannot afford. Political cycles may push you toward short-term fixes over long-term cultural shifts. Peers or superiors may resist. And yes, there will be times when holding the line on what you know is right feels impossibly difficult.

But history shows us that the most transformative leaders are those who hold firm on what matters, even when it's difficult. They are the ones who, years later, look back and see that their small decisions—to listen differently, to reward differently, to take calculated risks—rippled outward in ways they could barely have imagined.

You have more power than you think. And this book exists to help you use it well.

The Creative Energy Equation: Your Roadmap

Throughout this book, we have explored the intricate interplay of conditions necessary for creativity to flourish across all levels of the organisation. This understanding sits at the heart of the Creative Energy Equation—a concise and powerful model that provides a practical framework for assessing and amplifying creative potential.

Creativity = Emotion × Meaning × Connection (self and others)

$$C = EMC^2$$

C—Creativity: The foundational belief that creativity is essential, that everyone has creative potential, and that making space for its flourishing is core to public service effectiveness.

E—Emotion: The emotional landscape that either fuels creative energy (through courage, joy, psychological safety and confidence) or depletes it (through fear, self-doubt and emotional unsafety).

M—Meaning: The clarity of purpose and connection between individual work and the broader mission—the compass that directs creative energy toward what truly matters.

C—Connection with Self: Self-awareness, authenticity and alignment between personal values and daily work—the foundation from which genuine creativity and resilience emerge.

C—Connection with Others: The quality of relationships, collaboration and genuine human connection that either amplifies or diminishes collective creative potential.

Together, these elements support one another to develop synergy, where the sum of the parts provides far greater creative potential than they can individually. The energy of creativity multiplies when all components are present and aligned.

You can use this framework (and the reflection questions provided) to identify where improvements can be made to encourage creative energy to flow—in your team, your department, across your entire community.

The Systemic View: How It All Works Together

What makes the Creative Energy Equation powerful is that it captures a fundamental truth: creativity is not a solo endeavour confined to individual brilliance. Rather, it is a systemic phenomenon that flows across all boundaries—individual, team, organisation, and sector.

Each layer can either enhance or hinder creative energy. A team member may be bursting with creative confidence, but if their organisation sends signals that failure is not tolerated, that creativity signals disloyalty, or that the work lacks meaning, that individual energy will be dampened. Conversely, an individual with lower creative confidence can be lifted by a team culture, an organisational structure, and leadership messaging that all reinforce that creative contribution is valued, safe and purposeful.

> This is where leaders play a unique and critical role. Leaders must take a helicopter view of their organisation and actively work to ensure alignment of capabilities and cultures across all levels.

They must ask:

- Are we building creative confidence?
- Are we supporting people to be courageous?
- Are we connecting people to meaning?
- Are we fostering authentic relationships?
- And critically, are all these elements working together in concert, or are they working at cross-purposes?

But we must also look beyond the organisation to understand the creative supports and constraints that live in the outer layers— oversight bodies, communities and societal norms.

The effectiveness of public sector creativity depends on the alignment of beliefs and approaches across all levels of influence. There must be dedicated attention to fostering creativity across the broader system.

Leaders who grasp the systemic nature of creativity can orchestrate conditions that allow creative energy to flourish fully. They become architects of possibility.

Two Critical Investments And Two Harsh Realities

If there is one clear and consistent call from this book, from the OECD, the Productivity Commission, and from citizens themselves, it is that government must get better at creativity. Getting there requires two key investments:
1. Development of creative confidence
2. Building a better balance between risk and reward.

1. Development of Creative Confidence

Public servants can be creative, but this skill is suffering from severe neglect. We need to arm them with three complementary abilities:

- Creative growth mindset: The belief that creativity is a skill that can be developed with dedicated effort and practice.
- Creative self-efficacy: The belief in their ability to come up with new and valuable ideas and overcome the challenges involved in implementing them.
- Intellectual risk-taking: The willingness to bear discomfort in order to share ideas and deliver something of value.

Together, these contribute to creative confidence—ensuring that when we need our people to be creative, they can be. Moreover, creative confidence means people will be on the lookout for improvements and compelled to share their ideas, reshaping culture over time to become more creative.

2. Building a Better Balance Between Risk and Reward

Both recent research and the Productivity Commission agree that risk aversion is a barrier to creativity. But here's what's critical: risk aversion is not simply a personal characteristic. It is also a response to the context. The emotion of fear (which is what a risk-aversion is basically about) is based on past experiences and current social conditions, and so the environment in which a person is making risk/reward decisions is crucial to consider.

Asking people to simply be less risk-averse and more courageous is akin to asking them to swim in crocodile-infested waters. Leaders must recognise their duty to reduce the number of crocodiles in the first place. You cannot demand that your people be more creative and innovative if you do not ensure supportive conditions.

The contextual nature of emotions and the resultant risk/reward decisions means it is imperative to identify and unravel those cultural elements that signal that creativity is not welcome, that impose personal and professional costs, and where a lack of compelling communication around vision and mission makes rewards almost invisible.

While developing individual creative ability is advantageous, leaders must also identify and address conditions that create a sense of danger and diminish the meaningfulness of acting creatively.

Why Psychological Safety Alone Is Not Enough

Psychological safety—the belief that you can take interpersonal risks without fear of negative consequences—is essential for reducing perceived risk and supporting people in moving forward with innovations. Conversely, a lack of safety stifles creativity.

There has been much concentration on this concept lately, which is to be congratulated. But here's the critical truth: psychological safety, while beneficial, is not sufficient.

In addition to people feeling supported, they also need to feel able and willing to act creatively. This requires dedicated attention building creative confidence. Psychological safety is one part of the puzzle, but it must be paired with creative confidence and genuine meaning for any significant shift in public sector creative capability to occur.

Emotion Must Be Acknowledged

Additionally, the reality is that you cannot advance creativity without acknowledging and working with emotions. There seems to be a general belief in the public sector that emotions are beneath the important work of government—too trivial and distracting from the serious issues we deal with.

But as this book has shown, every single innovation intervention is aimed at either enhancing positive emotions or reducing the negative ones. This is because emotions are the deciding factor in whether people will adopt the programs you develop and whether your people will deliver the changes necessary for your communities to thrive.

Your customers, clients, stakeholders and citizens are all judging your work based on how they *feel* about it. Their emotions determine whether they will adopt or resist the innovations and improvements you're offering.

Your people also share ideas or hold back based on their emotional response to the situation. When they feel confident in their creativity and in their ability to make a difference, they innovate and improve productivity. Where they fear repercussions—whether criticism or the extensive effort required to make a change—they do not engage.

Until emotion is recognised as fundamental to the creativity puzzle, efforts to enhance it will always be compromised.

Ultimately, It's About Being Human

Creativity is an inherent human trait. We are born from the ultimate creative process, and our bodies and brains are continually changing to keep us alive and flourishing. Creativity is critical for our physical and mental health—with it we become more whole and well; without it, we slip into disengagement, disease and despair.

We cannot continue to think that our workplaces are somehow separate from life—that they are rational, logical little cocoons where creativity is not necessary. Doing so denies us all the ability to achieve our fullest potential and spend our work hours making the contribution that only we can make.

Increasing creativity and innovation is not about introducing fancy new tricks or implementing expensive new programs. It is about making our government and its agencies more human and humane, and in doing so, allowing our inherent creativity to rise.

It's For the People—All People

This understanding—that we can honour and hone our inherent creativity—was my main motivation for writing this book.

I have witnessed the traumatic and destructive outcomes of creativity being denied. It is damaging to the people who turn up to work every day seeking to make a difference. And it is downright unjust to the people in our neighbourhoods and communities who are looking to government for support now and who trust government to help ensure the prosperity of their children into the future.

> I do not doubt that we all want the best for those we serve—our families, constituents, communities and nations. I truly believe we can only deliver on this desire if we allow ourselves to be our fullest, creative selves.

Covering over creativity with politically correct terms or denying its nature—both as humans and as producers of public value—serves no one. It is time to call this capability exactly what it is. It is time to put creativity in its rightful place in the public service lexicon.

It is time for all of us to find the courage we claim as a core public service value and to release the stigma and false assumptions about creativity that are constraining our effectiveness. It is time to accept our role as creators and arm ourselves with the ability and the environments that will let this thrive. It is time to give ourselves permission to be creative people.

For You—And For What Comes Next

For you are a creator.
And so are all those who work for you.

And so are all those in the communities you serve.
This is not the end of the conversation. It is the beginning.

Throughout this book, I have shared frameworks, evidence, and insights drawn from decades of research and lived public-sector experience. But the real work—the transformative work—happens in *your* context, with *your* people, in *your* community. It happens when you take these ideas and adapt them, test them, challenge them, and make them real.

Your Next Steps

This book is meant to be engaged with, not just read and shelved. It's a conversation starter. Here's how you might begin:

Reflect: Use the $C=EMC^2$ framework to assess your current context. Where is creative energy flowing freely? Where is it constrained? What emotions are you seeing? What part of their work do people find meaningful? What relationships need strengthening?

Connect: Share these insights with your leadership team, your colleagues, and your staff. Spend some time considering where you see these concepts playing out in your organisation. And take some time to wonder—what would change if you invested deliberately in creative capability?

Act: Start small. Choose one element of the Creative Energy Equation to focus on. It might be building psychological safety or helping people connect their daily work to a larger purpose. It might be creating space for people to bring their authentic selves to work. Or it could be breaking down some silos and sharing information and inspiration with other organisational or community groups.

Reach Out: I would genuinely love to hear from you. Share your stories—your obstacles, your breakthroughs, the moments when you saw creative energy shift in your team or organisation. Tell me what you're learning. Tell me where you're struggling. Tell me how you're reimagining what's possible in the public sector. You can connect with me at belinda@btcreative.agency.

Building a Creative Country

Given the chaos occurring in our world, there is a consistent call for leaders to rise to the moment. I want to make it clear that this is the moment.

> Our communities are facing challenges that demand the best of our creative thinking. Our citizens are looking to us not just to manage what exists, but to imagine and create what could be. Our public servants are seeking work that matters, environments where they can bring their full selves, and the chance to contribute their creativity.

Let's celebrate the creative people we are. Let's build the conditions for creativity to thrive. Let's use this reality to build a creative country.

For it is only through this comprehensive view of creativity, and intentional investment in it, that we will achieve the sustainable prosperity we seek, the wellbeing our communities deserve, and the future our children are counting on us to build.

The energy is already there, lying in wait for your leadership. Your job is to let it flow.

ACKNOWLEDGEMENTS

This book would not have been possible without the groundbreaking research and unwavering commitment of scholars and thought leaders who have dedicated their careers to understanding creativity—not as an abstract concept, but as a practical, transformative capability essential to how we live and work.

To Teresa Amabile and her colleagues, I send my deepest appreciation. Your work was what first inspired me to continue learning about creativity and to more fully understand the intricate relationship between organisational context and creative potential.

To Glenn Houtgraaf and his team of researchers: thank you for bringing nuance and rigour to understanding how creativity manifests—and too often, struggles—within the public sector. Your work is profound and powerful.

To Charles Landry and Margie Caust: your passionate advocacy for a more humane approach to public sector workplaces has been a compelling and inspirational call at a time when our organisations need it most. Your vision of institutions that honour the creativity inherent in all people has motivated me to pursue this book and to believe that change is possible.

To Professor Peter Coaldrake: your precise insights into the public sector experience captured what so many public servants have felt but struggled to articulate. With your words, we felt heard. Your willingness to hold leaders and policymakers to account for the atmospheres they create, and the consequences on our people and institutions, has been both sobering and sustaining. Your work reminds us that culture is not accidental; it is created, and it matters.

I send a special thanks to the OECD, and in particular the Observatory of Public Sector Innovation (OPSI), for their visionary work in championing innovation within public services and for their commitment to helping governments address the most complex societal challenges of our time. Your work deeply matters.

I would also like to thank ANZSOG—the Australia and New Zealand School of Government—for their dedication to growing public sector leadership capability and bridging the gap between research and real-world practice. You challenge us to think differently about what is truly important, and this is vital.

And to all the researchers, practitioners, and thought leaders who appear in these pages but who I have not mentioned in person— my most heartfelt gratitude. I wish I had the space to thank you all, because your work, wisdom, and genuine commitment to advancing human potential have been a source of constant motivation.

This book is, in many ways, a conversation with all of you—which one day I would cherish having in person. It is my honour to amplify your great work and to merely repeat what you have so carefully demonstrated: that creativity is not a luxury, but a necessity; not a risk, but the foundation upon which meaningful and sustainable change is built. Thank you for your scholarship, your courage, and your unwavering belief that a more creative public sector is possible.

And last, but certainly not least, thank you to my daughters. Thank you for your quiet support as I sat with my head down for hours on end. Thank you for tolerating the endless sighs and repeated rhetorical question— "why am I doing this again?". I also deeply appreciate your reminders not to take myself too seriously. Through this process you have taught me an incredibly valuable lesson—that love looks like consistently showing up, even if you don't yet fully understand the mission. You'll figure it out. Just have faith.

ABOUT THE AUTHOR

Belinda Tobin holds a BCom from the University of Wollongong and an MBA from the University of Queensland. She spent her early career consulting on governance and strategy to multi-national corporations and implementing change projects in governments across Australia. Over the last 20 years, she has shaped the governance, strategy, and performance systems in various Queensland state government agencies, providing her with deep insights into the practical challenges of driving innovation in large-scale organisations.

Through her personal creative pursuits, Belinda has realised the power of creativity as a fundamental driver of meaningful change. To this end, she has spent the last few years researching and writing about the nature and preconditions of creativity, integrating her extensive public sector expertise with lived experience and academic investigation.

Through her consultancy, Belinda helps organisations of all kinds understand the power of creative confidence and supports individuals to foster it for themselves. Her unique combination of governance and strategy expertise, public and private sector experience, and deep creative research positions her to understand the practical barriers meaningful change, as well as the creative confidence solutions needed to overcome them.

Belinda also passionately pursues her own creative practice. She has self-published 14 books, both fiction and non-fiction titles. Additionally, she is a series executive producer for an acclaimed film project and curates events to celebrate the courage and creativity within our indie author community.

Other Publications

Non-Fiction (Understanding Press)	Fiction (Bel House Books/ Curiosity)
Understanding Creativity	Crucifixus
Create Your Classroom	The Emptiness Algorithm
Understanding Violence	The Love Life of a Chameleon
Understanding Addiction	I'm Sorry Juno
Understanding Monogamy	To The Heart of The Man
Understanding Sexuality	

Reports and submissions

Creative Confidence - Essential Economic Infrastructure. (2025). A submission to the Productivity Commission's Five Pillar Inquiry into building a skilled and adaptable workforce.

Creative Confidence - Essential Reform Infrastructure. (2025). A submission to the Productivity Commissions Five Pillar Inquiry into building a dynamic and resilient economy.

REFERENCES

Ackoff, R. L. (1971). Towards a system of systems concepts. *Management Science*, 17(11), 661-671. https://doi.org/10.1287/mnsc.17.11.661

Ahmad, A., Achmad, G. N., & Adhimursandi, D. (2025). Mediating effect of creative self-efficacy in the relationship between knowledge sharing and perceived organisational support. *International Journal of Multidisciplinary Approach Research and Science*, 3(2), 635–651. https://doi.org/10.59653/ijmars.v3i02.1661

Alblooshi, M. (2024). Assessing creativity training as New Public Management Reforms in public sector organizations. *European Journal of Business and Management*, 16(5), 1-12.

Amabile, T. M. (1996). *Creativity in context: Update to the social psychology of creativity*. Westview Press.

Amabile, T. M., Conti, R., Coon, H., Lazenby, J., & Herron, M. (1996). Assessing the work environment for creativity. *Academy of Management Journal*, 39(5), 1154–1184.

Amabile, T. M. (1998). How to kill creativity. *Harvard Business Review*, 76(5), 76–87. https://hbr.org/1998/09/how-to-kill-creativity

Amabile, T., & Kramer, S. (2011). *The progress principle: Using small wins to ignite joy, engagement, and creativity at work*. Harvard Business Review Press.

An, S., Song, R., & Carr, M. (2016). A comparison of two models of creativity: Divergent thinking and creative expert performance. *Personality and Individual Differences, 90*, 78-84. https://doi.org/10.1016/j.paid.2015.10.040

Anderson, S., Cameron, C. D., & Beaty, R. E. (2023). Creative Empathy. *Creativity Research Journal*, 37(1), 71–93. https://doi.org/10.1080/10400419.2023.2229649

Angelou, M. (2006). Maya Angelou and Dave Chappelle. *Iconoclasts*, Sundance Channel

Ansell, C., & Gash, A. (2008). Collaborative governance in theory and practice. *Journal of Public Administration Research and Theory*, 18(4), 543–571. https://doi.org/10.1093/jopart/mum032

ANZSOG. (2017, April 10). What is public value? Public admin explainer. Melbourne: Australia and New Zealand School of Government. https://anzsog.edu.au/research-insights-and-resources/research/what-is-public-value/

ANZSOG. (2018, May 30). Why creativity is the key to managing conflict and leading successfully. https://anzsog.edu.au/news/why-creativity-is-the-key-to-managing-conflict-and-leading-successfully/

ANZSOG. (2022). Joined-up government: what works and when. *ANZSOG Research*. https://anzsog.edu.au/research-insights-and-resources/research/joined-up-government-what-works-and-when/

ANZSOG. (2023b, 27 June). How to think outside the box to solve complex public problems. https://anzsog.edu.au/news/how-to-think-outside-the-box-to-solve-complex-public-problems/

ANZSOG. (2023c, 4 July). Creativity in policy capacity. https://anzsog.edu.au/research-insights-and-resources/research/creativity-in-policy-capacity/

Australian Parliament. (2015). *Australia's Innovation System: Report of the Senate Economics References Committee*. Commonwealth of Australia. https://www.aph.gov.au/Parliamentary_Business/Committees/Senate/Economics/Innovation_System/Report/c02

Australian Public Service Commission. (2024). *Strategic context and objectives: APS hierarchy and classification review report*. Commonwealth of Australia. https://www.apsc.gov.au/initiatives-and-programs/workforce-information/aps-hierarchy-and-classification-review-report/strategic-context-and-objectives

Australian Public Service Commission. (2025). *Trust in Australian public services: 2025 annual report*. https://www.apsc.gov.au/sites/default/files/2025-10/Trust%20in%20Australian%20public%20services%20Annual%20Report%202025%20-%20Accessible.pdf

Baer, J. (2016). *Domain specificity of creativity*. Academic Press.

Bandura, A. (1977). *Social learning theory*. Prentice Hall.

Bandura, A. (1997). *Self-efficacy: The exercise of control*. W. H. Freeman.

Barrett, L. F. (2017). *How emotions are made: The secret life of the brain*. Houghton Mifflin Harcourt.

Barsade, S. G. (2002). The ripple effect: Emotional contagion and its influence on group behavior. *Administrative Science Quarterly, 47*(4), 644-675.

Basadur, M., Basadur, T., & Calic, G. (2023). Organizational development. In R. Reiter-Palmon & S. T. Hunter (Eds.), Handbook of organizational creativity: Leadership, interventions, and macro level issues (2nd ed., pp. 239–255). Academic Press. https://doi.org/10.1016/B978-0-323-91841-1.00015-4

Beaty, R. E., Benedek, M., Silvia, P. J., & Schacter, D. L. (2016). Creative cognition and brain network dynamics. *Trends in Cognitive Sciences*, 20(2), 87-95.

Beaty, R. E., Kenett, Y. N., Christensen, A. P., Rosenberg, M. D., Benedek, M., Chen, Q., Fink, A., Qiu, J., Kwapil, T. R., Kane, M. J., & Silvia, P. J. (2018). Robust prediction of individual creative ability from brain functional connectivity. *Proceedings of the National Academy of Sciences, 115*(5), 1087–1092. https://doi.org/10.1073/pnas.1713532115

Beck, A. T. (1979). *Cognitive therapy and the emotional disorders*. New York: New American Library.

Beck, U. (1995). *Ecological Politics in an Age of Risk*. Cambridge: Polity Press. (Original work published 1988 as *Gegengifte: Die organisierte Unverantwortlichkeit*).

Beghetto, Ronald A. 2019. *Beautiful Risks. Having the Courage to Teach and Learn Creatively*. Lanham: Rowman & Littlefield.

Benedetti, F., Carlino, E., & Pollo, A. (2011). How placebos change the patient's brain. *Neuropsychopharmacology*, 36(1), 339-354. https://doi.org/10.1038/npp.2010.81

Benington, J., & Moore, M. H. (Eds.). (2011). *Public value: Theory and practice*. Palgrave Macmillan.

Beyers, F. (2024). Collaborative governance and personal relationships for sustainability transformation in the textile sector. *Scientific Reports, 14*, Article 13347. https://doi.org/10.1038/s41598-024-64373-1

Blumberg, M., & Pringle, C. D. (1982). The missing opportunity in organizational research: Some implications for a theory of work performance. *Academy of Management Review, 7*(4), 560–569. https://doi.org/10.5465/amr.1982.4285240

Boden, M.A. (2004), *The creative mind: Myths and mechanisms*, Routledge, London, UK.

Borins, Sandford. (2001). Encouraging Innovation in the Public Sector. *Journal of Intellectual Capital*. 2. 310-319. 10.1108/14691930110400128.

Bos-Nehles, A. (2023). Examining the Ability, Motivation, and Opportunity (AMO) framework in HRM research: Conceptualization, measurement and interactions. *International Journal of Management Reviews, 25*(2), 274–298. https://doi.org/10.1111/ijmr.12332

Boston Consulting Group. (2024). *From purpose to trust to lasting value: How stakeholders' perceptions create a roadmap to company value*. https://www.bcg.com/publications/2024/driving-company-value-with-stakeholders-perceptions

Boyatzis, R., & McKee, A. (2005). *Resonant leadership: Renewing yourself and connecting with others through mindfulness, hope, and compassion*. Harvard Business Review Press.

Boyatzis, R., Passarelli, A., Koenig, K., Lowe, M., Mathew, B., Stoller, J., & Phillips, M. (2012). Examination of the neural substrates activated in memories of experiences with resonant and dissonant leaders. *The Leadership Quarterly*, 23(2), 259-272.

Brewster, A. L., Lee, Y. S. H., Linnander, E. L., & Curry, L. A. (2021). Creativity in problem solving to improve complex health outcomes: Insights from hospitals seeking to improve cardiovascular care. *Learning health systems, 6*(2), e10283. https://doi.org/10.1002/lrh2.10283

Buckingham, M., & Clifton, D. O. (2001). *Now, discover your strengths*. Free Press.

Butler, C., Kwantes, C., & Boglarsky, C. (2014). The effects of self-awareness on perceptions of leadership effectiveness in the hospitality industry. *Journal of Human Resources in Hospitality & Tourism, 13*(1), 89–112.

Cai, W., Fan, X., & Wang, Q. (2023). Linking visionary leadership to creativity at multiple levels: The role of goal-related processes. *Journal of Business Research, 167*, Article 114182. https://doi.org/10.1016/j.jbusres.2023.114182

Carey, G., & Crammond, B. (2015). What Works in Joined-Up Government? An Evidence Synthesis. *International Journal of Public Administration, 38*(13–14), 1020–1029. https://doi.org/10.1080/01900692.2014.982292

Carey, G., & Buick, F. (2019, December 19). ANALYSIS: What do Morrison's changes to The APS mean for public servants and policy? UNSW Newsroom. https://www.unsw.edu.au/news/2019/12/analysis--what-do-morrisons-changes-to-the-aps-mean-for-public-s

Cederberg, K. (2018). Building creative confidence: A review of literature and implications for beginning design studios. *National Conference on the Beginning Design Student, 34*(1). https://journals.uc.edu/index.php/ncbds/article/view/840

Černe, M., & Škerlavaj, M. (2012). *Authentic leadership, creativity, innovation: A multilevel perspective.* Paper presented at the OLKC Conference, University of Ljubljana.

Cirella, S. (2021). Managing collective creativity: Organizational variables to support creative teamwork. *European Management Review, 18*(3), 269-287. https://doi.org/10.1111/emre.12475

Coaldrake, P. (2022, June 28). *Let the sunshine in: Review of culture and accountability in the Queensland public sector* (Final report). Queensland

Government.
https://www.coaldrakereview.qld.gov.au/assets/custom/docs/coaldrake-review-final-report-28-june-2022.pdf

Creative Systems Theory. (2022). *Overview*.
https://csthome.org/overview/

Csikszentmihalyi, M. (1988). Society, culture, and person: A systems view of creativity. In R. J. Sternberg (Ed.), *The nature of creativity* (pp. 325-339). Cambridge University Press.

CX Today. (2025, October 18). Gartner: *No Fortune 500 firms will fully replace customer support staff with AI by 2028*. https://www.cxtoday.com/customer-analytics-intelligence/gartner-no-fortune-500-firms-will-fully-replace-customer-support-staff-with-ai-by-2028/

Dahl, C. J., Wilson-Mendenhall, C. D., & Davidson, R. J. (2020). The plasticity of wellbeing: A training-based framework for the cultivation of human flourishing. *Proceedings of the National Academy of Sciences*, 117(51), 32197–32206. https://doi.org/10.1073/pnas.2014859117

Daley, J. (2021). *Gridlock: Removing barriers to policy reform*. Grattan Institute.

Dawahdeh, A. M. A., & Mai, M. Y. (2021). The mediating effect of creative thinking on multiple intelligence and thinking patterns among 10th-grade students in Abu Dhabi private schools. *European Journal of Education*, 4(2), 107–125.

DemocracyCo. (2016). *A joined-up policy guide*. Government of South Australia. https://www.democracyco.com.au/wp-content/uploads/2016/02/JUP-smaller.pdf

Doshi, A. R., & Hauser, O. P. (2024). Generative AI enhances individual creativity but reduces the collective diversity of novel content. *Science Advances*, *10*, eadn5290. https://doi.org/10.1126/sciadv.adn5290

Duarte, A. P., Ribeiro, N., Semedo, A. S., & Gomes, D. R. (2021). Authentic Leadership and Improved Individual Performance: Affective Commitment and Individual Creativity's Sequential Mediation. *Frontiers in psychology, 12*, 675749. https://doi.org/10.3389/fpsyg.2021.675749

Edmondson, A. (1999). Psychological safety and learning behavior in work teams. *Administrative Science Quarterly, 44*(2), 350-383.

Edmondson, A. C. (2011). Strategies for learning from failure. *Harvard Business Review*, 89(4), 48-55.

Edelman Trust Institute. (2025). *2025 Edelman Trust Barometer Global Report [Australia report version]*.
https://www.edelman.com.au/sites/g/files/aatuss381/files/2025-03/2025%20Edelman%20Trust%20Barometer_Australia%20Report.pdf

Einstein, A. (1929, October 26). What life means to Einstein: An interview by George Sylvester Viereck. *The Saturday Evening Post*, 117(43), 17, 110–111.

Eldor, L. (2025). The relationship between organisational authenticity perceptions and employees' work performance: Evidence from a field experiment. *Journal of Management*, 51(1), 326–353.
https://doi.org/10.1177/01492063241310153

Ernst, C., Lee, L., & Horth, D. M. (2025). *Why you should collaborate across boundaries*. Center for Creative
Leadership. https://www.ccl.org/articles/leading-effectively-articles/boundary-spanning-the-leadership-advantage/

Eurich, T. (2018). What self-awareness really is (and how to cultivate it). *Harvard Business Review*, 96(1), 136-143.

Fancourt, D., & Finn, S. (2019). *What is the evidence on the role of the arts in improving health and well-being? A scoping review* (Health Evidence Network synthesis report 67). World Health
Organization. https://apps.who.int/iris/handle/10665/329834

Frankl, V. E. (1946). *Man's search for meaning: An introduction to logotherapy*. Boston, MA: Beacon Press.

Fredrickson, B. L. (2001). The role of positive emotions in positive psychology: The broaden-and-build theory of positive emotions. *American Psychologist*, 56(3), 218-226.

Gardner, H. (1993). *Frames of mind: The theory of multiple intelligences*. Basic Books.

Gerlich, M. (2025). AI tools in society: Impacts on cognitive offloading and the future of critical thinking. *Societies*, 15(1), 1-28.

Gigerenzer, G. (2023). Heuristics: The tools of intuition. In *The intelligence of intuition* (Chapter 5). Cambridge University.

Glăveanu, V. P. (2014). *Distributed creativity: Thinking outside the box of the creative individual*. SpringerBriefs in Psychology. Springer Publishing Company. https://doi.org/10.1007/978-3-319-05434-6

Global Government Forum, & PA Consulting. (2023). *Responsive Government Survey 2023*. Global Government Forum. https://rgs.globalgovernmentforum.com/wp-content/uploads/Global_Government_Forum_Responsive_Government_Survey_2023.pdf

Goncalo, J. A., & Katz, J. H. (2020). Your Soul Spills Out: The Creative Act Feels Self-Disclosing. *Personality & social psychology bulletin*, 46(5), 679–692. https://doi.org/10.1177/0146167219873480

Gong, Y., Huang, J. C., & Farh, J. L. (2009). Employee learning orientation, transformational leadership, and employee creativity: The mediating role of creative self-efficacy. *Academy of Management Journal*, 52(4), 765–778. https://doi.org/10.5465/amj.2009.43670890

Gürbüz, S., Schaufeli, W. B., Freese, C., & Brouwers, E. P. M. (2024). Fueling creativity: HR practices, work engagement, personality, and autonomy. *The International Journal of Human Resource Management*, 35(22), 3770–3799. https://doi.org/10.1080/09585192.2024.2429125

Han, S. J., Lee, Y., & Beyerlein, M. (2019). Developing team creativity: The influence of psychological safety and relation-oriented shared leadership. *Performance Improvement Quarterly*, 32(2), 159-182. https://doi.org/10.1002/piq.21293

Hatfield, E., Cacioppo, J. T., & Rapson, R. L. (1994). *Emotional contagion*. Cambridge University Press.

Hawkins, D. R. (2012). *Power vs. force: The hidden determinants of human behavior* (Author's official authoritative ed.). Hay House.

Heard, J., Ramalingam, D., Scoular, C., Anderson, P., & Duckworth, D. (2025). *Creative thinking: Skill development framework.* 2nd ed. Australian Council for Educational Research. https://doi.org/10.37517/978-1-74286-753-3

Houtgraaf, G., Kruyen, P., & van Thiel, S. (2022). Public servants' creativity: salient stimulators and inhibitors a longitudinal qualitative digital diary study. *Public Management Review*, 26(3), 591–612. https://doi.org/10.1080/14719037.2022.2103175

Houtgraaf, G. (2022). Public sector creativity: triggers, practices and ideas for public sector innovations. A longitudinal digital diary study. *Public Management Review*, 25(8), 1610–1631. https://doi.org/10.1080/14719037.2022.2037015

Houtgraaf, G., Kruyen, P. M., & van Thiel, S. (2023). Public sector creativity as the origin of public sector innovation: A taxonomy and future research agenda. *Public Administration*, 101(2), 539–556. **https://doi.org/10.1111/padm.12778**

Houtgraaf, G., & Ropes, E. (2024). Thinking "Outside the Box" Whilst Remaining "Inside the Box": Do Rules and Procedures Demotivate Creativity and Innovation in the Public Sector? *Review of Public Personnel Administration*, 0(0). https://doi.org/10.1177/0734371X241266117

HR Executive. (2022, October 13). *What the explosion of non-routine work means for HR.* https://hrexecutive.com/what-the-explosion-of-non-routine-work-means-for-hr/

Huang, L. (2016). Leader creative self-efficacy and follower creativity: A moderated mediation model of leader creative expectation and follower creative role identity. *The Leadership Quarterly*, 27(1), 109-128.

Hughes, D. J., Lee, A., Tian, A. W., Newman, A., & Legood, A. (2018). Leadership, creativity, and innovation: A critical review and practical recommendations. *The Leadership Quarterly*, 29(5), 549-569.

IBM Corporation. (2010). *Capitalising on complexity: Insights from the global chief executive officer study* (Full report). https://www.ibm.com/downloads/cas/1VZV5X8J

IDM. (2023, November 1). *Public sector still battling data silos*: Survey. IDM Magazine. https://idm.net.au/article/0014600-public-sector-still-battling-data-silos-survey

Jaiswal, N. K., & Dhar, R. L. (2017). Transformational leadership, innovation climate, creative self-efficacy and employee creativity: A multilevel study. *International Journal of Hospitality Management, 63*, 44–53. Johnson, W., & Proudfoot, D. (2024). Greater variability in judgements of the value of novel ideas. *Nature Human Behaviour 8(1), 1-9.* http://dx.doi.org/10.2139/ssrn.4769688

Jørgensen, T. B., & Bozeman, B. (2007). Public values: An inventory. *Administration & Society, 39*(3), 354-381. **https://doi.org/10.1177/0095399707300703**

Jung, R. E., Mead, B. S., Carrasco, J., & Flores, R. A. (2013). The structure of creative cognition in the human brain. *Frontiers in Human Neuroscience, 7*, 330. https://doi.org/10.3389/fnhum.2013.00330

Kahneman, D., & Tversky, A. (1979). Prospect theory: An analysis of decision under risk. *Econometrica, 47*(2), 263–291. https://doi.org/10.2307/1914185

Karwowski, M. (2014). Creative mindsets: Measurement, correlates, consequences. *Psychology of Aesthetics, Creativity, and the Arts, 8*(1), 62–70.

Kashdan, T. B., & Rottenberg, J. (2010). Psychological flexibility as a fundamental aspect of health. *Clinical psychology review, 30*(7), 865–878. https://doi.org/10.1016/j.cpr.2010.03.001

Kastelle, T. (2015, June 30). Why national culture should be at the heart of innovation management. *Technology Innovation Management Review, 5*(6), 42-48. http://www.timreview.ca/article/978

Kattel, R., & Mazzucato, M. (2020). COVID-19 and public-sector capacity. *Oxford Review of Economic Policy, 36*(1), S256-S269.

Kaufman, J. C., & Beghetto, R. A. (2009). Beyond big and little: The Four C model of creativity. *Review of General Psychology, 13*(1), 1–12. https://doi.org/10.1037/a0013688

Kaufman, S. B., & Gregoire, C. (2015). *Wired to create: Unraveling the mysteries of the creative mind*. Perigee Books.

Kelley, T., & Kelley, D. (2012, November 30). Reclaim your creative confidence. *Harvard Business Review*. https://hbr.org/2012/12/reclaim-your-creative-confidence

Kirchner, J. (2025, September 25). This underrated trait is quietly separating top leaders from the rest. *Entrepreneur*. https://www.entrepreneur.com/leadership/this-underrated-trait-is-quietly-separating-top-leaders/494917

Kniffin, K. M., Narayanan, J., Anseel, F., Antonakis, J., Ashford, S. P., Bakker, A. B., & Vugt, M. V. (2021). COVID-19 and the workplace: Implications, issues, and insights for future research and action. *American Psychologist*, 76(1), 63-77.

Korthagen, Fred A. J. 2004. In search of the essence of a good teacher: Towards a more holistic approach in teacher education. *Teaching and Teacher Education* 20: 77–97.

Krekel, C., Ward, G., & De Neve, J. E. (2019). Employee well-being, productivity, and firm performance: Evidence and case studies. In Global Happiness Council (Ed.), *Global Happiness and Wellbeing Policy Report 2019* (pp. 73–94). Global Happiness Council. https://www.hbs.edu/ris/Publication%20Files/gh19_ch5_9e171d71-db54-4e08-a2eb-3cf1587daf4a.pdf

Land, G., & Jarman, B. (1992). *Breakpoint and beyond: Mastering the future today*. New York, NY: HarperBusiness.

Landry, C., & Caust, M. (2017). *The creative bureaucracy & its radical common sense*. Comedia.

Larson, E. (2017). New research: Diversity + inclusion = better decision making at work. *Forbes*. https://www.forbes.com/sites/eriklarson/2017/09/21

/new-research-diversity-inclusion-better-decision-making-at-work/

Larson, E. (2023, October 25). *Five reasons why innovation decisions succeed 2.5X more often at top companies*. Forbes. https://www.forbes.com/sites/eriklarson/2023/10/25/five-reasons-why-innovation-decisions-succeed-25x-more-often-at-top-companies/

Lerner, J. S., Li, Y., Valdesolo, P., & Kassam, K. S. (2015). Emotion and Decision Making. *Annual Review of Psychology, 66*, 799–823. https://doi.org/10.1146/annurev-psych-010213-115043
Lindstrom, P. (2024). *Purpose at work: How purpose and innovation drive transformational change*. Routledge.

Liu, X., Yu, Y., Zhao, X., & Zhang, N. (2022). Top management team boundary-spanning leadership: Measurement development and its impact on innovative behaviour. *Frontiers in psychology, 13*, 988771. https://doi.org/10.3389/fpsyg.2022.988771

Liu, P., Xie, J., Hu, D., Chen, X., & Xie, L. (2022). Employee growth mindset and innovative behaviour. *Frontiers in Psychology, 13*, 814154. https://doi.org/10.3389/fpsyg.2022.814154

Liu, L., Long, J., Liu, R., & Wan, W. (2024). Influencing mechanism of the combination of creative self-efficacy and psychological safety on employees' bootleg innovation. *Frontiers in Business Research in China, 18*(4), 441–464. https://doi.org/10.3868/s070-009-024-0021-7

Liu, C., Zhuang, K., Zeitlen, D. C., Zhou, J., Wang, Z., Yuan, Y., & Beaty, R. E. (2024). Neural, genetic, and cognitive signatures of creativity. *Communications Biology, 7*, Article 1324. https://doi.org/10.1038/s42003-024-07007-6

Lusiani, M., & Langley, A. (2019). The social construction of strategic coherence: Practices of enabling leadership. *Long Range Planning, 52*(5), Article 101840. https://doi.org/10.1016/j.lrp.2018.05.006

Lyubovnikova, J., Legood, A., Turner, N., & Mamakouka, A. (2017). How authentic leadership influences team performance: The mediating role of team reflexivity. *Journal of Business Ethics, 141*(1), 59–70. https://doi.org/10.1007/s10551-015-2692-3

Ma, G., Wu, W., Liu, C., Ji, J., & Gao, X. (2024). Empathetic leadership and employees' innovative behavior: examining the roles of career adaptability and uncertainty avoidance. *Frontiers in psychology*, *15*, 1371936. https://doi.org/10.3389/fpsyg.2024.1371936

Manyika, J., Lund, S., Chui, M., Bughin, J., Woetzel, J., Batra, P., Ko, R., & Sanghvi, S. (2017). *Jobs lost, jobs gained: Workforce transitions in a time of automation*. McKinsey Global Institute.

Marin-Garcia, J. A., & Tomas, J. M. (2016). Deconstructing AMO framework: a systematic review. *Intangible Capital*, 12(4), 1040-1087.

Marrocu, E. and Paci, R. (2012), Education or Creativity: What Matters Most for Economic Performance?. *Economic Geography*, 88: 369-401. https://doi.org/10.1111/j.1944-8287.2012.01161.x

Maslow, A. H. (1943). A theory of human motivation. *Psychological Review*, 50(4), 370–396. https://doi.org/10.1037/h0054346

Massie, M.-H., Capron Puozzo, I., & Boutet, M. (2022). Teacher Creativity: When Professional Coherence Supports Beautiful Risks. *Journal of Intelligence*, *10*(3), 62. https://doi.org/10.3390/jintelligence10030062

Maté, G. (2003). *When the Body Says No: Understanding the Stress-Disease Connection*. Toronto, Canada: Vintage Canada.

Mayer, E. A. (2011). Gut feelings: The emerging biology of gut–brain communication. *Nature Reviews Neuroscience*, 12(8), 453–466. https://doi.org/10.1038/nrn3071

McCracken, M. (2024). *Understanding the role of growth mindset on innovative thinking in working professionals* [Doctoral dissertation, Purdue University]. Purdue e-Pubs. https://hammer.purdue.edu/articles/thesis/27941673

McCraw, T. K. (2007). *Prophet of Innovation: Joseph Schumpeter and Creative Destruction*. Harvard University Press.

McGuire, J., De Cremer, D., & Van de Cruys, T. (2024). Establishing the importance of co-creation and self-efficacy in creative collaboration with artificial intelligence. *Scientific Reports*, 14(1), 18525. https://doi.org/10.1038/s41598-024-69423-2

McKinsey & Company. (2020). *The hidden perils of unresolved grief: How leaders can anticipate and address loss to unlock transformation.* https://www.mckinsey.com/~/media/mckinsey/business%20functions/organization/our%20insights/the%20hidden%20perils%20of%20unresolved%20grief/the-hidden-perils-of-unresolved-grief-vf.pdf

McCraty, R., Atkinson, M., & Bradley, R. T. (2004). Electrophysiological evidence of intuition: part 1. The surprising role of the heart. *Journal of alternative and complementary medicine (New York, N.Y.), 10*(1), 133–143. https://doi.org/10.1089/107555304322849057

Moore, M. H. (1995). *Creating public value: Strategic management in government.* Harvard University Press.

Mueller, J. S., Goncalo, J. A., & Kamdar, D. (2011). Recognizing creative leadership: Can creative idea expression negatively relate to perceptions of leadership potential? *Journal of Experimental Social Psychology, 47*(2), 494–498. https://doi.org/10.1016/j.jesp.2010.11.010

Mumford, M. D., Mobley, M. I., Uhlman, C. E., Reiter-Palmon, R., & Doares, L. M. (1991). Process analytic models of creative capacities. *Creativity Research Journal, 4*(2), 91–122. https://doi.org/10.1080/10400419109534380

Mumford, M. D., Baughman, W. A., Supinski, E. P., & Maher, M. A. (1996). Process-based measures of creative problem-solving skills: II. information encoding. *Creativity Research Journal, 9*(1), 77–88. https://doi.org/10.1207/s15326934crj0901_7

Mumford, M. D., Zaccaro, S. J., Harding, F. D., Jacobs, T. O., & Fleishman, E. A. (2000). Leadership skills for a changing world: Solving complex social problems. *Leadership Quarterly, 11*(1), 11–35. https://doi.org/10.1016/S1048-9843(99)00041-7

NSW Government. (2023). *Creative, Community, Wellbeing and Resilience Hub: Executive Summary Report.* New South Wales Department of Communities and Justice. https://banc.org.au/wp-content/uploads/2024/09/Final-summary-report-HUB-project.pdf

OECD (2015), *The Innovation Imperative in the Public Sector: Setting an Agenda for Action*, OECD Publishing, Paris, https://doi.org/10.1787/9789264236561-en

OECD. (2017). *HR and leadership strategies for building innovative public sector organisations*. Observatory of Public Sector Innovation. https://oecd-opsi.org/wp-content/uploads/2019/03/HR-and-Leadership-Catalyst-for-Innovation-Capabilities.pdf

OECD. (2017a). *Core skills for public sector innovation: A beta model*. OECD Observatory of Public Sector Innovation. https://oecd-opsi.org/wp-content/uploads/2018/07/OECD_OPSI-core_skills_for_public_sector_innovation-201704.pdf

OECD. (2017b). *Innovation skills in the public sector: Building capabilities in Chile*. OECD Public Governance Reviews. https://www.oecd.org/content/dam/oecd/en/publications/reports/2017/04/innovation-skills-in-the-public-sector_g1g7847d/9789264273283-en.pdf

OECD. (2017c). *Fostering innovation in the public sector*. OECD Publishing. https://www.oecd.org/content/dam/oecd/en/publications/reports/2017/04/fostering-innovation-in-the-public-sector_g1g75c6c/9789264270879-en.pdf

OECD. (2019). *Declaration on Public Sector Innovation*. OECD Legal Instruments. https://legalinstruments.oecd.org/en/instruments/OECD-LEGAL-0450

OECD. (2021a). *Public sector innovation facets: Innovation portfolios*. OECD Publishing.

OECD. (2021c). *Economic and social impact of cultural and creative sectors*. https://www.oecd.org/content/dam/oecd/en/publications/reports/2021/08/economic-and-social-impact-of-cultural-and-creative-sectors_6d8452e4/4d4e760f-en.pdf

OECD. (2024, June). *New PISA results on creative thinking: Can students think outside the box?* (PISA in Focus 2024/125). OECD Publishing. https://www.oecd.org/content/dam/oecd/en/publications/repo

rts/2024/06/new-pisa-results-on-creative-thinking_7dccb55b/b3a46696-en.pdf

Oh, S., & Pyo, J. (2023). Creative Self-Efficacy, Cognitive Reappraisal, Positive Affect, and Career Satisfaction: A Serial Mediation Model. *Behavioral sciences (Basel, Switzerland), 13*(11), 890. https://doi.org/10.3390/bs13110890

Oliver Wyman. (2024). *A resilient Australian public sector*. https://www.oliverwyman.com/our-expertise/insights/2024/jun/boost-resilience-in-public-sector-australia.html

Parliamentary Library. (2025). *Australia's flagging productivity growth*. Australian Parliament. https://www.aph.gov.au/About_Parliament/Parliamentary_departments/Parliamentary_Library/Research/Policy_Briefs/2025-26/Australiasflaggingproductivitygrowth

Pink, D. H. (2018). Drive: The surprising truth about what motivates us. Canongate Books.

Pretz, J. E., & Nelson, D. (2017). Creativity is influenced by domain, creative self-efficacy, mindset, self-efficacy, and self-esteem. In M. Karwowski & J. C. Kaufman (Eds.), *The Creative Self* (pp. 155-170). Academic Press. https://doi.org/10.1016/B978-0-12-809790-8.00009-1

Kerrissey, M. J., Satterstrom, P., & Edmondson, A. C. (2020). From member creativity to team creativity? Team information elaboration as moderator of the additive and disjunctive models. *PLOS ONE, 15*(12), e0243289. https://doi.org/10.1371/journal.pone.0243289

Paulus, P. B., & Yang, H. C. (2000). Idea generation in groups: A basis for creativity in organisations. *Organisational Behavior and Human Decision Processes, 82*(1), 76-87. https://doi.org/10.1006/obhd.2000.2888

Productivity Commission. (2023a). *Advancing Prosperity: 5-Year Productivity Inquiry*. Volume 1, Inquiry Report no. 100, Canberra. https://assets.pc.gov.au/inquiries/completed/productivity/report/productivity-recommendations-reform-directives.pdf
Productivity Commission. (2023b). *Advancing Prosperity: 5-Year Productivity Inquiry – Factsheet 3: Innovation for the 98%*.

https://assets.pc.gov.au/inquiries/completed/productivity/report/productivity-factsheet3-innovation-diffusion.pdf

Productivity Commission. (2025a). *Annual productivity bulletin 2025* (PC productivity insights). Australian Government. https://www.pc.gov.au/ongoing/productivity-insights/bulletins/bulletin-2025/productivity-bulletin-2025.pdf

Productivity Commission. (2025b). *Growth mindset: how to boost Australia's productivity* (5 productivity inquiries). Australian Government. https://www.pc.gov.au/inquiries-and-research/five-productivity-inquiries/growth-mindset/

Project ROAR. (2023, May 23). *Growth mindset in the workplace: Benefits and strategies for leaders.* https://www.projectroar.com.au/blog/tax-ec298-dta3c

Public Sector Network. (2025, August 29). Collaborative governance: Breaking barriers, building bridges – Part 1. *Public Sector Network.* https://publicsectornetwork.com/insight/collaborative-governance-breaking-barriers-building-bridges-part-1

Rawlings, A., & Cutting, C. (2025). Divergent thinking is linked with convergent thinking: Meta-analytic evidence for the independence-involvement paradox. *Thinking & Reasoning, 31*(1), 1-35. https://doi.org/10.1080/13546783.2025.2485059

Rego, A., Sousa, F., Marques, C., & e Cunha, M. P. (2012). Authentic leadership promoting employees' psychological capital and creativity. *Journal of Business Research, 65*(3), 429–437. **https://doi.org/10.1016/j.jbusres.2011.10.003**

Reserve Bank of Australia. (2017, December 1). *Skills for the modern workforce* [Speech]. https://www.rba.gov.au/speeches/2017/pdf/sp-so-2017-12-01.pdf

Ricoh Australia. (2019, January 30). Australia's innovation paradox. *Ricoh News.* https://www.ricoh.com.au/news/australias-innovation-paradox

Ringel, M., Taylor, A., & Zablit, H. (2019). *The most innovative companies 2019: The rise of AI, platforms, and ecosystems.* Boston Consulting Group.

Rittel, H. W. J., & Webber, M. M. (1973). Dilemmas in a general theory of planning. *Policy Sciences*, 4(2), 155-169.

Rock, D. (2008). SCARF: A brain-based model for collaborating with and influencing others. *NeuroLeadership Journal*, 1(1), 44-52.

Rock, D., & Grant, H. (2016). Why diverse teams are smarter. *Harvard Business Review*, 4(4), 2–5.

Sawyer, R. K. (2017). *Group genius: The creative power of collaboration*. Basic Books.

Schein, E. H., & Schein, P. (2017). *Organizational culture and leadership* (5th ed.). Jossey-Bass.

Sharma, S., & Mehta, S. (2023). Psychological safety and creativity in teams: A mediated moderation model of shared leadership and team diversity. *Business Perspectives and Research*. https://doi.org/10.1177/22779752231163356

Schuckert, M., Kim, T. T., Paek, S., & Lee, G. (2018). Motivate to innovate: How authentic and transformational leaders influence employees' psychological capital and service innovation behavior. *International Journal of Contemporary Hospitality Management*, 30(2), 776–796.

Scotney, V. S., Weissmeyer, S., Carbert, N., & Gabora, L. (2019). The Ubiquity of Cross-Domain Thinking in the Early Phase of the Creative Process. *Frontiers in psychology*, *10*, 1426. https://doi.org/10.3389/fpsyg.2019.01426

Seligman, M. E. P. (2011). *Flourish: A visionary new understanding of happiness and well-being*. Free Press.

Sinek, S. (2009). *Start with why: How great leaders inspire everyone to take action*. Portfolio.

Steger, M. F., & Dik, B. J. (2012). Work as meaning: Individual and organizational benefits of engaging in meaningful work. In P. A. Linley, S. Harrington, & N. Garcea (Eds.), *Oxford handbook of positive psychology and work* (pp. 131–142). Oxford University Press.

Sternberg, R. J. (2015, October 27). Standardized tests "narrow," don't assess creative skills. *Hamilton College News*. https://www.hamilton.edu/news/story/standardized-tests-narrow-dont-assess-creative-skills-sternberg-contends

Sun, M., Wang, M., & Wegerif, R. (2020). Effects of divergent thinking training on students' scientific creativity: The impact of individual creative potential and domain knowledge. *Thinking Skills and Creativity, 37*, 100682. https://doi.org/10.1016/j.tsc.2020.100682

Thabit, S., Sancino, A., & Mora, L. (2025). Strategic public value(s) governance: A systematic literature review and framework for analysis. *Public Administration Review*, 85(3), 885–906.

Tierney, P., & Farmer, S. M. (2002). Creative self-efficacy: Its potential antecedents and relationship to creative performance. *Academy of Management Journal, 45*(6), 1137–1148. https://doi.org/10.2307/3069429

Torfing, J., & Ansell, C. (2017). Strengthening political leadership and policy innovation through the expansion of collaborative forms of governance. *Public Management Review*, 19(1), 37-54.

Treasury. (2025). Productivity overview. Australian Government. https://treasury.gov.au/sites/default/files/2025-08/productivity-overview.docx

UN DESA. (2014). *Whole of government and collaborative governance.* United Nations Department of Economic and Social Affairs. https://publicadministration.un.org/egovkb/portals/egovkb/documents/un/2014-survey/chapter4.pdf

UNDP. (2019). *Design thinking for public service excellence.* United Nations Development Programme. https://www.undp.org/sites/g/files/zskgke326/files/publications/GPCSE_Design%20Thinking.pdf

United Nations Office for Sustainable Development. (2011). *Introduction to the whole-of-government approach* [Presentation]. https://unosd.un.org/sites/unosd.un.org/files/session_10-2_mr._samuel_danaa.pdf

U.S. Department of Energy. (1992). *DOE fundamentals handbook: Classical physics* (DOE-HDBK-1010-92). Washington, DC: U.S. Department of Energy. https://engineeringlibrary.org/reference/energy-work-power-doe-handbook

Van Bommel, T. (2025). The power of empathy in times of crisis and beyond (2nd edition). *Catalyst*. (2021).

Victorian Public Sector Commission. (2015). *Organisational Culture: A Framework for the Victorian Public Sector*. Victorian Government. https://vpsc.vic.gov.au/wp-content/uploads/2015/03/Organisational-Culture_Web.pdf

Wageman, R., Nunes, D. A., Burruss, J. A., & Hackman, J. R. (2008). *Senior leadership teams: What it takes to make them great*. Harvard Business School Press.

Ward, T. B. (2008). The role of domain knowledge in creative generation. *Learning and Individual Differences, 18*(4), 363-366. https://doi.org/10.1016/j.lindif.2007.07.002

WIPO (World Intellectual Property Organization). (2024). *Global innovation index 2024: Australia ranking*. https://www.wipo.int/edocs/gii-ranking/2024/au.pdf

World Economic Forum. (2025, October 6). *The future of jobs report 2025*. https://www.weforum.org/publications/the-future-of-jobs-report-2025/digest/

Wróbel, A. E., Johansen, M. K., Jørgensen, M. S., & Cash, P. (2021). Facilitating creativity: Shaping team processes. *Creativity and Innovation Management, 30*(4), 742–762. https://doi.org/10.1111/caim.12465

Yates, J. (2003). An interview with Ulrich Beck on fear and risk society. *The Hedgehog Review, 5*(3), 96-107.

Yavich, R., & Rotnitsky, I. (2020). Multiple intelligences and success in school studies. *International Journal of Higher Education, 9*(6), 107–115. https://doi.org/10.5430/ijhe.v9n6p107

Zabelina, D. L., & Robinson, M. D. (2010). Child's play: Facilitating the originality of creative output by a priming manipulation. *Psychology of Aesthetics, Creativity, and the Arts*, 4(1), 57–65. https://doi.org/10.1037/a0015644

Zhang, Y., Zhang, J., Gu, J., & Tse, H. M. (2022). Employee radical creativity: the roles of supervisor autonomy support and employee intrinsic work goal orientation. *Innovation: Organization and Management*, 24(2), 272-289. https://doi.org/10.1080/14479338.2021.1885299

Zhou, J., & George, J. M. (2001). When job dissatisfaction leads to creativity: Encouraging the expression of voice. *Academy of Management Journal*, 44(4), 682-696.

Zhou, Q. (2020). Exploring role of personal sense of power in facilitation of proactive behavior and creativity. *Frontiers in Psychology*, 11, 1102.

Zhou, X., Zhong, J., & Zhang, L. (2024). Action speaks louder: The role of proactive behavior between creative leadership and employees' creativity. *Behavioral Sciences*, 14(3), 257.

www.ingramcontent.com/pod-product-compliance
Lightning Source LLC
Chambersburg PA
CBHW071728270326
41928CB00013B/2603